LAW, CRIME AND LAW ENFORCEMENT

CRIMINAL HISTORY RECORDS AND BACKGROUND CHECKS

ELEMENTS, CONSIDERATIONS AND RECOMMENDATIONS

LAW, CRIME AND LAW ENFORCEMENT

Additional books in this series can be found on Nova's website
under the Series tab.

Additional e-books in this series can be found on Nova's website
under the e-book tab.

LAW, CRIME AND LAW ENFORCEMENT

CRIMINAL HISTORY RECORDS AND BACKGROUND CHECKS

ELEMENTS, CONSIDERATIONS AND RECOMMENDATIONS

BRIAN WILKINS
EDITOR

nova publishers
New York

Library of Congress Cataloging-in-Publication Data

ISBN: 978-1-63483-438-4

Published by Nova Science Publishers, Inc. † New York

CONTENTS

PREFACE

There is widespread interest in obtaining access to criminal history record information from reliable sources for the purpose of screening an individual's suitability for employment, licensing, or placement in positions of trust. The interest is based on a desire or perceived need to evaluate the risk of hiring or placing someone with a criminal record in particular positions and is intended to protect employees, customers, vulnerable persons, and business assets. Employers and organizations are subject to potential liability under negligent hiring doctrines if they fail to exercise due diligence in determining whether an applicant has a criminal history that is relevant to the responsibilities of a job and determining whether placement of the individual in the position would create an unreasonable risk to other employees or the public. This book addresses to what extent states conduct FBI record checks for selected employment sectors and face any challenges; states have improved the completeness of records, and remaining challenges that federal agencies can help mitigate; and private companies conduct criminal record checks, the benefits those checks provide to employers, and any related challenges.

In: Criminal History Records and Background Checks
Editor: Brian Wilkins
ISBN: 978-1-63483-438-4

Chapter 1

THE ATTORNEY GENERAL'S REPORT ON CRIMINAL HISTORY BACKGROUND CHECKS*

U.S. Department of Justice

I. EXECUTIVE SUMMARY

Interest in Criminal History Screening

There is widespread interest in obtaining access to criminal history record information from reliable sources for the purpose of screening an individual's suitability for employment, licensing, or placement in positions of trust. The interest comes from private and public employers, as well as non-profit organizations that place employees and volunteers to work with vulnerable populations such as children, the elderly, and disabled persons. The interest is based on a desire or perceived need to evaluate the risk of hiring or placing someone with a criminal record in particular positions and is intended to protect employees, customers, vulnerable persons, and business assets. Employers and organizations are subject to potential liability under negligent hiring doctrines if they fail to exercise due diligence in determining whether an applicant has a criminal history that is relevant to the responsibilities of a job and determining whether placement of the individual in the position would create an unreasonable risk to other employees or the public. In addition to addressing this litigation risk, employers want to assess the risks to their assets and reputations posed by placing persons with criminal histories in certain positions. To meet these business needs, employers can and frequently do ask applicants whether they have a criminal history. Such employers and organizations want access to criminal history records to determine whether applicants are answering the question about their criminal history truthfully and completely. They believe that having access to good sources of criminal history information is the only way the interest in performing due diligence to protect employees, assets, and the public can be served. Public employers' need for the information often goes beyond considering job suitability and includes security

* This is an edited, reformatted and augmented version of a report issued June 2006.

clearance determinations. There also has been a growing use of criminal history screening in certain sectors of the economy related to counterterrorism efforts.

Privacy and Fair Information Practice Interests

Competing interests also enter the criminal background screening picture. Individuals have a strong interest in ensuring that fair information practices are followed when employers and other organizations obtain and use criminal history information to screen a person for employment or volunteer suitability. No one wants to be wrongly associated with someone else's criminal record, particularly when applying for a job. Individuals who do have a criminal record want reasonable assurance that the information is accurate and complete, that they have a meaningful opportunity to see the information and correct any inaccuracies, and that the information is used fairly in the screening process and does not unfairly exclude them from employment opportunities when they are otherwise qualified for a position.

Fair Use of Criminal History – Reentry and Anti-Discrimination Interests

The individual's interest in the fair use of criminal history information is mirrored by the broader social policy of facilitating the reentry of ex-offenders into the workforce. Steady gainful employment is a leading factor in preventing recidivism. The unfair use of or discrimination based upon criminal records can raise barriers to employment by ex-offenders and, as a result, undermine the reentry that makes us all safer. This social interest is reflected in federal and state consumer reporting and anti-discrimination laws, as well as guidance from the Equal Employment Opportunity Commission, that limit the reporting of criminal history information by consumer reporting agencies or the use that can be made of such information by public and private employers for employment or licensing purposes. The limits generally seek to ensure that criminal records are only used to deny employment to an otherwise qualified applicant when the conduct underlying the conviction or arrest is relevant to the responsibilities of the job and takes into account an ex-offender's efforts at rehabilitation. Some jurisdictions also do not allow employers to use information about arrests that do not lead to a conviction.

Private Sector Criminal History Databases and Background Screening Services

Most private employers' demand for criminal history background checks is currently met by private sector enterprises that provide professional background screening services and/or commercial databases that aggregate criminal records that are available to the public from government agencies. The commercial databases are not complete because not all states, and not all agencies within individual states, make their records available to such databases; nor does the FBI make its federal or state criminal records available to such databases. In addition, the information in the commercial databases may only be updated periodically. The commercial databases may also be missing important disposition information that is relevant to a conviction record's use for employment suitability purposes, such as sealing and expungement orders or entry into a pre-trial or post-trial diversion program. Checks of these databases are based not upon positive, biometric identification (such as fingerprints), but upon personal identifiers such as names and other information that can help confirm a person's identity. Nevertheless, these databases provide a source of information that is significantly broader than going to individual county courthouses in the counties where an applicant indicates that he or she has lived. Professional background screening services also provide overall screening services to employers, performing the function of going to all appropriate data sources, whether primary sources (such as a courthouse) or secondary sources (such as public and private databases) to gather criminal history records and other information, such as financial history, that an employer may be seeking to evaluate a candidate. These services also assist in obtaining the current status of a record at the primary source when it may not necessarily be reflected in a database.

The private data providers and screening services are considered consumer reporting agencies under the federal Fair Credit Reporting Act (FCRA) and state consumer reporting laws. The activities of consumer reporting agencies in providing information on individual consumers are regulated under these federal and state laws. Some state consumer reporting laws are more restrictive than the FCRA. All of these laws impose fair information-practice requirements by consumer reporting agencies that report public record information, such as criminal history records, for employment purposes. The privacy protections provided to consumers under these laws include the right to consent (including opportunities to opt-in or opt-out), the right to access information about themselves in databases, the right to notice about reporting disclosures that have been made, and the right to challenge the accuracy of the information before adverse action is taken by the user based on the information. They also restrict the reporting of certain types of information, such as, in the case of the FCRA, records of arrests that did not result in a conviction that are older than seven years. Some states restrict the reporting of any arrest-only records by consumer reporting agencies.

Non-Criminal Justice Use of FBI-Maintained Criminal History Record Information

The Federal Bureau of Investigation (FBI) maintains a criminal history record repository, known as the Interstate Identification Index (III or "Triple I") system, that contains records from all states and territories, as well as from federal and international criminal justice agencies. The state records in the III are submitted to the FBI by central criminal record repositories that aggregate criminal records submitted by most or all of the local criminal justice agencies in their jurisdictions. The records in the III are all based on 10 rolled fingerprints, which provide a positive, biometric match between the individual and his or her record. Although it is quite comprehensive in its coverage of nationwide arrest records for serious offenses, the III is still missing final disposition information for approximately 50 percent of its records.

The FBI record system was initially created for the use of government agencies involved in the administration of criminal justice functions, such as investigations, prosecutions, and sentencing. Over time, however, the use of this information has been authorized for numerous non-criminal justice purposes, such as background screening for employment and licensing in industries that either state governments or the federal government have decided to regulate in some fashion. Non-criminal justice screening using FBI criminal history records is typically done by a government agency applying suitability criteria that have been established by law or the responsible agency. Non- criminal justice checks of the III have generally been required to be supported by fingerprints in order to substantially reduce the twin risks posed by name checks, which can result in false positives (when a person with a common name is associated with another person's record) or false negatives (when a record is missed because an individual provides false identifying information). This requirement is now embodied in the National Crime Prevention and Privacy Compact, enacted by Congress in 1998, which provides a structure for establishing rules regarding the interstate sharing of FBI-maintained criminal history information for non-criminal justice purposes.

The number of fingerprint submissions to the FBI for non-criminal justice checks, including visas and other federally required checks for public safety and national security, has grown to a point at which they now exceed fingerprint submissions to the FBI for criminal justice checks. The FBI processed approximately 10 million non-criminal justice fingerprint checks in 2005. As of June 2005, the FBI has begun accepting flat, as opposed to rolled, fingerprints for non-criminal justice background checks, making the capture of fingerprints for these checks faster, easier, and less expensive. The FBI charges a fee for fingerprint-based checks of the III for non-criminal justice purposes. Submission of flat prints does not affect the FBI's fingerprint processing or the fees charged.

State Record Repository Data

State record repositories have also made their records available for non-criminal justice checks for a fee. Some states do so more broadly than others, allowing any person for any purpose to do name-based and, in some cases, fingerprint-based checks of their repository records on the theory that they are public records and should therefore be open to the public. Some states have even made name checks of their repositories records available on the Internet for a fee. Other states are more restrictive with their records, limiting their use for non-criminal justice purposes to those specifically authorized by state law. Thus, in some states, private employers can obtain access to state criminal history records, but cannot get access to criminal history records from other states through a check of FBI-maintained records unless they have a separate statutory authority to do so. State records are also more complete and up-to-date than the FBI-maintained records. For that reason, checks of state databases, in addition to an FBI check, are considered necessary to get more comprehensive data. State repositories also charge a fee for non-criminal justice background checks.

Existing Authorities for Access to FBI Criminal History Records

Under current law, access to FBI-maintained criminal history information is governed by a patchwork of state and federal statutes. The main vehicle for gaining access for non-criminal justice purposes has been state statutes that take advantage of the provisions of Public Law (Pub. L.) 92-544 (enacted in 1972), which allow sharing of FBI-maintained criminal history records in certain licensing and employment decisions, subject to the approval of the Attorney General. These checks are processed through state record repositories and, in order to provide more complete information, include a check of state records. These statutes generally require background checks in certain areas that the state has sought to regulate, such as persons employed as civil servants, day care, school, or nursing home workers, taxi drivers, private security guards, or members of regulated professions. The results of these checks are supplied to public agencies that apply their own suitability criteria or those established under state law. There currently are approximately 1,200 state statutes that are approved by the Attorney General under Pub. L. 92-544. In addition, the National Child Protection Act/Volunteers for Children Act (NCPA/VCA) allows state governmental agencies, without requiring a state statute, to conduct background checks and suitability reviews of employees or volunteers of entities providing services to children, the elderly, and disabled persons.

Other access has been authorized by federal statutes allowing particular industries or organizations to go directly to the FBI for an employment, licensing, or volunteer check, without first going through a state repository and also checking state records. These laws, some of which were passed after the terrorist attacks on September 11, 2001, seek to promote public safety and national security by either authorizing access to a check by certain industries or affirmatively regulating an industry or activity by requiring background checks and risk assessments by government agencies. They include authority for discretionary access by the banking, nursing home, securities, nuclear energy, and private security guard industries, as well as required security screenings by federal agencies of airport workers, HAZMAT truck drivers and other transportation workers, persons seeking access to nuclear facilities and port facilities, and aliens visiting the United States.

This existing framework for providing authority to access FBI-maintained criminal history records for non-criminal justice purposes, requiring separate statutes for each new authorized use, has created inconsistencies in access to the information across industries and states. It has also created inconsistencies in the scope of the records checked, with some checks accessing both state and FBI records and others checking just FBI records. For example, depending on whether the state has passed a Pub. L. 92-544 statute, an industry may, in some states, be allowed access to state criminal history records (where the check stops at the state level), but not to FBI records reflecting criminal records originating in other states. Also, an industry may be able to get access to both state and FBI records when screened by agencies in some states, but have no access to state or FBI records in other states. Industries with authority to obtain checks directly from the FBI get checks of FBI maintained records, but not of records maintained at the state level.

Private Sector Interest in Access to FBI-Maintained Criminal History Record Information

Because of the limitations on the convenience, completeness, and reliability of the information on criminal history records from state and local public agencies and commercial databases, strong interest has been expressed in broadening authority to access FBI-maintained criminal information for the purpose of suitability screening by private employers and organizations placing individuals in positions of trust. There are two primary reasons for this interest. First, because the FBI has fingerprint-based records from all states and territories, it can identify a person's record created in states other than those of self-disclosed past residences or where the employment is located. This is important in a mobile society where many persons may have lived in or traveled to more than one state. Second, the FBI records are based on the positive identification of a person to a record through fingerprints, significantly reducing the risks to privacy (false positives) and security (false negatives) posed by strictly name-based searches.

This interest is demonstrated, in part, by the many bills introduced in Congress each year to authorize access to FBI-maintained criminal history records for background checks in particular industries or settings. Private employers and other private entities seeking such access authority wish it to be nationwide, without the need to obtain such authority in each state through separate state statutes under Pub. L. 92-544. Frequently, private employers would also like to have the access to the records themselves, giving them the ability to make their own determinations about the suitability of a candidate. In other words, they would like the information without necessarily having a state or federal government agency establishing inflexible suitability criteria and making suitability determinations about their prospective employees. It should also be noted that there are undoubtedly many positions in the private sector today for which checks of FBI-maintained records are not available because they are unregulated, yet those positions may involve greater degrees of trust and security risk (such as in critical infrastructure industries) than positions that are subject to such background checks because they are regulated. Broader access by the private sector would help address this anomaly.

Data Quality Issues and the Opportunity to Correct Information

No single source exists that provides complete and up-to-date information about a person's criminal history. The FBI-maintained criminal history database, however, is certainly one of the better sources because it is based on positive identification and can provide, at a minimum, nationwide leads to more complete information. If provided such access, however, users may not want to rely exclusively on an FBI and state repository check and may also want to check other record sources, such as commercial databases and local courthouses to obtain more complete and up-to-date information in support of criminal history background screening.

In addition to the data quality issue of obtaining comprehensive criminal record information, there is the issue of ensuring that users are provided information that is accurate and up-to-date. Public comments received by the Department on the questions that Congress asked to be addressed in this report cited many examples of the adverse consequences to individuals caused by inaccurate or incomplete criminal history information reported to employers by consumer reporting agencies. Issues of information quality in criminal history databases, whether commercial, state, or FBI, therefore require adequate privacy safeguards that provide individuals a meaningful opportunity to correct inaccurate or incomplete information before it has an adverse effect on an employment opportunity.

Summary of Recommendations

Section 6403 of the Intelligence Reform and Terrorism Prevention Act of 2004 calls upon the Attorney General to "make recommendations to Congress for improving, standardizing, and consolidating the existing statutory authorizations, programs, and procedures for the conduct of criminal history record checks for non-criminal justice purposes." This report responds to the congressional interest in these issues expressed in section 6403 and seeks to provide insight on possible ways that the law can be changed to create a framework for providing broader private sector access to state and FBI-maintained criminal history records without the need to enact separate statutes that create inconsistent levels and rules for access. As called for by the Act, we obtained input from the state record repositories, the National Crime Prevention and Privacy Compact Council, and representatives from the private sector and labor, as well as other interested members of the public. The following summarizes our major recommendations:

- When a private employer or entity can inquire into whether an applicant or employee has a criminal history, a process should be available that allows the employer to determine whether the response to the question is truthful and complete. We think that the fingerprint-based criminal history information maintained by the FBI and state record repositories should be one of the authorized sources of information for this purpose, as system capacity allows, so long as the process provides appropriate privacy protections to the individual and respects state and federal laws designed to ensure that criminal records are not used to unfairly deny employment.
- The expanded access to this information should take advantage of the existing private sector infrastructure for employment screening and background checks on consumers and, therefore, consumer reporting agencies, under conditions specified in law and by the Attorney General, such as certification of training on record handling and data security requirements, should also be authorized access when acting on behalf of an authorized user. Employer access to records directly from the FBI or participating states should be permitted, but made manageable by allowing the Attorney General and participating states to set minimum threshold requirements for such direct access. The checks should be based on fingerprints.
- When possible, these fingerprint checks should involve states that agree to participate in an expanded program for non-criminal justice checks. The participating states should be required to meet minimal standards for processing these checks, including a response time of no more than three business days from the date the fingerprints are received by a repository. The Attorney General should establish a means for doing the checks in states that do not opt-in to the program. Regardless of whether the checks go through a state or the FBI, the checks should include a check of as many federal and state records as possible.
- The Attorney General should be allowed to prioritize access under this new authority to enable the scaling of the system to meet private sector demand and to do so in a way that does not interfere with use of the system for criminal justice or national security purposes (which are the original reasons the system was established). The Attorney General should also be authorized to expand access to

additional individuals or entities when he finds that doing so promotes public safety or national security.

- Given the competing law enforcement and national security demands on the FBI's system and resources, implementation of all-employer access is likely to be, at best, many years away. Therefore, if Congress's goal is to create a means by which all qualified private employers can obtain a national fingerprint check of criminal history information, then other solutions besides relying exclusively on the FBI should be explored, such as relying more directly on private sector resources without requiring significant new government resources to help service the private sector's need for this information. The privacy and civil liberties issues discussed in our recommendations, as well as issues of governance, accountability, information security, and information control by the agencies that own the data, would have to be addressed in deciding how to create such alternative solutions and whether they are feasible. In the meantime, the FBI should be authorized to provide access to priority employers as capacity allows.
- Users should be enrolled with agreements that specify the requirements for access, including security of the information, certified training on the interpretation of criminal records, and notice to individuals concerning record access and correction and fair use of the information.
- The checks should include appropriate privacy safeguards to protect the individual. These protections should include informed consent and the opportunity to review a record before an application is made, before the record is provided to the user, and before adverse action is taken by the user. Moreover, a streamlined process for appealing incorrect records must be implemented. Because of the likely public concerns about privacy relating to fingerprint retention, limits regarding the retention and deletion of fingerprints by the FBI, participating states, consumer reporting agencies, and authorized users should be established by statute.
- The FBI and participating state repositories disseminating records directly to employers and other users under this new authority should be required, as consumer reporting agencies disseminating the records will be required, to screen the records in accordance with limits applicable to consumer reporting agencies and employers under federal and state laws in order to respect the reentry policies promoted by those laws. The law of the state of employment should be applied in the screening. Appropriate exceptions to the screening requirements should be made when consistent with state open records laws or where users are serving vulnerable populations.
- Employers and organizations with access under this authority should be required to certify that they will not use the information obtained in violation of any applicable federal or state equal employment opportunity laws or regulations, just as users must do when obtaining criminal history information from consumer reporting agencies under the FCRA for employment suitability purposes. Congress should also consider whether employers should be provided guidance on appropriate time limits when establishing specific disqualifying offenses and on allowing individuals an opportunity to seek a waiver from such disqualifications.
- The infrastructure for collecting fingerprints under this new authority should be exclusively through electronic, live-scan devices. Such devices should be fast and

unobtrusive where possible. The fingerprint collection should be decentralized at locations other than law enforcement agencies, including at the place of employment or through a consumer reporting agency, and should take advantage of outsourcing where necessary. User fees should be used to develop any additional system capacity for processing the additional demand for fingerprint checks.

- Appropriate criminal and civil penalties should be established for the unauthorized use of information by those provided access under this authority.
- A new commitment should be made to improving the completeness of records held by the FBI and state record repositories. A realistic assessment should be made of the funds – state and federal – necessary to meet the national goals for criminal history record improvement. A means should be found for conducting a consolidated fingerprint check of the FBI and all state repository records.
- Consideration should be given to amending the FCRA to make the rules on reporting and using name-based criminal history records for employment purposes more consistent, regardless of the source of the information. Steps to improve the accuracy of name-based checks should also be considered.

In sum, we believe that new authority should be established allowing broader access by private sector users to the fingerprint-based criminal history record information maintained by the FBI and the state repositories. The Attorney General should be able to prioritize the access to allow for the development of system capacity as necessary resources are made available and in order to avoid interference with use of the system for criminal justice and national security purposes. The new rules should provide access in a way that is both controlled and accountable and that respects the privacy interests of individuals in accurate information and the social interests in encouraging reentry and preventing unlawful discrimination in employment. If the information is handled properly, we believe allowing dissemination of FBI-maintained records to employers and other entities can not only provide more accurate and reliable information for use in the suitability screening, but also enhance individual protections for privacy and fair use of the information.

II. INTRODUCTION

A. Congressional Reporting Requirement

On December 17, 2004, the President signed the Intelligence Reform and Terrorism Prevention Act of 2004 (hereinafter the "Act"), Pub. L. No. 108-458, 118 Stat. 3638 (2004). Section 6403 of the Act calls for the Attorney General to report to Congress on a number of matters associated with record checks using Department of Justice maintained criminal history information. For example, the Act calls for the Department of Justice to provide information regarding the number of criminal history record checks requested, the type of information requested, the usage of different terms and definitions regarding criminal history information, and the variation in fees charged for such information and who pays such fees.

In addition, the Act calls for the Attorney General to "make recommendations to Congress for improving, standardizing, and consolidating the existing statutory authorizations, programs, and procedures for the conduct of criminal history record checks for non-criminal justice purposes." Section 6403(d), 118 Stat. 3638, 3759 (2004). Section 6403(d) set forth the following factors that the Attorney General was to consider in making his recommendations:

1. The effectiveness and efficiency of utilizing commercially available databases as a supplement to fingerprint checks of FBI-maintained criminal history information;
2. Any security concerns created by the existence of these commercially available databases concerning their ability to provide sensitive information that is not readily available about law enforcement or intelligence officials, including their identity, residence, and financial status;
3. The effectiveness of utilizing State databases for criminal history record checks;
4. Any feasibility studies by the Department of Justice of the resources and structure of the Federal Bureau of Investigation to establish a system to provide criminal history information;
5. Privacy rights and other employee protections, including employee consent, access to the records used if employment was denied, the disposition of the fingerprint submissions after the records are searched, an appeal mechanism, and penalties for misuse of the information;
6. The scope and means of processing background checks for private employers utilizing data maintained by the Federal Bureau of Investigation that the Attorney General should be allowed to authorize in cases where the authority for such checks is not available at the state level;
7. Any restrictions that should be placed on the ability of an employer to charge an employee or prospective employee for the cost associated with the background check;
8. Which requirements should apply to the handling of incomplete records;
9. The circumstances under which the criminal history information should be disseminated to the employer;
10. The type of restrictions that should be prescribed for the handling of criminal history information by an employer;
11. The range of federal and state fees that might apply to such background check requests;
12. Any requirements that should be imposed concerning the time for responding to such background check requests;
13. Any infrastructure that may need to be developed to support the processing of such checks, including the means by which information is collected and submitted in support of the checks and the system capacity needed to process such checks at the federal and state level;
14. The role that states should play in such background checks; and
15. Any other factors that the Attorney General determines to be relevant to the subject of the report.

B. Consultation Requirement and Solicitation of Public Comments

Section 6403(e) of the Act called for the Department to consult with certain parties when preparing the report, including representatives of state criminal history record repositories, the National Crime Prevention and Privacy Compact Council (Compact Council), appropriate representatives of private industry, and representatives of labor, as determined appropriate by the Attorney General. On June 6, 2005, the Department published in the Federal Register a notice seeking public comment on the report described in section 6403 of the Act. Specifically, the Department sought comments on the fifteen factors Congress asked the Department to consider in preparing the report. The Department invited comments not just from the specific parties identified in section 6403(e) of the Act, but from any person who may be able to provide responsive information that the Department may consider when drafting the report. The Department reviewed the comments received on the Congressional factors when drafting the report, but did not solicit comments on the report itself.

We received 55 comments from a wide range of entities with experience and interest in criminal history checks. They include professional background screeners, commercial data aggregators, representatives of private sector businesses, employers and trade associations, security companies, labor representatives, privacy advocates, ex-offender and employment law advocates, the National Consortium for Justice Information and Statistics (SEARCH) (an organization representing state criminal history record repositories), and the Compact Council. The comments are posted on the website of the Department's Office of Legal Policy, which can be found at www.usdoj.gov. We also met personally with several interested groups at their request, including representatives of private sector businesses and labor, labor advocacy groups, ex-offender advocacy groups, the professional background screening industry, the consumer data industry, SEARCH,[1] and the Compact Council. The information, knowledge, experience, and concerns shared by the commenters provided valuable input for this report and we are grateful for the efforts made by those submitting comments. We encourage those with interest in the issues discussed in this report to read the comments that we received as well.

We agree that there is a need to revisit the authorities under which checks can be made of FBI-maintained criminal history information for non-criminal justice purposes. For that reason, we have developed the recommendations below on how the authority of the private sector to access such information can be broadened and standardized. While we have considered the factors specified by Congress, we have structured the recommendations in a way that we believe makes the most sense.

III. Background

A. FBI-Maintained Criminal History Record Information

The FBI maintains an automated database that integrates criminal history records, including arrest information and corresponding disposition information, submitted by state, local, and federal criminal justice agencies. Each state has a criminal records repository responsible for the collection and maintenance of criminal history records submitted by law enforcement agencies in its state. The state record repositories are the primary source of criminal history records maintained at the FBI. Currently, the FBI maintains criminal history records on more than 48 million different individuals, with many of the individuals having multiple entries of separate encounters with the criminal justice system.

1. Authority

The basic federal authority for the Attorney General to maintain criminal history information is found at 28 U.S.C. 534, which provides that the Attorney General shall "acquire, collect, classify, and preserve identification, criminal identification, crime, and other records." That law also provides for the sharing of the information by requiring that the Attorney General "exchange such records and information with, and for the official use of, authorized officials of the federal government, including the United States Sentencing Commission, the States, cities, and penal institutions." The states are not required to provide this information to the Attorney General, but do so voluntarily in order to gain the mutual benefit of having ready access to criminal history information on an individual arising in other states.

2. FBI Criminal History Records

An FBI criminal history record is a listing of information on individuals collected and submitted with fingerprints by agencies with criminal justice responsibilities, such as descriptions of arrests, detentions, informations, or other formal criminal charges and any dispositions of the charges, such as dismissal, acquittal, conviction, sentencing, correctional supervision, release, and expungement or sealing orders. The record includes the name of the agency that submitted the fingerprints to the FBI, the date of arrest, the arrest charge, and the disposition of the arrest, if known to the FBI.

B. Fingerprint Identification

1. The FBI CJIS Division

Fingerprint identification has been a major responsibility of the FBI since 1924 and fingerprints have been a key part of the FBI's national criminal history record system. The FBI's Criminal Justice Information Services (CJIS) Division was established in February 1992 to serve as the focal point and central repository for criminal justice information services in the FBI. It is the largest Division within the FBI and is responsible for administering several programs, including the Integrated Automated Fingerprint Identification System (IAFIS), the National Crime Information Center (NCIC) (including the national criminal history record index (the III) and other files of interest to law enforcement, such as those relating to wanted persons, civil protection orders, registered sex offenders, and missing persons), and the National Instant Criminal Background Check System (NICS) (which processes background checks on prospective purchasers of firearms from federal firearm licensees).

2. IAFIS

For most of the life of the FBI criminal history record system, record submissions and record requests were supported by ink and paper fingerprints. During the 1980s, however, technology was developed allowing state repositories to collect fingerprints and search against fingerprint databases digitally. To meet the growing demand for fingerprint identification, the FBI developed and implemented the IAFIS, which became operational on July 28, 1999. IAFIS integrates fingerprint records that have been sent to the FBI by the states and territories and federal law enforcement agencies, all of which have established their own Automated Fingerprint Identification Systems (AFIS). IAFIS provides automated fingerprint search capabilities, latent fingerprint searching capability, electronic image storage, and electronic exchange of fingerprints and responses 24 hours a day, 365 days a year. IAFIS allows for the automated submission and amendment of fingerprint- based criminal history records by the state record repositories, as well as automated fingerprint searches of the records. Paper fingerprint submissions are digitally scanned into the system. A large percentage of fingerprints, however, now are "live-scanned" into the system, which means the original fingerprint is collected on a machine that captures the fingerprint image digitally, without the involvement of paper prints.

The FBI is currently in the planning stage of making improvements and enhancements to the capabilities of IAFIS. This initiative is known as "Next-Generation Identification (NGI) System" and, among other things, will provide advanced fingerprint identification technology, enhanced terrorist identification services, improved disposition reporting services, "Rap-Back" services (providing users with updates of subsequent criminal history record activity), interstate photo system ("mug shot") enhancements, and an FBI national palm print system.

C. The Interstate Identification Index

1. The III

The Interstate Identification Index (III or "Triple-I") segment of IAFIS is the national system designed to provide automated criminal history record information. The III is an index-pointer system that allows for the exchange of criminal history records. The III stores the criminal history records of federal offenders and records of offenders submitted by all states and territories. Under the III, the FBI maintains an index of persons arrested for felonies or misdemeanors under either state or federal law. The index includes identification data such as name, birth date, race, and sex. In addition, the index contains FBI and state identification numbers (SIDs) from each state that has information about an individual. Search queries using names and other identifiers are made by law enforcement agencies throughout the country. The automated name search process takes about two seconds and, if a hit occurs, record requests are made using the associated SIDs or FBI numbers. Data are automatically retrieved from the appropriate repositories, including state repositories, and forwarded to the requesting agency. As of December 2005, 48 states were participating in III.[2]

2. III Standards

In order for the exchange of criminal history record information to occur, standards for the submission of fingerprints and records had to be set. The FBI, in cooperation with the state record repositories and the law enforcement users of the information, developed certain standards that record contributors must meet to ensure the accuracy, completeness, currency, integrity, and security of the criminal history information maintained in the III. The states are audited by the FBI for compliance with these standards.

3. Fingerprint-Supported Records

Each criminal history record indexed in the III is created through the submission of fingerprint images to IAFIS. The III-participating states establish and update records within III through the submission of first and subsequent fingerprint images of arrested subjects. The fingerprints and the criminal history records indexed in the III are kept in an FBI Privacy Act system of records named the Fingerprint Identification Record System (FIRS).

The requirement of 10 rolled fingerprints from the record subject for submission and acceptance of the information in the III allows for the later positive identification of the person to his or her record. It also allows for the comparison of the fingerprints of record subjects with latent fingerprint impressions obtained from crime scenes for possible leads in criminal investigations. While criminal records in the III can be accessed either via name-based searches or fingerprint-based searches, as explained below, name-based searches are limited to searches conducted for criminal justice purposes.

4. The National Fingerprint File and Record Decentralization

Once records are entered into the III, the III-participating states provide requested criminal history records when an electronic inquiry for a state-maintained record is processed by the III system. States participating in the III's National Fingerprint File (NFF) submit only the first arrest fingerprint images on a subject to establish a pointer record within the III. Any subsequent activity related to the person whose fingerprints have been placed in the NFF, such as disposition reports, expungements, or subsequent arrests, are maintained solely at the state level by the NFF participating state. This is in lieu of having the state forward all of its records to the FBI for retention and dissemination from the FBI's centralized repository. Within the NFF, the FBI need only maintain the fingerprints on a person's first arrest. All subsequent criminal history information concerning the person about that arrest and any subsequent arrests are maintained at the state level and disseminated by that state, rather than the FBI. This record management approach avoids the redundancy of the state keeping records at the state level and also having to update its records at the FBI level. The NFF also has the advantage of allowing a state to share all records that it has on a subject in response to a national record search, some of which have never been submitted to or accepted by the FBI. In other words, full participation in the NFF program would enable a national fingerprint check to respond with the records held at the state level by all 50 states.

The National Crime Prevention and Privacy Compact[3] requires the FBI to participate in the NFF. As of January 2006, eight states are participating in the NFF,[4] and the FBI is working with additional states that intend to participate in the NFF. Certain states, however, have indicated that they do not intend to become NFF participants, primarily because, by doing so, they would have to agree to disseminate some of their records for employment and licensing purposes in response to queries from other states when they are not authorized to disseminate the records for those purposes to users in their state under their own state law.

5. Limited Completeness of III Records

Contrary to common perception, the FBI's III system is not a complete national database of all criminal history records in the United States. Many state records, whether from law enforcement agencies or courts, are not included or have not been updated. For example, not all the state criminal history records or associated fingerprints meet the standards for inclusion in the III. Because of inconsistent state reporting requirements, some criminal history records involve offenses that are not submitted to the FBI. Other records that were submitted to the FBI do not have fingerprints of sufficient quality to be entered into the system. Moreover, many criminal history records may contain information regarding an arrest, but are missing the disposition of that arrest. Currently, only 50 percent of III arrest records have final dispositions. The records of more recent arrests, however, have a higher rate of completeness. Nevertheless, the III, while far from complete, is the most comprehensive single source of criminal history information in the United States, and provides users, at a minimum, with a pointer system that assists in discovering more complete information on a person's involvement with the criminal justice system.

6. The National Criminal History Records Improvement Program

The National Criminal History Improvement Program (NCHIP), administered by the Department of Justice's Bureau of Justice Statistics (BJS), is designed to improve the nation's public safety by enhancing the quality, completeness, and accessibility of the nation's criminal history and sex offender record systems. NCHIP is part of the Department's overall effort to help ensure that states have the capability to compile accurate and complete criminal record information and that the criminal records systems designed are compatible with FBI standards and practices. Through cooperative agreements with the states, BJS provides NCHIP funding to facilitate their participation in the FBI's NICS, a system designed under the permanent provisions of the Brady Handgun Violence Prevention Act[5] as a means for determining whether prospective firearms transferees are prohibited from receiving or possessing a firearm under the 1968 Gun Control Act, as amended. NCHIP provides funding to improve the quality of states' criminal history records and increase the number of complete records that will be immediately available to all states through the FBI's III. The III is the primary system through which the FBI accesses state-held data for background checks of firearm purchasers. NCHIP awards totaled $465 million between 1995 and 2005, and the states have spent approximately $30 million in matching funds since the matching requirement was imposed in 2000. NCHIP allows states:

- to develop and enhance automated adult and juvenile criminal history record systems, including arrest and disposition reporting;
- to implement and upgrade their AFIS systems, which must be compatible with the FBI's IAFIS;
- to establish programs and systems to facilitate full participation in the III and the FBI's NICS;

- to support court-based criminal justice systems that report dispositions to the state repositories and the FBI and are compatible with other criminal justice systems;
- to support the development of accurate and complete state sex offender identification and registration systems that interface with the FBI's Sex Offender Registry; and
- to identify, classify, collect, and maintain records of protection orders, warrants, arrests, and convictions of persons violating protection orders to protect victims of stalking and domestic violence.

NCHIP accomplishments include:

- Accessibility of records: From among the estimated 71 million criminal records in the U.S., about 9 out of 10 are now automated and 3 out of 4 of these are accessible for a firearms check. Over the last decade, increases in the number of records available for a background check has increased at twice the rate of increase in the number of records held by repositories.
- III participation: All but two states are now III participants, which entails compliance with rigorous FBI standards. Over the last 10 years, the number of States participating in III has roughly doubled.
- Automating fingerprints: Nearly all states are now participating in IAFIS, dramatically reducing the time required to conduct fingerprint-based checks and to match latents from crime scenes.
- NICS Checks: The annual total of between 8 and 9 million presale firearms checks are by and large conducted instantly or within the parameters of state law, and the number of records available to the system on firearms disabilities other than a prior felony conviction, such as protection orders, misdemeanor crimes of domestic violence, and records of mental illness, is growing rapidly.
- Domestic violence records and protection orders: Two new NCIC files, protection orders and registered sex offenders, now have nearly one million records and 400,000 records, respectively, available for background checks.

Despite the tremendous progress made toward criminal record improvements since 1995, significant shortcomings in record completeness remain, most significantly the fact that approximately one half of III arrest records are missing dispositions. More also needs to be done to obtain full participation in the NCIC Protection Order File and the flagging of protection orders that prohibit firearm purchases.

D. Non-Criminal Justice Purpose Checks of the III

The FBI-maintained criminal history records kept in the III can be accessed for a number of purposes. The principal searches are those conducted in support of the administration of criminal justice and those conducted for non-criminal justice purposes. The term "administration of criminal justice" is defined in the applicable regulation to include activities relating to the detection, apprehension, detention, pretrial release, post-trial release, prosecution, adjudication, correctional supervision, or rehabilitation of accused persons or criminal offenders.[6] Checks in connection with employment by a law enforcement agency are also considered a criminal justice purpose. The term "non-criminal justice purposes" is defined by the National Crime Prevention and Privacy Compact (discussed below) as uses of criminal history records for purposes authorized by federal or state law other than purposes relating to criminal justice activities, including employment suitability, licensing determinations, immigration and naturalization matters, and national security clearances.[7]

1. The Authority for Non-Criminal Justice Checks

Most of the non-criminal justice checks using FBI-maintained criminal history records are done under the authority of Pub. L. 92-544, a federal law originally passed in 1972, that allows for the sharing of FBI-maintained criminal history information for licensing and employment background checks by state or local governmental agencies. These statutes generally require background checks in certain areas that the state has sought to regulate, such as individuals employed as civil servants, day care, school, or nursing home workers, taxi drivers, private security guards, or members of regulated professions. The results of these checks are supplied to public agencies that apply suitability criteria established by those agencies or under state law. There currently are approximately 1,200 state statutes that are approved by the Attorney General under Pub. L. 92-544. In addition, the National Child Protection Act (NCPA)[8] and the Volunteers for Children Act (VCA)[9] allow state governmental agencies without requiring a state statute to conduct background checks and suitability reviews of employees or volunteers of entities providing services to children, the elderly, and disabled persons.

In addition to qualified state statutes authorizing access to FBI-maintained criminal history information, there are federal statutes that authorize access or require background checks for certain industries. These laws seek to promote public safety and national security by either authorizing access to a check by certain industries or affirmatively regulating an industry or activity by requiring background checks and risk assessments by government agencies. They include authority for discretionary checks by federally insured or chartered banking institutions,[10] the nursing home industry, the securities industry, public housing authorities, and nuclear facilities. Since the terrorist attacks of September 11, 2001, Congress has also required criminal history background checks and security screening in a number of contexts with an eye toward preventing terrorism, including checks on persons seeking employment as airport screeners or unescorted access to certain areas at airports, hazardous materials endorsements on their commercial drivers licenses, access to restricted biological agents and toxins, access to nuclear facilities and port facilities, or visas and passports. federal law also requires background checks and screening of aliens seeking entry or exit from the United States or flight school training within the United States. A list is provided at Appendix 1 of the federal laws authorizing access to FBI-maintained criminal history information for certain industries or purposes.

2. The Freedom of Information and Privacy Acts

Criminal history record information maintained by the FBI is protected by the federal Privacy Act.[11] As such, its disclosure is prohibited absent consent from the individual who is the subject of the information or a statutory exception authorizing disclosure. The Privacy Act allows individuals to request and obtain copies of information concerning themselves from federal agencies. The federal Freedom of Information Act (FOIA)[12] allows an individual to consent to the disclosure to third parties of information about the individual from federal agencies. This includes access to an individual's criminal history record maintained by the FBI. There are no restrictions regarding the purpose of a FOIA request and, therefore, an individual could make such a request for his or her FBI criminal record and either provide it to an employer or specify that the record be sent directly to an employer. This has not, however, been a widely used means for employers to obtain criminal history information about applicants or employees. Widespread use of FOIA as a means for criminal screening would raise privacy concerns and undermine employment discrimination policies, since the records furnished in response to a FOIA request may not be complete or up to date and are not screened in any way (*see infra* discussion at pages 94-111, Explanations of Privacy Protection and Screening Standards Recommendations). This potential means of access for criminal history record screening purposes shows, however, that current federal law does permit individuals to obtain and use criminal history record information about themselves from the FBI for employment suitability purposes.

3. The Growth of Non-Criminal Justice Checks

The use of FBI-maintained criminal history records in background checks for licensing, employment, and volunteer activities has grown in recent years. In addition to the majority of non- criminal justice checks which are conducted under approved state statutes, in the few years since the terrorist attacks against the United States on September 11, 2001, there have been several federal laws relating to homeland security that also require the checking of FBI-maintained CHRI in connection with risk assessments performed by federal agencies. As a result, the FBI has seen an increase of the number of checks that it processes for such non-criminal justice purposes over the past 4 years. The FBI processed approximately 9.8 million civil fingerprint-based background checks in FY 2005, while processing approximately 6.8 million such checks in FY 2001.[13]

This does not mean, however, that FBI criminal history record checks are widely available. As noted above, under current law, expanding access to FBI-maintained criminal history records for particular employment and licensing purposes generally requires the enactment of a state or federal statute. This requirement has resulted in wide disparity in the access provided for these purposes within particular industries and across the 50 states. While uniform nationwide access is available to a few industries authorized access directly through the FBI pursuant to federal statute, such as the banking, securities, and nuclear industries, other industries are only able to get FBI checks done in states where a Pub. L. 92-544 statute has been passed. We also note that the VCA's amendment to the NCPA, allowing state to perform NCPA checks of FBI data without passing a Pub. L. 92-544 statute, did not have the intended effect of broadening the availability of NCPA checks. This suggests that the participation of states in making such checks available includes issues not just of authority but also of resources.

4. Fees

The FBI and the states charge fees for processing fingerprint-based background checks that they conduct for non-criminal justice purposes. The FBI's authority for charging its fees is found in Public Law 101-515. That law allows the FBI to include a surcharge, currently set at $6.00 per check, to support the automation and improvement of its record system. The FBI's current fees (including the surcharge), depending on the user and form of payment, range from $16 to $24. A detailed breakdown of FBI fees is set forth in Appendix 2. State fees for civil fingerprint checks can vary widely, ranging from $5 to $75, with the average state fee being $20.

5. Record Response Times

The FBI has prioritized its responses to fingerprint checks, depending on whether they have a criminal justice or a non-criminal justice purpose. The FBI performance goal for a criminal justice check is a response within 2 hours, while non-criminal justice checks should receive a response within 24 hours, provided the fingerprints are submitted electronically. When fingerprints are submitted electronically, the FBI's response is generally much quicker than these time frames. The paper submission of fingerprints, however, substantially slows the process for completing a check, even if they are later digitally scanned, as they typically involve first transmitting the prints through the mail.

State response times to a non-criminal justice fingerprint check vary widely, from 1 to 42 days, depending largely on whether the fingerprints are collected on paper and submitted by mail or collected and submitted electronically.

6. Searching Records with Flat Fingerprints

The fingerprints associated with criminal history records that populate the III database must be 10 rolled fingerprints. As of June 2005, the fingerprints submitted for civil checks used to determine if a match exists within the III database (a "one-to-many" search) may be 10 flat, or "slap," fingerprints. The use of flat fingerprints for matching is expected to greatly reduce the cost and inconvenience of capturing fingerprints for non-criminal justice purposes. This is because the devices for capturing flat prints are not as expensive and do not require a fingerprint technician to grasp the person's fingers, as is currently necessary for rolled fingerprints. The use of flat prints instead of rolled prints does not affect the FBI's fingerprint process or costs.

7. Current Procedures for Conducting FBI Non-Criminal Justice Checks

The following tasks are typically considered the core components of the FBI non-criminal justice background check process:

- Organization enrollment
- Fingerprint capture and submission
- State background check of state-held records
- National background check of FBI-maintained records in the III
- Error resolution
- Record review and analysis
- Suitability determination
- Notification
- Appeals
- Billing

The process for conducting civil background checks varies from state to state. To avoid a full, one-to-many fingerprint search of the database when not necessary, some states conduct a name- based search using the personal information contained on the fingerprint card. If the search results in a match, the state makes a one-to-one comparison of the subject's fingerprints to the applicant's fingerprints to determine if the individuals are identical. Other states conduct a name-based search and a fingerprint-based search. If either search results in an identification, the state retrieves the national criminal history record using the III. If the search does not result in an identification, the state forwards the fingerprints to the FBI for a search of IAFIS. Additionally, some states conduct auxiliary name searches on fingerprint submissions in attempts to locate other criminal record information, such as outstanding warrants, sex offenders, and protection orders.

When using the III to retrieve a copy of a previously identified criminal history record, the state uses the subject's FBI number or SID. The use of III for licensing and employment purposes is limited to one agency in the state, usually the state repository. Currently, only 29 states and the District of Columbia respond to a III request for licensing and employment purposes. If the state does not respond, then the FBI CJIS Division provides a copy of the subject's criminal history.

Some states forward all fingerprints to the FBI regardless of the state criminal history background checks results. Fingerprints may be submitted to the FBI by mail or electronically. If the state mails the fingerprint cards to the FBI, the cards must be converted to an electronic format prior to processing. Currently, 6 states and two territories submit less than 10 percent, 9 states submit between 10 and 49 percent, and 8 states and the District of Columbia submit between 50 and 89 percent of their fingerprint cards for civil background checks electronically, while 27 states submit 90 percent or more of their civil fingerprint checks electronically. *See* Table 1.

In FY 2005, the CJIS Division received approximately 83 percent of all civil fingerprint submissions (federal and non-federal) and 74 percent of state civil fingerprint submissions electronically. *See* Table 2.

Table 1. Percentage of Checks Electronically Submitted by Jurisdictions

Percentage of checks Electronically submitted	Number of States
Less than 10%	6 states and 2 territories
10 - 49%	9 states
50 - 89%	8 states and D.C.
> 90%	27 states
Total	**53**

Table 2. Percentages of Federal and State Civil Fingerprint Submissions in FY 2005 Received by the FBI Electronically

	Number (FY 2005)	Number of States
Federal Submissions	3,836,531	96%
State Submissions	5,976,900	74%
Other (Territories and Canada)	2,430	16%
Total	**9,815,861**	**83%**

E. The National Crime Prevention and Privacy Compact

After 15 years of cooperative effort by the state repositories and the FBI, the National Crime Prevention and Privacy Compact[14] was signed into law October 10, 1998, establishing a legal structure by which states can exchange criminal records for non-criminal justice purposes according to the laws of the requesting state and provide reciprocity among the states to share records without charging each other for the information. The Compact became effective April 28, 1999, after Montana and Georgia became the first two states to ratify it. Currently, in addition to the United States, 27 states are members of the Compact.[15] Three states and one territory have pending legislation to ratify the Compact and become members.[16] In addition, eight states and two territories that have not yet become members by passing statutes ratifying the Compact have nonetheless signed Memoranda of Understanding (MOU) indicating that they agree to follow the rules established under the Compact governing the exchange of criminal history information for non-criminal justice purposes.[17] There are 15 states and one territory in which there is no known action to adopt the Compact.[18]

1. The Compact Council

The Compact established a 15-member Council whose members are appointed by the Attorney General and represent state and federal agencies that are providers and users of FBI-maintained criminal history record information for non-criminal justice purposes.[19] The Council promulgates rules and procedures governing the exchange and use of III criminal history records for non-criminal justice purposes. Since the Council was established in 2000, it has promulgated several such rules, which are found at 28 CFR Chapter IX. The rules address matters such as the timing of fingerprint submissions, requirements for repositories to screen records for civil purposes, sanctions for rule violations, and standards that allow authorized users to outsource administrative functions relating to civil background checks. The Council holds public meetings twice a year at which it discusses and votes on business. It also publishes its proposed rules in the Federal Register for public comment. The Council's activities are administratively supported by the FBI.

2. The Compact's Fingerprint Requirement

Article V(a) of the Compact requires that all searches conducted of the III for non-criminal justice purposes must be based on fingerprints or other approved forms of positive identification. Even before the passage of the Compact, fingerprints in support of civil checks was a general policy requirement imposed by the FBI for approving state statutes under Pub. L. 92-544. There is a strong rationale for imposing this requirement for checks made for non-criminal justice purposes, while allowing name-based checks of the III for criminal justice purposes when fingerprints cannot be collected or when time is of the essence. Name-based searches of the III present the risk of false positives (incorrectly associating a record with a person with a common name) and false negatives (missing a record associated with a person because he or she provided false identifying information).

This risk was confirmed in the 1998 Report of the National Task Force to the U.S. Attorney General on Interstate Identification Index Name Check Efficacy. The study was based upon data developed by parallel name checks (using names and other personal identifiers submitted by the applicant, such as date of birth, sex, race, and state of residence) and fingerprint checks on approximately 93,000 applicants for public housing in the State of Florida. The Task Force found that based on name checks alone, 5.5 percent of the checks produced false positives and 11.7 percent resulted in false negatives. These results would have translated into large absolute numbers of false positives (380,000) and false negatives (807,000) if the 6.9 million civil applicant background checks processed by the FBI in 1997 had been processed by III name checks alone. It is significant to note that the individuals involved in the study who provided the incorrect name data did so knowing that they were also providing fingerprints.[20]

Typically, name-based searches of the III are allowed when fingerprints cannot be collected and when time is of the essence. For example, during a roadside stop, the law enforcement official cannot take the fingerprints of the driver, but for his or her safety, the official needs to know whether the driver has a criminal record. The performance of a name-based search of criminal records for criminal justice purposes balances the need for expediency with the added risk that the name-based search will result in a false positive or false negative match. Moreover, if a name-based search results in a hit warranting an arrest, the arrest generally is followed up by the collection of fingerprints, allowing for positive identification. In contrast, non-criminal justice checks, such as those performed for employment, licensing, or the granting of governmental benefits, do not present the same risk or urgency. As a result, a policy decision was made, now embodied in the Compact, that non-criminal justice checks of the III should be performed based only on the positive identification provided by fingerprints, significantly reducing the twin risks of false positives and false negatives.[21]

3. The Compact's Requirement for State Background Checks

The role of the states in civil background checks was also strengthened with the passage of the Compact. Article V, Record Request Procedures, of the National Crime Prevention and Privacy Compact provides in pertinent part:

> (b) Submission of State Requests. – Each request for a criminal history record check utilizing the national indices made under any approved State statute shall be submitted through that State's criminal history record repository. A State criminal history record repository shall process an interstate request for noncriminal justice purposes through the national indices only if such request is transmitted through another State criminal history record repository or the FBI.
>
> (c) Submission of Federal Requests. – Each request for criminal history record checks utilizing the national indices made under Federal authority shall be submitted through the FBI or, if the State criminal history record repository consents to process fingerprint submissions, through the criminal history record repository in the State in which such request originated. Direct access to the National Identification Index by entities other than the FBI and State criminal history records repositories shall not be permitted for noncriminal justice purposes.

The rationale for requiring the submission of fingerprints through a state record repository is based on the fact that the FBI-maintained records are not as complete as the records maintained at the state level. As noted above, the states have records of offenses that have not been forwarded to the FBI because of the FBI's previous limitation of III submissions to records relating to misdemeanors or felonies. Some state records may also have not been accepted by the FBI because the supporting fingerprints do not meet III quality standards. The FBI's records also have limited information about dispositions of arrest records, with only 50 percent of the arrest records in the III containing the final disposition. State records, in contrast, have a higher percentage of dispositions, ranging between 70 and 80 percent. The inclusion of a check of state records therefore is regarded as a way of obtaining a more complete search, as well as a way of obtaining more complete and accurate records.

It should be noted, however, that membership in the Compact does not have an impact on the completeness of a state's records. Rather, because Compact membership entails an agreement to disseminate records for non-criminal justice purposes according to the laws of the requesting state, Compact membership generally results in a more complete dissemination of the records the member state does have when responding to requests originating from other states.

F. Fingerprint Capture and Processing Infrastructure

Fingerprint capture involves collecting the applicant's personal descriptors and fingerprints for use in performing the criminal history background check. This information may be captured by a state or local law enforcement agency, a private vendor, or the employer or volunteer organization. Prior to fingerprinting the applicant, the capturing entity usually requires the applicant to provide proof of identity in the form of a photo ID, such as a driver's license or state identification card. The capturing entity then collects the applicant's personal information (e.g., name, sex, race, and date of birth) by printing or typing the information on a fingerprint card, typing the information into a database, or capturing the information electronically from a magnetic strip. The applicant's fingerprints may be captured on a fingerprint card using the ink and roll method or on a live-scan device. After the entity takes the applicant's fingerprints, it returns the fingerprint card to the applicant or forwards the card to the central repository. If the entity took the applicant's fingerprints on a live-scan device, the fingerprint images may be printed on a fingerprint card or forwarded electronically to the central repository. To ensure data integrity, some states require local law enforcement agencies to forward the fingerprint submissions to the central repository rather than returning the fingerprint cards to the applicant.

1. Infrastructure Findings of the FBI's Survey Supporting the PROTECT Act's Feasibility Study Requirement

On April 30, 2003, the President signed into law the PROTECT Act (the Prosecutorial Remedies and Other Tools to end the Exploitation of Children Today Act of 2003), Pub. L. 108-21. Section 108 of the PROTECT Act required the Attorney General to establish a pilot program for volunteer organizations providing services to children to obtain background checks on prospective volunteers.[22] The purpose of the pilot program, implemented by the FBI on July 29, 2003, is to evaluate methods for conducting such checks. In conjunction with the pilot, the Act also required the Attorney General to conduct a feasibility study that was to provide recommendations, taking into account the available state and federal infrastructure for fingerprint checks, on how a national system could be established for making these checks available to organizations that provide care to children, the elderly, or the disabled.[23]

In support of the feasibility study required by the PROTECT Act, and to obtain information regarding the current state of civil fingerprint processing at the state and local level, the CJIS Division surveyed each state in 2003 to determine its procedures for processing civil background checks, including the primary method for fingerprint capture and submission to the FBI. Agencies may submit civil fingerprints to the CJIS Division either electronically or by mail. The 2003 survey revealed:

- Twenty-six states and the District of Columbia accept paper fingerprint cards only for civil background checks. Twenty-two states accept paper fingerprint cards and electronic live-scan fingerprint submissions. One state and one territory do not process civil fingerprint submissions. *See* Table 3.
- Fourteen states and the District of Columbia indicated they submit civil fingerprint background checks to the FBI by mail. Thirty states only submit civil fingerprint-based background checks electronically. Five states submit civil fingerprint-based background checks either by mail or electronically, depending on the method of submission to the state. *See* Table 3.

The CJIS survey also asked each state to consider how many fingerprint submissions it currently processes and estimate the number of additional fingerprint submissions it could potentially process each year.

- Twelve states and the District of Columbia indicated that they are operating at full capacity; fifteen states said that their additional system capacity is between 2,000 and 100,000 fingerprints, five states claimed their additional capacity is over 100,000 fingerprint submissions, and one state described its additional capacity as "significant." Five states indicated their additional system capacity is unlimited if provided additional space and resources. Three states indicated their capacity is unknown, and 10 states did not answer the question. *See* Table 4.

Additionally, the CJIS survey asked each state to estimate the time it takes to process a civil applicant submission from the date of receipt from the contributor to the date of submission to the FBI. The results of the survey revealed that the time for a state to process a fingerprint-based criminal background check, from date of receipt to date submitted to the FBI, ranged from 1 day to 42 days, with the average response time dependant on the method of submission:

Table 3. Form of Acceptance and Transmission of Fingerprints by States

Form Accepted	Number of States	Form Transmitted	Number of States
Fingerprint Cards Only	27	Mail Only	14
Electronic and Cards	22	Electronically Only	30
		Mail or Electronically	5
Total	**49**		**49**

Table 4. Annual Additional Fingerprint Processing Capacity of the States

Annual Additional Capacity	Number of States
2,000 - 100,000	15
More than 100,000	5
Significant/Unlimited	4
Sub-total	**24**
None (Operating at Capacity)	12
No Report (Unknown)	13
Total	**49**

- The average processing time for a card-scan submission is 10 days.
- The average processing time for a live-scan submission is 1 day.
- The average processing time for a manual mail-in submission is 5 days.

The survey also developed information on the procedures states use to capture fingerprints, some of which do not rely on the historical model of sending employment and licensing applicants to police stations to submit rolled-only, ink and paper fingerprints. Examples of new approaches are described below:

- Tennessee, Florida, and New Jersey have established privately-operated fingerprint centers throughout the state to provide live-scan fingerprint services to applicants and volunteers.
- The Ohio Bureau of Criminal Identification and Investigation (BCI&I) WebCheck program enables participating agencies to request state criminal background checks by submitting applicant fingerprint images and other data over the Internet using a single-digit fingerprint scanner (to capture each index finger and each thumb) and a magnetic reader strip. The BCI&I has also implemented a pilot program, in cooperation with the FBI, that enables participating agencies to submit state and national criminal history background applicant checks using 10-finger flat impressions instead of 10-fingerprint rolled impressions. Flat impressions are captured by laying one or more fingers on a live-scan surface and capturing the fingerprint image without rolling the fingers across the surface. Flat fingerprints are easier to capture than rolled fingerprints and do not require an experienced individual to assist in capturing the fingerprints.
- The California Department of Justice (DOJ) has installed 1,585 live-scan devices throughout the state. Of these, 638 are dedicated for use by government agencies to facilitate applicant processing. Applicants are provided with a "Request for Live-scan Service" form to complete and a list of nearby live-scan locations where they can be fingerprinted. At these locations, a trained operator enters the information from the "Request for Live-scan Service" form into the live-scan terminal and initiates the live-scan fingerprinting process. After successful electronic capture of the fingerprint images and the accompanying data, the information is electronically transmitted to the California DOJ.[24]

- The Vermont Department of Public Safety (DPS) has partnered with a law enforcement agency in each county to create a center that provides fingerprint identification services to the public.[25] The Vermont DPS and the FBI provided each service center with specialized training in the capture and review of fingerprints. Half of the service centers are equipped with live-scan devices.

2. The Increasing Use of Outsourcing in Support of Non-Criminal Justice Checks

More states are beginning to use private vendors to perform some of the functions relating to the processing of civil criminal history record checks. The Compact Council published, on December 15, 2005, a final rule authorizing the outsourcing of administrative functions in support of non-criminal justice background checks, along with the Security and Management Control Outsourcing Standards that vendors must meet in order to perform these functions on behalf of authorized recipients doing the outsourcing.[26] In June 2005, the FBI published a Request for Information from private vendors on the creation of channeling agents to act for the FBI in the collection and submission of fingerprints for non-criminal justice checks.[27] The FBI's request for proposal for the selection of channelers pursuant to the Compact Council's Outsourcing Rule and Standards was published in Federal Business Opportunities on June 21, 2006.[28]

The DHS's Transportation Security Administration (TSA) has made use of non-criminal justice outsourcing for fingerprint collection in its implementation of the threat assessment program for commercial truck drivers with HAZMAT endorsements required by the USA PATRIOT Act. Under its final rule implementing this program, TSA required states to declare whether they would use a TSA agent or conduct the collection of fingerprints, applicant information, and fees themselves.[29] Thirty-four states have initially opted to use the TSA agent.

3. The Increasing Use of Live-scan Technology

The use of live-scan technology to capture fingerprints for non-criminal justice purposes is growing rapidly as states and client agencies find funds to acquire live-scan devices. Many states allow private vendors to contract with authorized agencies to electronically capture and submit fingerprints to the state repository. For example, California currently has 237 privately-operated fingerprint centers throughout the state that provide fingerprinting services to applicants and volunteers. Live-scan technology enables agencies to submit fingerprints to the state repository electronically and reduces the time it takes to obtain a background check.

The Tennessee Bureau of Investigation (TBI) has established privately-operated fingerprinting centers throughout the state to provide live-scan fingerprinting services to applicants and volunteers. Applicants and volunteers must call a toll-free number to schedule an appointment to be fingerprinted at one of the centers. The operator asks the applicant for certain identifying information, the reason the applicant is being fingerprinted, and the agency or organization for whom they are being fingerprinted. At the time of the appointment, the applicant must provide a photo identification and pay the appropriate fee, unless other payment arrangements have been made by the organization. After taking the applicant's personal descriptors and fingerprints, the fingerprinting center forwards them electronically to the TBI.

4. The Further Development of Live-scan Technology

The Department of Justice, in conjunction with the Department of Homeland Security (DHS), the Department of State (DOS), and the Department of Defense (DOD), is pursuing a research and development initiative for an imaging device to capture 10-rolled fingerprints in less than 15 seconds and both palms in less than one minute. This would be a substantial change from the three to five minutes that it currently takes a fingerprint technician to capture 10 fingerprints, one-by-one. The program will remove the need for a technician to grasp the individual's fingers, allow multiple rolled fingers to be captured simultaneously, and advance new technologies to collect finger and palm images from excessively dry or wet fingers. In September 2005, the National Institute of Justice announced the award of more than $7 million dollars in grants by the Department of Justice and the Department of Homeland Security to four grantees who are taking different technological approaches to developing such a device. The initiative's aim is to develop devices that are not only fast and user-friendly but also more affordable and portable. Prototype devices should be available in 18 to 24 months from project initiation.

In addition, in September 2005, the DHS, DOJ, DOS, DOD Biometric Fusion Center (DOD/BFC), and National Institute of Standards and Technology (NIST), jointly defined an urgent, near-term demand for faster, smaller, more mobile, 10 fingerprint slap capture devices to meet critical needs for civil background checks. These departments organized a unified User Group in order to develop standardized requirements and to co-sponsor a "Challenge to Industry" as a first step towards meeting these common needs. The User Group issued its "Challenge to Industry" through a formal request for information to develop by the fall of 2006 a small device (no larger than 6" x 6"x 6" in size) that will capture 10 flat fingerprint images in less than 15 seconds.[30] Such devices are needed to support the DHS and State Department's plans to capture 10 flat fingerprints when enrolling individuals in the U.S. VISIT program it has established under federal law to track the entry and exit of alien visitors into and from the United States as well as a number of other needs in each of the participating agencies. Each of the interested contractors had the opportunity to attend an open briefing on the needs and requirements in the document, to submit a five-page paper describing their current capabilities and approach to meeting the requirements, and to participate in a one-on-one debrief following a review of their submission. Based on the responses, the industry appears prepared to respond to the near-term requirements of the User Group (one vendor has already obtained FBI certification of a device now on the market that meets the size requirements and is reportedly able to capture 10 flat fingerprints in 10 seconds) and can meet additional more challenging application requirements in the coming years with additional applied research and development.

Based on these efforts, it appears that biometric capture technology is on the verge of significant improvements in speed, convenience, affordability, and reliability. Such improvements should make fingerprint capture less obtrusive and stigmatizing for persons when they are having a civil criminal history record check performed or are otherwise involved in identity management efforts. Further research and development will produce devices that meet additional mobility and cost requirements in time for technology refresh of devices currently being put into use.

G. Examples of Programs Implementing Criminal History Check Authorities

1. Outsourcing to Channeling Agencies – The American Bankers Association

The majority of civil applicant fingerprints submitted to the FBI are collected by state or local law enforcement agencies because such agencies are recognized by the FBI as qualified to collect both paper and digital fingerprints. In addition, many such agencies have invested in digital fingerprint scanning technology and have electronic connections to the FBI for submitting the prints. Private agencies, however, also can and do serve as channeling agents to the FBI for fingerprint submissions.

The American Bankers Association (ABA) is a good example of the functions that private companies can perform in the collection and submission of fingerprints. The ABA channels fingerprint submissions to the FBI for many financial institutions submitting under Pub. L. 92-544. The ABA is not authorized to receive criminal history records on behalf of submitting agencies and does not perform fitness or suitability determinations. Instead, the company serves as a "channeling agency" for authorized financial institutions to submit fingerprints, thus providing a solution for consolidating billing and connectivity issues that can arise from a large, diversified pool of customers.

The ABA has established an infrastructure to support the channeling of fingerprint requests to the FBI. Authorized financial institutions establish fingerprint programs within their organizations and perform fingerprinting and fitness determinations as a routine part of their background screening processes. Authorized financial institutions registered with the ABA may choose to submit hard- copy paper fingerprints or to establish connectivity with the ABA for the transmission of electronic 10-print submissions. Although institutions may request a formal contract, the ABA only requires user agreements for the establishment of electronic connectivity.

Financial institutions complete manual paper fingerprint cards and forward them with direct payment to the ABA. The ABA then mails the submissions to the FBI for IAFIS processing. Financial institutions can forward electronic submissions to the ABA via three methods: dial-up connection, virtual private network, or compact disc. All electronic submissions must be sent to the ABA in IAFIS Electronic Fingerprint Transmission Specification format. Both paper and electronic fingerprint submissions forwarded to the ABA must include a valid Originating Agency Identifier (ORI), which the CJIS Division previously assigned to the financial institution for reference of agency location information.

The ABA submits fingerprints to the FBI by mail or electronically via the CJIS Wide Area Network (WAN). Electronic submissions received by the ABA are forwarded to the FBI with minimal interaction. The ABA also serves as a card scanning service for a limited number of paper fingerprint submissions, converting them to electronic format, thus providing expeditious processing to financial institutions that lack electronic submission capabilities. The ABA randomly scans and enters the data of approximately 300 manual fingerprint cards per day, sending the remaining manual submissions to the FBI by mail. Upon completion of processing, the FBI returns all responses to electronic and paper fingerprint card submissions to the requesting financial institution in hard-copy paper format via metered mail.

The ABA currently charges $3 per fingerprint submission in addition to the FBI's fee of $22. Financial institutions that submit fingerprints electronically must provide payment to the ABA at the time of service by credit card or draw-down account. Direct payments in the form of business checks, which are processed by a separate financial institution contracted out by the ABA, must accompany paper submissions. The CJIS Division bills the ABA for services provided to the banking institutions on a monthly basis by generating a user fee billing report. This report sorts transactions and fees by banking institution, providing the ABA with an organized listing of submissions channeled for each institution for a one-month period.

Some states also have expressed an interest in outsourcing non-criminal justice functions to a private vendor. The Compact Council's outsourcing rule and standards should accelerate the use of private vendors by the states to perform functions in the civil background check process similar to those performed for the FBI and the banking industry by the ABA.

2. State Dissemination of FBI Records to the User – Florida's VECHS Program Implementing the National Child Protection Act

In 1999, the Florida Department of Law Enforcement (FDLE) established the Volunteer & Employee Criminal History System (VECHS) program to perform criminal history background checks on employees and volunteers who work with children, the elderly, or individuals with disabilities. The VECHS program was established under Florida law [31] as part of Florida's effort to implement the NCPA/VCA. Florida had long allowed such organizations to obtain Florida state criminal history records under Florida's open records law. By establishing controls on access and use of the information, Florida created a system that includes the dissemination of FBI-maintained criminal history records to qualified organizations under the authority of the NCPA/VCA.

Generally, any organization (public, private, profit, or non-profit) that resides in Florida and provides care to children, the elderly, or the disabled is qualified to participate in the VECHS program. The VECHS program is not available to organizations that are required to obtain criminal history record checks on their employees and/or volunteers under other statutory provisions. If the statute, however, only requires or allows the organization to obtain state and national checks on specific types of employees and volunteers, then the VECHS may be able to process requests for state and national checks on the organization's other employees or volunteers who are not otherwise covered by the statute providing background check authority.

In order to become a qualified entity, an organization must submit an application to FDLE explaining what functions the organization performs that serve children, the elderly, or disabled persons and sign a VECHS User Agreement with the FDLE that delineates the terms and conditions under which criminal history background checks shall be performed.

The qualified entity must obtain a completed and signed Waiver Agreement and Statement from every current or prospective employee and volunteer who is subject to a criminal history background check. The Waiver Agreement and Statement must include the following information: (a) the person's name, address, and date of birth that appear on a valid identification document (as defined at 18 U.S.C. Section 1028); (b) an indication of whether the person has or has not been convicted of a crime, and, if convicted, a description of the crime and the particulars of the conviction; (c) a notification that the individual may request a criminal history background check on the person as authorized by section 943.0542, F.S. and the NCPA/VCA; (d) a notification to the person of his or her rights; and (e) a notification that, prior to the completion of the background check, the qualified entity may choose to deny him or her unsupervised access to a person to whom the qualified entity provides care. The qualified entity must retain the original of every Waiver Agreement and Statement and provide the FDLE with a copy.

To request a criminal history background check, a qualified entity must submit a completed fingerprint card and a copy of a completed Waiver Agreement and Statement for each employee and volunteer. The FDLE will perform a state background check and forward the fingerprints to the FBI for a national background check.[32] Once the background check process is completed, the FDLE will provide the qualified entity with the following:

- An indication that the person has no criminal history (i.e., no serious arrests in state or national databases), if applicable.
- The criminal history record that shows arrests and/or convictions for Florida and other states, if any.
- Notification of any warrants or domestic violence injunctions that the person may have.

Neither the NCPA/VCA nor the Florida law governing the VECHS program defines specific criteria to use during the evaluation of an employee or volunteer. The suitability or screening criteria may already be covered under other statutory provisions. If so, the qualified entity must comply with all of the required screening criteria under these laws. If not, the qualified entity is free to select its own screening criteria and use its own judgment in determining who is suitable to work in the organization.

In the event an individual's criminal history record contains an arrest without a disposition, the qualified entity is responsible for retrieving disposition data. The data may be obtained by contacting the appropriate Clerk of Court or, in the case of an out of state arrest, the State Identification Bureau.

The qualified entity must notify the current or prospective employee or volunteer of his or her right to obtain a copy of the criminal history records, if any, contained in the report. Every person who is subject to a background check is entitled to challenge the accuracy and completeness of any information contained in any such report, and to obtain a determination as to the validity of such challenge before a final determination regarding the person is made by the qualified entity reviewing the criminal history information.

The qualified entity must use criminal history information acquired under this process only to determine the suitability of current and/or prospective employees and/or volunteers to work with children, the elderly, or disabled persons. Florida law permits the qualified entity to share criminal history information with another qualified entity if authorized by the individual on the Waiver Agreement and Statement. The qualified entity must keep a written record of the dissemination. This exchange of information helps to reduce the cost of performing multiple criminal history background checks on the same person.

The qualified entity must keep all criminal history records acquired in a secure file, safe, or other security devices, such as locked file cabinet in an access-controlled area, and shall take such further steps as are necessary to insure that the records are accessible only to those employees who have been trained in their proper use and handling and have a need to examine such records. The qualified entity is also required to keep all records necessary to facilitate a security audit by FDLE and to cooperate in record audits as FDLE or other authorities may deem necessary. Examples of records that may be subject to audit are: criminal history records; notification that an individual has no criminal history; internal policies and procedures articulating the provisions for physical security; records of all disseminations of criminal history information; and a current executed User Agreement with FDLE.

H. Growing Private Sector Interest in Access to FBI- Maintained Criminal History Information

While the number of authorized non-criminal justice checks of FBI-maintained criminal history information has grown over the years, most of the private sector does not have authority to access that information. Yet many private employers are very interested in access to FBI criminal records to help evaluate the risk of hiring or placing someone with a criminal record in particular positions.

1. Due Diligence and Recidivism Concerns

Employers and organizations are, for example, subject to potential liability under negligent hiring doctrines if they fail to exercise due diligence in determining whether an applicant has a criminal history that is relevant to the responsibilities of a job and determining whether placement of the individual in the position would create an unreasonable risk to other employees or the public.[33] In addition to addressing this litigation risk, employers want to assess the risks to their assets and reputations posed by placing persons with criminal histories in certain positions. Employers cite the well-recognized problem of recidivism[34] as support for the reasonableness of doing criminal background checks for certain jobs to protect public safety. To meet these business needs, employers can and frequently do ask applicants whether they have a criminal history. Such employers and organizations want access to criminal history records to determine whether applicants are answering the question about their criminal history truthfully and completely. They believe that having access to good sources of criminal history information is the only way this interest in performing due diligence can be served.

2. Existing Sources for Private Sector Access to Criminal History Information

Most private employers pursue, through sources other than the FBI, criminal history information on applicants and employees for purposes of employment screening and risk assessment. Employers can perform these background checks themselves, but often use third-party background screening companies (which, as discussed below, are regulated as consumer reporting agencies under the Fair Credit Reporting Act (FCRA)) to conduct the criminal history search. For example, employers, or credit reporting agencies acting on their behalf, will conduct name-based searches of courthouses at the county level in an applicant's past places of residence. These searches have the advantage of obtaining the most recent records at the courthouse. They have the draw-back, however, of possibly missing a criminal record that an applicant may have in a jurisdiction other than his or her residence, such as a record in an adjacent jurisdiction. They may also miss a record if the applicant failed to disclose a past residence in a jurisdiction where he was involved with the criminal justice system.

Name-based searches may also be made by private employers of commercial databases, which are also regulated under the FCRA, that aggregate criminal history information from multiple states. The information in such databases is obtained from, for example, county courthouses, state correctional facilities, and state criminal history record repositories. These state agencies provide, for a fee, criminal history records in bulk to the commercial data compiler. Such commercial databases offer the advantage to users who cannot access FBI data of broadening the scope of records searched beyond the jurisdictions of past residence. Such commercial databases are not truly national in scope, however, since not all states make their public records available to such compilers and not all courts or agencies in particular states make the information available to the compilers. The commercial databases may also lack data currency because they are updated with additions or corrections to records from the source only periodically.

In some states, private employers can also conduct, for a fee, name-based searches over the Internet of state repository records, as can any member of the public.[35] A survey of the states by SEARCH in April 2006 showed that, of 34 states responding, 25 states make name-only searches of criminal history information available to the public, either through a website maintained by a repository (15 states) or the state court system (10 states), as well as variously through in-person, telephone, or mail-in queries. The average fee for a state repository website name-check query is approximately $13.00. The same survey showed that 25 of 34 responding states allowed fingerprint- based record searches of their records by the public, with 19 states providing such access to the general public at an average fee of $25.00. The 25 states allowing fingerprint checks also variously made them available for all employment, designated employment, volunteers, or housing purposes.

All of the name-based checks have the drawback of possible false positives and false negatives. As noted by some of the commenters, name-based searches of commercial criminal history databases have in some cases resulted in the incorrect association of an individual with a different person's criminal record.

3. Reasons for Private Sector Interest in FBI Criminal History Data

There are two primary reasons that employers and other entities placing persons in positions of trust have a strong interest in obtaining an FBI check. First, the FBI has fingerprint-based records from all states and territories. Thus, an FBI check can identify a record on a person created in a state other than those where the person has lived or where the employment is located. This is important in a mobile society where many persons may have lived in or traveled to more than one state. Second, the FBI records are based on the positive identification of a person to a record through fingerprints. This significantly reduces the twin risks posed by name-based searches of false negatives (missing a record in the database because of false or inaccurate name search criteria) and false positives (incorrectly identifying a person to a record because of similarity in name and other search criteria being used).

Because of the limitations on the convenience, completeness, and reliability of the information on criminal history records from local public agencies and commercial databases, private employers and entities placing persons in positions of trust have expressed strong interest in authority to access FBI-maintained criminal information for purposes of employment suitability screening. For example, during the 2003 Congressional hearings on the re-authorization of the FCRA, concerns about the inadequacy of existing criminal history data available to most employers and an interest in access to FBI criminal history records was expressed by the Labor Policy Association (LPA), an association of senior human resource directors of more than 200 leading employers that do business in the United States, collectively employ over 19 million people worldwide, and over 12 percent of the U.S. private sector work force.[36] The statement noted:

> Thus, [because of limited access to FBI criminal history information] for the vast majority of positions, employers and consumer reporting agencies they use are left with a jurisdiction-by-jurisdiction search, which is not always sufficient. For example, in a recent case in Virginia, a former employee of the Williams School was convicted of videotaping nude boys from the school. The school only ran a background check in Virginia, which, of course, failed to turn up a previous conviction for child molestation in North Carolina.[37]

Testimony by a representative of the private security guard industry in support of the Private Security Officer Employment Authorization Act of 2004, which appears in section 6402 of the Intelligence Reform and Terrorism Prevention Act of 2004, also emphasized the problems caused by limited access to FBI-maintained criminal history records, even when a state fingerprint check is available:

> In my home state of Illinois, a review of January 2004 applicants showed that the FBI criminal history check eliminated four times as many applicants as the Illinois State Police check for crimes committed within the State. Put another way, Illinois State Police clear 87% of all applicants while the FBI check clears only 64% – a 23% difference. . . . As the statistics cited above demonstrate, the State Police clear a large percentage of applicants (87%). However, if [the applicant] had committed a crime in neighboring states, such as Wisconsin, Iowa, Missouri or Indiana, the State Police check alone would not uncover those crimes. Nor would the check reveal whether the applicant had disclosed his/her true identity. Only a nationwide fingerprint search would ascertain the true identity and background of an applicant.[38]

Testimony at the same hearing noted the holes left in employers' risk assessment safety net left by the piecemeal approach to access to criminal history information for employment screening:

> By selectively identifying careers that will allow employers to seek access to public records containing criminal histories, we effectively preclude other equally deserving employers the same access. It is time for Congress to act and to do so with the recognition that it is in the best interest not only of business, but of our nation to craft a statute that allows for inclusive rather than exclusive access to these public records. . . .
>
> Employers are permitted by law to inquire if an applicant has ever been convicted of a crime, permitted to require a formal statement on a written application to this effect, permitted to deny employment if the listed criminal conviction bears a relationship with the job offered, and to discharge the employee if the written statement is false. But with selected exceptions, most employers have no way of determining whether the statement the employee has given is the truth, or is a lie. . . .
>
> The fact is that our laws in this area are a disjointed hodgepodge of narrow provisions, enacted one at a time on a position-by-position basis, with no attempt to rationalize why one sensitive position is subject to a criminal history check while a different, comparably sensitive position is not. At best, legislatures across this country are constantly closing the barn door after the horse has escaped: enacting legislation in the aftermath of a tragedy, limited to the singular situation that tragedy involved. . . .

> The issue here is not whether someone with a criminal past should be disqualified from all employment. Those who have been punished for breaking our laws should have every reasonable opportunity to progress toward a normal, law-abiding life. But when there is a relationship between the employee's criminal history and the job, employers should be allowed to make informed decisions.[39]

Private sector interest is also demonstrated in part by the many bills introduced in Congress each year to authorize access to FBI criminal history records for background checks in particular industries or settings. Those seeking such access generally do not want to have to obtain authority in each state through separate state statutes under Pub. L. 92-544. Frequently, private employers would also like to have the access to the records themselves, giving them the ability to make their own determinations about the suitability of a candidate. In other words, they would like the information without necessarily having the state or federal government regulating their activities by establishing inflexible suitability criteria and making suitability determinations about their employees.

I. Regulation of Criminal History Record Information Reported by Consumer Reporting Agencies

1. Consumer Reporting Agencies

Consumer reporting agencies are organizations that, for a fee or on a cooperative, non-profit basis, assemble or evaluate personally identifiable information obtained from third parties that bears on a consumer's credit worthiness, character, reputation, personal characteristics, or mode of living. The records that they collect and report include criminal history information, such as arrest and conviction information. Such information is generally obtained by consumer reporting agencies by going to original public sources of the information, such as courts, or from databases that have aggregated the information obtained in bulk, for a fee, from public agency sources.

2. The Fair Credit Reporting Act

The Fair Credit Reporting Act of 1970[40] (FCRA), as amended, regulates the use of criminal history record information by consumer reporting agencies for employment, credit, and certain other purposes. Under the FCRA, a consumer reporting agency may only provide a consumer report to a party when the agency has reason to make a credit determination, an employment determination, an insurance underwriting determination, or otherwise in connection with a legitimate business need in a transaction involving the consumer or pursuant to written instructions of the consumer. If a customer makes a false representation about its purpose for requesting the consumer report, there are penalties under the FCRA, although the penalties do not always deter persons from lying about their eligibility to receive a consumer report.

The FCRA includes safeguards relating to fair information practices and consumer privacy, including notice to consumers; consent, including opportunities to opt-in/opt-out of certain uses of the information; accuracy, relevance, and timeliness standards; confidentiality and use requirements; security requirements; consumer access and correction rights; content restrictions; and remedies, including administrative sanctions and private rights of action. The FCRA provides consumers with the following privacy rights:

- A consumer reporting agency that furnishes a consumer report for employment purposes containing public record information, including criminal history records, which is "likely to have an adverse effect upon a consumer's ability to obtain employment," must either provide the consumer with notice at the same time that the information is reported to the potential employer or "must maintain strict procedures" to ensure that the information is complete and up-to-date.[41]
- A consumer must be notified when information is used to take an action against him or her, such as the denial of employment. In such cases, the party denying the benefit must provide the consumer with information on how to contact the consumer reporting agency that provided the information.
- Consumer-reporting agencies must, upon request within any 12-month period, provide a consumer, without charge, with a copy of that consumer's file, as well as a listing of everyone who has requested it recently.
- Consumers are permitted to request a correction of information they believe to be inaccurate. The consumer reporting agency must investigate unless the dispute is frivolous. The consumer reporting agency must also send a written investigation report to the individual and a copy of the revised report, if changes were made. The consumer may also request that corrected reports be sent to recent recipients. If the dispute is not resolved in the consumer's favor, the consumer has the option of including a brief statement to the consumer's file, typically for distribution with future reports.
- Consumer reporting agencies must remove or correct unverified or inaccurate information from its files, typically within 30 days after the consumer disputes the information.
- In most cases, a consumer reporting agency may not report negative information that is more than seven years old (including arrest information in connection with positions where the salary is less than $75,000), or more than 10 years old for bankruptcies. A 1998 amendment to the FCRA permits inclusion of criminal conviction information without time limitations.
- Consumers can sue for violations or seek assistance from the Federal Trade Commission and other federal agencies responsible for the enforcement of the FCRA.

3. State Consumer Reporting Laws

In addition to the FCRA, there are state consumer reporting laws, such as in California, that are more restrictive than the FCRA in the criminal history information that may be reported by a consumer reporting agency. Such state laws may also have more stringent procedures for confirming the accuracy and currency of the information before it is reported to a user.

As explained in a recently published SEARCH report[42] on the commercial sale of criminal history record information:

Approximately one-half of the States have their own fair credit reporting statutes. Many include provisions similar to those in the Federal FCRA, but some are even more restrictive. State law is fully preempted with respect to certain specified FCRA provisions.[43] In the case of FCRA provisions that are not fully preempted, State law is preempted only to the extent that it is inconsistent with the FCRA.[44] This has been interpreted to mean that State law is preempted only when compliance with an inconsistent State law would result in violation of the FCRA.[45] In general, there is no inconsistency if the State law is more protective of consumers.[46] Many state fair credit reporting laws impose obligations on credit reporting agencies and end-users that differ from those imposed by the FCRA without being inconsistent, making compliance with all applicable laws complicated. For example, in at least four States (California, Montana, Nevada, and New Mexico), a consumer reporting agency may not report convictions that are more than 7 years old, even though the FCRA imposes such a time restriction only on the reporting of arrests, and has no limitation on convictions.[47] Also, unlike the FCRA, California, New Mexico, and New York preclude the reporting of arrests that do not result in convictions.[48]

In addition, some States set the employee's expected salary level, which governs the applicability of time limits on reporting arrest information, at levels differing from that set in the FCRA. Whereas the FCRA imposes the 7-year restriction on the reporting of arrest information if the expected salary is less than $75,000, the laws in at least four States impose the 7-year restriction on the reporting of arrests only if the employee or applicant is expected to earn less than $20,000 per year.[49] Unlike the FCRA, these States also impose the 7-year restriction limit on the reporting of convictions if the expected salary is less than $20,000. Some State laws also impose disclosure requirements that differ from those in the FCRA. For example, in some States, employers must provide employees/applicants with a copy of the consumer report they obtain for employment purposes, regardless of whether they take any adverse action in reliance upon the report.[50] In addition, California requires end-users, including prospective or current employers, to disclose to the consumer any information gathered on the person's character, general reputation, personal characteristics, or mode of living, including criminal justice information, even if the employer itself obtains the information directly without using a consumer reporting agency.[51]

J. Fair Information Practices

The requirements of the FCRA reflect what are widely known as fair information practices (FIPs). The FIPs are privacy design principles that have been developed since the 1960s to address privacy concerns that arose with the advent of new information technologies allowing for broader and easier dissemination and access to personal information.[52] To address these privacy concerns, the FIPs encourage appropriate restrictions on the collection, use, and disclosure of personal information. The FIPs principles were originally developed in the commercial context, but have also been relied upon by government agencies in developing policies for the management of their information about individuals. The goals of the FIPs include (1) limiting the collection and use of personal information to the purposes intended; (2) ensuring data accuracy; (3) establishing security safeguards; (4) being open about the practices and policies regarding personal data; (5) allowing individuals reasonable access and opportunity to correct errors in their personal data; and (6) identifying persons accountable for adhering to these principles. Those involved in the management of justice information systems also look to FIPs principles and goals in designing privacy practices for their information systems.[53]

K. The Regulation of the use of Criminal History Record Information by Employers

In addition to the FCRA and state consumer laws, federal and state laws prohibiting employment discrimination also may be applicable to the criminal background check process. These laws are intended to prevent the unfair exclusion of qualified persons with criminal backgrounds from employment opportunities. To address these issues and facilitate employment by ex-offenders, a number of states have enacted statutes and the federal government has issued guidance to prohibit employment discrimination against qualified people with criminal histories.

1. Title VII and Equal Employment Opportunity Commission Guidance

The relevant federal anti-discrimination laws include Title VII of the Civil Rights Act of 1964 (Title VII),[54] which prohibits employment discrimination based on race, color, religion, sex, or national origin, and the Civil Rights Act of 1991, which, among other things, provides monetary damages in cases of intentional employment discrimination. The U.S. Equal Employment Opportunity Commission (EEOC) enforces these laws and also provides oversight and coordination of all federal equal employment opportunity regulations, practices, and policies.

To assist employers in compliance with Title VII, the EEOC has provided policy guidance to employers on the general factors that should be considered in determining the relevance of convictions in hiring decisions.[55] The factors include: (1) the nature and gravity of the offense or offenses for which the individual was convicted; (2) the time that has passed since the conviction and/or completion of the sentence; and (3) the nature of the job held or sought. The EEOC guidance also provides that lifetime disqualifications from suitability should be applied only in special circumstances relating to either the nature of the position, the nature of the offense, or both. The EEOC also has issued guidance to employers on how arrests that have not resulted in a conviction should be considered in employment decisions, requiring additional inquiry about the arrest context and an opportunity for the applicant to explain.[56]

2. State Equal Employment Opportunity Laws

A number of states have also passed equal employment opportunity laws aimed at regulating the use of criminal history information by employers in order to provide a second chance to ex- offenders to obtain gainful employment. Currently, 14 states have statutes that prohibit discrimination against people with criminal records in employment and licensing. Nine of the states set out standards governing public employers' consideration of applicant's criminal records.[57] Five of the states require individualized assessments of criminal records by both public and private employers.[58] These laws do not require employers to hire people with criminal histories. Rather, like the EEOC guidance, they instruct employers on how to consider the relevance of the criminal history when the applicant is otherwise qualified for the position. Most statutes provide guidance by requiring that employers only consider convictions that are somehow related to the work expected in the position to be filled. The statutes may instruct employers to consider other factors, including the applicant's age at the time of his crime, the time that has elapsed since his arrest or conviction, and whether he has been rehabilitated. An applicant can demonstrate that he has been rehabilitated by showing that he has remained crime-free for an extended period of time, completed a sentence of incarceration or community supervision, completed a drug or alcohol rehabilitation program, etc.

Some state laws also prohibit or limit employers from inquiring about an applicant's arrest or conviction records, regardless of whether the employer's inquiry would in fact lead to unlawful employment discrimination. The above-cited Labor Policy Association testimony noted that while the EEOC's guidance allow employers to use arrest records under certain circumstances, many states' equal employment opportunity laws prohibit employers from seeking information on arrest records and some prohibit inquiries into certain convictions:[59]

> Indeed, at least 11 states have statutes explicitly prohibiting arrest records inquiries,[60] and as many as 13 states have issued administrative guidance declaring the inquiries unlawful.[61] Other states only permit arrest inquiries if the employer shows business necessity.[62]
>
> Some states even limit inquiries into conviction records, such as the District of Columbia (as noted), Hawaii, and Ohio, which prohibit inquiries into certain convictions more than 10 years old.[63] Other states impose different limitations. For example, Hawaii only permits inquiries into convictions for candidates who have been extended a conditional offer of employment.[64] California prohibits requests into marijuana convictions over two years old.[65] Similarly, Massachusetts prohibits inquiries into certain first-time convictions – including misdemeanor drunkenness, simple assault, and speeding.[66] Some states only allow inquiring into convictions when the employer proves it is job related.[67]

3. Private Sector Application of Regulatory Requirements

The EEOC guidelines regarding the relevance of a criminal record to an employment decision are reflected in a protocol published in 2003 by the Labor Policy Association, titled "LPA Background Check Protocol (2003)."[68] With respect to employer use of criminal justice information in employment decisions, the protocol states:

> Where not limited by state law, the employer may consider criminal convictions in making employment decisions. The mere presence of a criminal conviction should not necessarily render an individual ineligible for employment. In making such decisions, the employer should consider:
>
> - the circumstances and type of crime;
> - the length of time since the crime occurred;
> - whether the applicant has completed a rehabilitation program; and
> - the applicant's employment record since the commission of the crime.
>
> Determination of whether a crime is relevant to the job will generally be made on a case by case basis. For example, a conviction for driving while intoxicated may result in an adverse employment determination with regard to a delivery truck driver but not necessarily an accounting clerk. Similarly, a conviction for passing bad checks may

disqualify the latter but not the former. For positions where integrity is particularly essential to the job, such as a corporate ethics officer, any conviction may be relevant.

However, there are certain crimes that will be relevant to the vast majority of jobs, including crimes of violence, such as murder, rape, robbery, and assault; and dishonesty crimes, such as theft, burglary, embezzlement, forgery, and fraud. Un-rehabilitated drug-related crimes may also be considered, consistent with the Americans with Disabilities Act, for all positions. Multiple convictions, involving any combination of crimes, will also be considered as a factor in determining whether employment is appropriate.[69]

The LPA Background Check Protocol also provides guidance to employers on consideration of arrest records and pending criminal matters in employment decisions.[70]

At the same time, we note that the existence of this protocol does not necessarily mean that all businesses or employers are aware of or apply the EEOC guidelines on relevance when conducting a criminal screen.

L. Prisoner Reentry Considerations

According to information developed by the Bureau of Justice Statistics (BJS), approximately 630,000 individuals are released from state and federal prisons every year. In 2001, BJS estimated that over 64 million people in the United States had a state rap sheet, or about 30 percent of the Nation's adult population. Ex-offenders who are gainfully employed are generally considered to be much less likely to commit another crime. Successful reentry of ex-offenders into the workforce therefore has significant public safety benefits.

In his 2004 State of the Union Address, President Bush recognized the need to help ex-offenders reintegrate into society:

> Tonight I ask you to consider another group of Americans in need of help. This year some 600,000 inmates will be released into society. We know from long experience that if they can't find work, or a home, or help, they are much more likely to commit crime and return to prison. So tonight, I propose a four-year, $300 million prisoner re- entry initiative to expand job training and placement services, to provide transitional housing, and to help newly released prisoners get mentoring, including from faith-based groups. America is the land of second chance, and when the gates of the prison open, the path ahead should lead to a better life.[71]

These concerns about reentry need to be considered when deciding how to structure increased private sector access to FBI-maintained criminal history information.

IV. Commercial Databases

Section 6403(d) of the Act calls upon the Department to consider 15 factors when developing and making recommendations for improving, standardizing, and consolidating the existing statutory authorization, programs, and procedures for the conduct of criminal history record checks for non- criminal justice purposes. Before developing its recommendations, the Department solicited public comment on these factors. In addition, as called for in the Act, the Department consulted with representatives of state criminal history record repositories, the National Crime Prevention and Privacy Compact Council, and representatives of private industry and labor, as well as other interested members of the public.

The first two factors, relating to commercial databases of criminal history information, did not result in any specific recommendation and are discussed in this part of the report. The remaining 13 congressionally-defined factors are discussed, as relevant, in the Department's explanation in Part VI of its recommendations set forth in Part V.

A. Commercial Databases As a Supplement to Fingerprint Checks of FBI Data

One of the factors in Section 6403(d) seeks input on "the effectiveness and efficiency of utilizing commercially available databases as a supplement to IAFIS criminal history information checks." This refers to the databases compiled by private companies that are used for background checks. These commercial databases provide financial, employment, and residential information, as well as court, corrections and sex offender record information. They generally are considered consumer reporting agencies, since the information they collect is for resale, and are therefore regulated under the FCRA. These businesses gather criminal history records from various states, obtaining the information from county courthouses, state correctional facilities, and state criminal history record repositories. The amount of criminal history information available to these businesses can vary greatly by state. Some states and counties may not provide such information to these commercial enterprises, or may limit the use of such data by the business.

Because authority under federal or state law for background checks accessing FBI-maintained records is not available for most employment purposes, these commercial checks provide private employers a means of satisfying organizational due diligence requirements for screening an applicant's criminal history. The cost of a commercial database check also may be much less than fingerprint checks of the FBI and state repositories, depending on the scope of the search.

Unlike non-criminal justice background checks of the III, however, searches of commercially available databases are name-based and do not provide for positive identification through a fingerprint comparison. As a consequence, the matching of individuals to a record is not as reliable as a fingerprint check. In addition, in many instances the criminal history record information available through a commercial check is not as comprehensive as a III check because many states do not make criminal history records available to commercial database compilers. Also, states that do contribute criminal history records to commercial databases may not do so on a regular basis. As a result, some information in commercial databases may not be as timely as the information available through the III. These concerns were expressed by some commenters, who, despite the requirements and protections of the FCRA, cited cases where individuals have had problems with the accuracy and completeness of the records being disseminated from commercial databases. For example, several commenters were concerned about expungements that were not respected by commercial database reports that still note a conviction along with the fact that it was expunged.

Commercial databases, however, do offer other information that may not be available through state and FBI repository checks. A search of commercially available databases may reveal charges and dispositions not reported to the state or national repositories. As noted above, records relating to some offenses are not reported to the FBI, and some records submitted by a state to the III may be rejected because the fingerprints do not meet the standards set by the FBI. Even state repositories may not have records on less serious offenses that have not been forwarded by local law enforcement agencies. Some of this information may be available through certain commercial databases. Moreover, commercial databases may contain information on past residences, licenses, financial history, or other information in addition to criminal history background that may be pertinent in employment screening. More importantly for many organizations, the fee charged for commercial background checks can be much less than the fee charged for a governmental fingerprint-based check. Some consumer reporting agencies that provide professional background screening services also may do confirmatory checks of information at county courthouses to ensure that the information is complete and up-to-date.

The fact is that there is no single source of complete information about criminal history records. A check of both public and commercial databases and of primary sources of criminal history information such as county courthouses would, perhaps, provide the most complete and up- to-date information. Professional background screening companies can provide the clear value of a confirmatory search of the currency of records at a county courthouse. Even so, we do not have enough information to accurately assess the value added by a commercial criminal history database check as a supplement to fingerprint checks of the IAFIS and state repositories. In addition, there is not enough information to judge the accuracy and completeness of name-based commercial criminal history databases as compared to the fingerprint databases of the repositories. Many comments we received cited examples of commercial database checks incorrectly reporting an individual as having a criminal record or wrongly reporting convictions that were sealed or expunged. There certainly is not enough information to conclude that a check of commercial databases should be combined with the results of an IAFIS check. Employers, as well as consumer reporting agencies that may be handling the checks on their behalf, frequently decide, however, depending on the cost, to check both public and private sources in order to have the most complete check possible. Employers also can decide on their own whether they need to check the commercial databases for non-criminal information, such as financial history information.

We do think, however, that more information should be developed on the differences between the criminal history record results obtained by a name check of commercial databases and a fingerprint check of the FBI and state repositories. The Department's Bureau of Justice Statistics (BJS), in cooperation with SEARCH and several commercial database companies, is planning such a study, the results of which may be available in 2007. Information from this study should provide the Department and Congress and, most importantly, the users of criminal history information, a better basis to evaluate the cost/benefit of commercial criminal history database checks both as compared to and as a supplement to fingerprint checks of IAFIS and state repository records.

B. Security Concerns Created by Commercial Databases

Section 6403(d) also requested input on "security concerns created by the existence of these commercially available databases concerning their ability to provide sensitive information that is not readily available about law enforcement or intelligence officials, including their identity, residence, and financial status." This factor raises issues about the balance between the public's right to access public records and the risks posed when personal information regarding law enforcement officials is provided to the public. The FCRA regulates the use and dissemination of commercial data to ensure the fair and accurate reporting, and respect for an individual's right to privacy, but does not contain specific protections for law enforcement officials.

The FBI, the United States Marshals Service (USMS), the Drug Enforcement Administration (DEA), and the Bureau of Alcohol, Tobacco, Firearms, and Explosives (ATF) expressed concerns regarding the availability of personal information through commercial databases. First, sensitive information pertaining to law enforcement officials may be obtained from commercial databases. For example, an individual seeking retribution against a government official may obtain information such as the official's residential address, telephone number, or business address. The USMS has reason to believe that individuals seeking retribution do use these databases to gather personal information. This belief is based on their experience investigating inappropriate communications directed at judges, U.S. Attorneys, and other government officials.

The DEA also shares the concern that these databases will be used by individuals seeking retribution against government officials, or to compromise ongoing criminal investigations. There is existing potential for retribution against DEA personnel and Task Force Officers given their mission of enforcement of the Controlled Substances Act and related laws. There are already websites that operate with the apparent intent of exposing law enforcement officials (i.e., the website www.whosarat.com). The DEA believes that some information posted on that website comes from commercial databases.

In addition, over the last year, companies that house personal data had numerous instances where they lost significant amounts of data, whether through the theft or loss of data tapes, the "hacking" of information from the database, or individuals obtaining information under false pretenses. These data losses make many individuals vulnerable to identity theft.

Recently, a DEA Special Agent in Charge was named on a website utilized by marijuana legalization advocates, listing not only his name and position but also a residential address which is believed to have come from a commercial database. Shortly after this posting, a third party citizen, sharing the same last name as the DEA Agent received harassing telephone calls. The caller insisted he was calling the agent's residence, instead of an uninvolved, innocent citizen. In addition, the DEA Deputy Administrator recently learned that personal information about her was available in commercial databases, including a satellite photo of her residence. DEA foresees not only a potential for harassment and threats against our personnel but also against innocent third parties.

Second, commercial databases can be used in attempts to determine the true identity of undercover agents or to gather information on false identities agents may have assumed during their investigations. This information can compromise the safety of the agent. In addition, the information could have an adverse impact on other individuals working with law enforcement officials, including individuals in witness security programs. ATF is aware that outlaw motorcycle organizations often conduct sophisticated background investigations of new members, including instances involving undercover ATF Special Agents who were attempting to infiltrate the organization.

The commercial databases also could be used in attempts to determine the true identity of undercover agents or gather information on established false identities used to infiltrate drug trafficking organizations. DEA Agents and Task Force Officers involved in drug investigations have been exposed on websites providing their identities and personal information. Such exposure through information gleaned from these databases could result in the compromise of the agent's safety and that of co-workers involved in investigations. This type of exposure not only endangers the law enforcement officers but their families as well. Major traffickers are already known to conduct surveillance of law enforcement officers and DEA facilities when they suspect someone of being law enforcement members, and commercial databases could assist them in identifying law enforcement officers. They would then be in a position to conduct surveillance of those identified and potentially compromise on-going investigations.

The Department's law enforcement components are taking steps to reduce the risk to law enforcement officials. For example, USMS personnel use any means available to restrict the public availability of personal information, including use of opt out provisions, requesting unpublished numbers and addresses, the use of fictitious names, etc. In addition, ATF has a program for the protection of its employees from threats and harm from third parties. The mission of the ATF's Security and Emergency Programs Division (SEPD) includes assessing and responding to threats against ATF employees and members of their immediate families. Within SEPD, the Operations Security Office (OPSEC) is the primary point of contact on all matters relating to threats against employees, employees' families, ATF facilities and operations, and it facilitates any actions necessary to respond to such threats. OPSEC is responsible for assessing the validity and risk presented by all such threats and recommends appropriate countermeasures. The program includes a significant training and educational component, and ATF employees are briefed on the vulnerabilities associated with the inadvertent or deliberate release of personal information to third parties.

The Department believes that the concerns raised by the law enforcement agencies should be addressed, but further consultation with the consumer data industry is needed before specific remedies are proposed. Feasible remedies are likely to involve the implementation of new internal policies by law enforcement agencies and the cooperation of the consumer data reporting industry. For example, possible remedies may involve limiting searches relating to specific undercover agents, restricting access to certain personal information upon the request of a law enforcement agency, requiring commercial providers to notify law enforcement agencies when such information is requested, or providing the law enforcement agency with the identity of the person requesting such information. In addition, Congress also may want to consider strengthening criminal penalties aimed at those who wrongly use the personal information of law enforcement personnel.

It is important to note that the risk posed to government officials can be similar to the risk faced by the public. For example, stalkers or identity thieves could use commercial databases to gather personal information about their intended victims. Any restrictions on the dissemination of such information would have to be very carefully crafted so as not to violate the First Amendment to the United States Constitution. In addition, the regulation of information regarding federal law enforcement officers could raise other constitutional issues. For example, if the information was being sought by, or on behalf of, a criminal defendant for purposes of preparing his or her defense, restrictions on his or her ability to receive the information might be found to violate the Fifth and/or Sixth Amendments. Nonetheless, we believe that carefully drafted laws can protect the safety of federal law enforcement officers and other persons at risk of retaliation and harassment, without violating rights protected by the Constitution.

V. Recommendations for Standardizing Non-Criminal Justice Access Authority

Based on consideration of the congressionally-defined factors, the public comments received, and consultation with the state record repositories, the Compact Council, and representatives from private industry and labor, the Department of Justice has developed recommendations on how the authorities, programs, and procedures for obtaining FBI-maintained criminal history record information for non-criminal justice purposes can be improved, standardized, and consolidated. The recommendations are grouped into ten areas that address the following basic questions:

A. Who should have access to FBI-maintained criminal history records for non-criminal justice purposes?
B. What should be the process for access?
C. What privacy protections should be provided to individuals who are subject to such criminal history record checks?
D. How should records be screened before being disseminated to the user?
E. What requirements should be imposed regarding the suitability criteria applied by users in order to promote fair use of the information?
F. What kind of infrastructure is needed to support such checks?
G. Who should pay the fees charged for the cost of access and the associated improvements to infrastructure?
H. How should requirements regarding access and use be enforced? I. What should be done about improving record quality?
J. What other steps can be taken to improve the fairness and quality of criminal history checks for non-criminal justice purposes?

The ten sets of recommendations are set forth together here in Part V. The background discussion of each set of recommendations, together with explanations of the specific recommendations, follows in Part VI. A discussion of the congressional factors is incorporated in the explanations, where relevant.

A. Access to Criminal History Records Recommendations

(1) Subject to conditions specified in federal law and Attorney General regulations, authority to request FBI-maintained criminal history records should be broadened, under the priorities set forth in Access to Criminal History Records Recommendation # 2 and as system capacity and resources allow, to cover:

(A) priority employers, and subsequently, if capacity allows, all employers, for use in decisions regarding an individual's employment suitability;
(B) entities placing individuals in non-employment positions of trust, such as persons having access to vulnerable populations, client residences, significant organizational assets, or sensitive information;
(C) any person or entity when the Attorney General determines such access promotes public safety or national security; and
(D) consumer reporting agencies or other third parties that:
(i) are acting on behalf of one of the above authorized users of FBI-maintained criminal history record information;
(ii) meet data security standards established by the Attorney General, including being certified through a public or private program approved by the Attorney General as being trained in applicable federal and state consumer reporting laws and in Attorney General standards relating to the secure handling of criminal history record information; and
(iii) are prohibited, with limited exceptions, from aggregating the criminal history information obtained through these fingerprint-based checks for resale.

(2) To account for the need to develop FBI system capacity to handle the increased number of background check requests under this new authority, whether handled through a participating state or directly through the FBI, the Attorney General should prioritize access as follows:
(A) giving first priority to critical infrastructure industries, regulated industries and professions, and the placement of persons in positions of trust working with vulnerable populations;
(B) allowing the expansion of access, at the Attorney General's discretion and only as system capacity allows, to all employers or entities that meet the conditions of access; and
(C) allowing the FBI to manage access under the new authority to avoid a reduction in the level of service available for criminal justice, national security, and other governmental uses of IAFIS; and

(3) States should continue to be able to authorize background checks using FBI-maintained criminal history records for specific categories of employment or licensing pursuant to Pub. L. 92-544.

B. Process for Record Access Recommendations

(1) Access to records in the FBI repository should, when possible, be through states that agree to participate in processing these checks and should include a check of state records.
(A) In order to participate, states must meet standards specified by the Attorney General, within parameters set by statute, for the scope of access and the methods and time frames for providing access and responses to these checks.

(2) Access to FBI-maintained criminal history records should be available to employers and entities under this authority through an FBI-administered process when access is unavailable through the state level because the state has not opted to provide such access.

(A) In establishing an FBI-administered process for record access to IAFIS records by employers and other authorized entities, the Attorney General should:

(i) seek to create an efficient means by which the check will include a search, confirmed with fingerprints, of as many state and federal criminal history records as possible, including the records in the state where the check is being sought;

(ii) establish a means by which state repositories can be compensated when appropriate for efforts that they make in support of FBI-processed check requests; and

(iii) establish a means by which improvements required to provide such access to employers and other entities will be paid for from a fee or other appropriate charge to the requestor.

(3) State criminal history record repositories and the FBI should be authorized to disseminate FBI-maintained criminal history records directly to authorized employers or entities and to consumer reporting agencies acting on their behalf, subject to screening and training requirements and other conditions for access and use of the information established by law and regulation.

(A) Access through the state and FBI-administered process should be facilitated through:

(i) consumer reporting agencies meeting requirements specified by the Attorney General; or

(ii) direct access by employers that meet criteria established by the Attorney General or state repositories aimed at limiting direct access by employers to a manageable number, including requirements for meeting a minimum volume threshold of checks and for the electronic submission of fingerprints.

(4) The submission of fingerprints should continue to be required for positively identifying records in the FBI criminal history record repository to a record subject when a check is made for non-criminal justice purposes.

(A) The fingerprint submissions for criminal history record checks under this new authority should:

(i) be collected exclusively through electronic, live-scan capture and transmission of an individual's fingerprints on systems that have been certified by the FBI and submitted in the FBI standard format; and

(ii) use, when reasonably available, electronic fingerprint capture technology that is fast and unobtrusive.

(5) A participating state or the FBI should be required to respond to an enrolled employer, entity, or consumer reporting agency within three business days of the submission of the fingerprints supporting the request for the criminal history record check.

C. Privacy Protection Recommendations

(1) Authorized employers and consumer reporting agencies seeking access should be required to enroll under the program and enter into agreements concerning conditions and requirements for access to FBI-maintained criminal history record information, including:

(A) certifying that the information obtained from the FBI and state record repositories will be used solely for purposes of determining an individual's suitability for employment or placement in a position of trust, or another authorized purpose; and

(B) agreeing to:

(i) follow procedures established by the Attorney General to ensure data security and the privacy of the records obtained pursuant to this authority; and

(ii) maintain relevant records and be subject to audits by the FBI or another entity from which it receives criminal history records, e.g., an enrolled consumer reporting agency or a participating state repository, for compliance with record handling requirements.

(2) The limitation on the use of FBI-maintained criminal history information obtained under this authority exclusively for employment or placement suitability should be expressed in the law creating the authority.

(3) The Attorney General should establish standards for adequate identification and verification:

(A) of employers and consumer reporting agencies seeking to enroll as qualified to request background checks pursuant to the new authority; and

(B) of individuals subject to the background check.

(4) Privacy protections should be made applicable to enrolled employers and consumer reporting agencies obtaining under the new authority FBI- maintained criminal history information from a record repository, including:

(A) on a document that consists solely of a consent and notice document and that satisfies the requirements of the Privacy Act:

(i) obtaining written consent by the individual to the fingerprint- based criminal history record check of the applicable government record repositories; and

(ii) providing notice to the individual of the following:

(a) the scope of the databases that will be searched based on the request;

(b) his or her rights relating to confidential access to and the opportunity to review and challenge a criminal history record returned by a fingerprint check before it is provided to the enrolled employer or entity or, if not so reviewed, before the employer takes any adverse action based on the information in the record; and

(c) the fact that information in the record returned from the check may only be re-disseminated by the user in accordance with conditions specified by the Attorney General;

(B) the right of the individual to review and challenge the accuracy of a criminal history record produced by the repository search:

(i) before the record is provided to the employer; or

(ii) before adverse action is taken, if the individual has not availed him- or herself of the right to see the record before it is provided to the employer.

(5) Participating state repositories and the FBI should establish a process by which prospective applicants with enrolled employers or entities can obtain fingerprint check results about themselves once during any twelve-month period, allowing for review and correction in advance of application, but in a way that prevents passing such information on to employers or others as official record check results.

(6) Participating state repositories and the FBI should establish a stream-lined, automated appeal process for applicants seeking to challenge a record's accuracy, without requiring a separate set of fingerprints and an additional fingerprint fee, and ensure that appeal information is provided to applicants when reviewing their records during the check process.

(7) Limits should be established governing the use, retention, and deletion of fingerprint submissions under this new authority:

(A) collected by enrolled users, or third party consumer reporting agencies acting on their behalf; and

(B) received by the FBI or a participating state repository, and channelers acting on their behalf.

D. Screening Standards Recommendations

(1) "No record" responses may be disseminated by a repository to an enrolled consumer reporting agency or a direct access employer or authorized entity.

(2) Searches that result in a "hit" on a record should be screened by the enrolled consumer reporting agency or, in the case of direct access employers, by the participating state repository or the FBI before the record is reported to an enrolled employer or entity.

(A) Such screening should include:

(i) a reasonable effort by the participating state repository or the FBI to find missing dispositions of arrest records before disseminating the record to an enrolled consumer reporting agency or a direct access employer or entity; and

(ii) screening in accordance with FCRA and applicable state law requirements in the state of employment that limit the dissemination to or use by employers of criminal history record information.

(B) Congress should consider providing that the screening requirements under the FCRA should not apply to the dissemination of records under this authority:

(i) of a record from the state of employment when the record can be disseminated by the state repository under applicable state law;

(ii) of a record when the law of the state of record origin would allow public access to the record and the law of the state of employment allows use of the record by employers for employment suitability determinations; and

(iii) of records relating to violent or sexual offenses to employers or entities that provide care, as that term is defined in section 5 of the National Child Protection Act, for children, the elderly, or individuals with disabilities.

(3) Records disseminated to a user under this new authority by a consumer reporting agency, the FBI, or a participating state repository should identify whether an offense is a felony, a misdemeanor, or some lesser violation under the law of the charging jurisdiction.

(4) Except as noted below, the screened record may be disseminated to an enrolled employer or entity by consumer reporting agencies, a participating state repository, or the FBI:

(A) when as part of the enrollment process, the employer presents a certificate that it has received training, through a public or private program (including programs administered by consumer reporting agencies enrolling employers) recognized by the Attorney General, in the reading and interpretation of criminal history record information;

(B) however, only enrolled consumer reporting agencies should disseminate the screened record to the user when the law of the state of employment requires that before the record is reported to an employer by a third party, the record must be confirmed as complete and up-to-date as reflected in the current status of the record at the agency from which it originates.

(5) All disseminations of records to users under this authority should include an appropriate disclaimer that the response may not necessarily contain all possible criminal record information about the individual, either because it has not been entered in the repository database or because the responses have been screened in accordance with the above limitations on dissemination.

(6) In reporting information to an enrolled employer or entity, an enrolled consumer reporting agency should clearly separate the fingerprint-based criminal history information from other information reported.

(7) The enrolling entity (e.g., a consumer reporting agency or an outsourced agent acting on behalf of a participating state repository or the FBI) should be required to establish a toll-free number and a web-site that enrolled users, entities, or consumer reporting agencies can use for assistance in interpreting criminal history records.

E. Suitability Criteria Recommendations

(1) Enrolled users seeking access to criminal history information under this new authority should certify that the information obtained will not be used in violation of any applicable federal or state equal employment opportunity law or regulation.

(2) Congress should consider whether guidance should be provided to employers on appropriate time limits that should be observed when applying criteria specifying disqualifying offenses and on providing an individual the opportunity to seek a waiver from the disqualification.

F. Supporting Infrastructure Recommendations

(1) Electronic, live-scan fingerprint submissions should be collected:

(A) at the place of business of an enrolled employer or entity or an enrolled consumer reporting agency acting on their behalf, or through an authorized channeling agent; or

(B) at service centers established by a participating state, either through a governmental agency or through outsourcing, that are:

(i) at a location other than a law enforcement agency; and

(ii) at least as convenient to access as places where state identification documents, such as driver's licenses, are obtained.

(2) An appropriate number of channeling agents should be established to receive the fingerprints from the large number of service centers and enrolled employers, entities, and consumer reporting agencies that will be collecting fingerprints.

(3) Additional capacity at both the FBI and state repositories must be developed to enable the processing of these newly authorized checks.

G. Fee Recommendations

(1) A new fee-funded business model should be developed to streamline the processing and funding of federal and state non-criminal justice criminal history background checks with the goal of:

(A) reducing the costs of the checks;

(B) establishing greater consistency in the state fees charged for such checks;

(C) providing states appropriate compensation for the support they give to checks processed by the FBI in circumstances where the state does not charge a fee because it is not handling the check; and

(D) ensuring that all state repositories and the FBI have the funding necessary to support the technology required for improved data quality and efficient processing of check requests.

(2) The question of who should bear the cost of checks under this new authority should generally be decided between the employer and the individual, although Congress may wish to consider requiring that the cost of fingerprint checks for lower paying jobs be borne by the employer.

H. Enforcement Recommendations

(1) Penalties should be established for the unauthorized access to or misuse of records of government record repositories under this new authority, including:

(A) Criminal penalties for persons who knowingly:

(i) obtain criminal history record information through this authority under false pretenses; or

(ii) use criminal history record information obtained through this authority for a purpose not authorized under this authority; and

(B) Civil penalties, including monetary penalties and discontinued access, for violations of required security and privacy procedures resulting in the disclosure of information obtained under this authority to unauthorized persons.

(2) The Attorney General should be authorized to establish an administrative process, to be administered by the FBI and participating state repositories, for sanctions, including termination of access, against enrolled employers, entities, and consumer reporting agencies for violations of requirements regarding access to and security of the information, including failure to observe the required procedural rights of individuals.

I. Record Improvement Recommendations

(1) There should be a renewed federal effort to improve the accuracy, completeness, and integration of the national criminal history records system.

(2) Federal funds should be targeted at reaching national standards established by the Attorney General relating to disposition reporting and record completeness, including declinations to prosecute and expungement and sealing orders, so that there is uniformity in improvements by repositories nationwide.

(3) Accelerate the standardization of rap sheets to make them more readily understood by non-criminal justice purpose users.

(4) Congress should consider requiring state repositories to establish procedures meeting national standards to remedy the adverse affects on individuals who are wrongly associated with criminal records because they are victims of identity theft.

(5) Establish a national accreditation process for criminal history record repositories, much the same way that crime laboratories are accredited, to better ensure data quality by measuring repository performance against national standards.

(6) Seek to integrate the repository systems in ways that will allow a single fingerprint check to return all information on an individual maintained by all states rather than the current process for obtaining such complete information of requiring separate fingerprint checks of 50 stove-piped record systems.

(7) Develop a realistic assessment of the cost to achieve these record improvement goals.

(8) Develop a comprehensive ongoing data collection and research program by BJS that includes:

(A) study of the extent of automation and accessibility of state and FBI criminal records;

(B) data collection documenting the accuracy, completeness, and timeliness of state and FBI criminal history records;

(C) assessment of the completeness and timeliness of local agency criminal records submissions to state and federal databases;

(D) trends in state and national records quality indices; and

(E) monitoring statistical trends in public and private criminal background checks in terms of the types of records examined, the number and results of checks done, costs, timeliness of responses, and other relevant factors.

J. Additional Recommendations

(1) Congress should consider whether employers that have suitability determinations made by a governmental agency under Public Law 92-544 should also have the option of seeking the records under this authority.

(2) Congress should consider steps that would improve and create additional consumer protections relating to name checks of criminal history records used for employment purposes, such as:

(A) Amending the FCRA to:

(i) require a consumer reporting agency, before reporting name- based criminal history information along with fingerprint- based information to:

(a) confirm the accuracy and completeness of criminal history records obtained solely through a name-based search; or

(b) disclose the name-based information to the individual along with the fingerprint information and allow the individual to challenge the accuracy of the information before it is reported to the user;

(ii) as an alternative to subparagraph (I), require a consumer reporting agency, whenever it is reporting criminal history information, to provide the consumer the opportunity to see and challenge the accuracy of the information before it is reported to the user;

(iii) require notice to an individual by an employer prior to adverse action of criminal history information obtained from public or non-FCRA sources;

(iv) establish a choice of law provision providing that the consumer reporting laws of the state of employment should apply to reports made by consumer reporting agencies; and

(v) if adopted, provide for the exceptions discussed in Screening Standards Recommendation # 2(B); and

(B) establishing national standards for courts to confidentially maintain personal identifiers in criminal case dockets and to allow access to those identifiers for authorized purposes, such as record confirmations in connection with criminal history background checks sought with the written consent of the defendant.

VI. EXPLANATION OF RECOMMENDATIONS

A. Access to Criminal History Records Recommendations

Background

Access to criminal history record information maintained by the FBI in the III for non-criminal justice purposes is currently determined by a patchwork of federal and state statutes. The current process for providing employers and licensees with access to criminal history record information requires that a state or federal statute must be enacted each time access is provided. This approach has led to a great disparity in the level of access by specific industries and within specific states. While the National Crime Prevention and Privacy Compact of 1998 established rules for the interstate sharing with authorized non-criminal justice users of information in the III by the FBI and state record repositories that are Compact members, the Compact does not itself provide affirmative authority for access to information in the III.

As noted above, the main vehicle for creating authority for access to FBI-maintained criminal history records for non-criminal justice purposes has been state statutes, approved by the Attorney General under Pub. L. 92-544, authorizing the sharing of criminal history records from the III to a government agency for use in licensing and employment decisions. These checks are processed through state record repositories and include a check of state records. Other access has been authorized by federal statutes allowing particular industries or organizations to go directly to the FBI for an employment, licensing, or volunteer check, without first going through a state and also checking state records. In addition to creating inconsistencies in access to the information across industries, this framework has also created inconsistencies in the scope of the records checked, with some checks checking both state and FBI records and others checking just FBI records. For example, depending on whether the state has passed a 92-544 statute, an industry may in some states be able to obtain checks of criminal history records maintained by that state, but not of FBI records reflecting criminal records originating in other states. At the same time, an industry may be able to get access to both state and FBI records in some states, and no access to state or FBI records in other states.

When a private employer or entity can inquire about the existence of a criminal record of an applicant or employee, we believe that it is reasonable to provide the employer a means to check maintained criminal history records to determine whether the response to the question is truthful and complete. There is no one complete source of criminal history information, and users need to access many sources to ensure the search is comprehensive. FBI-maintained criminal history records are not complete and may serve only as a good, but not comprehensive, source of information for those performing employment screening functions. Nevertheless, the FBI-maintained criminal history database is one of the best sources because it is based on positive identification and can provide, at a minimum, nationwide leads to more complete information.

At the same time, we believe that any process allowing such access to traditionally restricted FBI criminal history information must establish conditions for access and use that: (1) protect the privacy rights of the applicant, including requirements for informed consent and the right to challenge the accuracy of the records reported; and (2) respect state and federal laws designed to ensure that criminal history records are not used to unfairly deny employment.

Accordingly, we believe that a more uniform and standardized set of rules should be established for private sector access to criminal history information maintained by the FBI and the state repositories. The rules should provide access in a way that is both controlled and accountable. We think that fingerprint-based criminal history information should be available, depending on system capacity and the availability of resources, to all employers and to entities placing persons in positions of trust.[72] We believe that the access should take advantage of the existing private sector infrastructure for employment screening and background checks on consumers and, therefore, consumer reporting agencies and other third parties, under certain conditions, should also be authorized access. The Attorney General should be allowed to prioritize access under this new authority to enable the scaling of the system to meet private sector demand without interfering with the criminal justice or national security uses of the system. The Attorney General should also be allowed to expand access to other individuals or entities when he finds that doing so promotes public safety or national security.

It must be emphasized that, given competing law enforcement and national security demands on the FBI's system and resources, implementation of all-employer access by the FBI is likely to be at best many years away. Therefore, if Congress's goal is to create a means by which all qualified private employers can obtain a nationwide fingerprint check of criminal history information, then solutions other than relying exclusively on the FBI to reach the goal should be explored, such as using private sector resources to establish the connectivity needed to service the private sector's need for this information. The privacy and civil liberties issues discussed in our subsequent recommendations, as well as issues of governance, accountability, information security, and information control by the agencies that own the data, would have to be addressed in deciding how to create such alternative solutions and whether they are feasible. In the meantime, the FBI should be authorized to provide access to priority employers as capacity allows.

Explanations of our recommendations for broadened authority to access FBI-maintained criminal history records are set forth below.

Access to Criminal History Records Recommendation #1

> ***(1) Subject to conditions specified in federal law and Attorney General regulations, authority to request FBI-maintained criminal history records should be broadened, under the priorities set forth in Access to Criminal History Records # 2 and as system capacity and available resources allow, to cover:***
>
> ***(A) priority employers, and subsequently, if capacity allows, all employers, for use in decisions regarding an individual's employment suitability;***

Explanation

To avoid the pitfalls of uneven access experienced under existing authorities that grant only certain industries or employers access to FBI-maintained criminal history records, the new general access authority should extend to all employers that meet the conditions for access and use. We do not think that this will lead to every job applicant being fingerprinted for a criminal history check. Only those employers willing to meet the conditions of access and use of the information and to pay the fee for the check are likely to take advantage of this authority. They will do so, presumably, only when they believe that the benefit of the check to the risk management need being addressed is worth the cost and inconvenience associated with the fingerprint- based check. If an employee is asked to consent to a fingerprint check of FBI criminal history records as part of a background check, it is because the employer wants to do a background check for that position that is national in scope and has the benefit of positive identification. We think the private sector is in the best position to identify the unregulated jobs that require this level of criminal history screening and merit the associated cost and inconvenience.

Expanded access will need to be prioritized based on system capacity, according to the priorities set forth in Access to Criminal History Records #2. First priority should be given to critical infrastructure industries, regulated employers, and employers placing persons in positions of trust working with vulnerable populations, and other checks that the Attorney General determines will promote public safety or national security. There are today undoubtedly many positions in the private sector for which checks of FBI- maintained records are not available because they are unregulated, yet those positions may involve greater degrees of trust and security risk (such as in critical infrastructure industries or persons working with vulnerable populations) than positions that are subject to such background checks because they are regulated. This recommendation would help address that anomaly.

As discussed in greater detail below in Access to Criminal History Records Recommendation #2, access by all employers will be available only when system capacity allows, as determined and managed by the Attorney General. Because of the higher priority projects currently being implemented by the FBI and the competing demands those projects place on its resources, even with the requirements for this new access being fully fee-funded, it is likely that "all-employer" access implementation would be at best many years away. Nevertheless, even with these capacity limitations, access within particular industries provided priority access will be more uniform through this approach than is currently the case.

(B) entities placing individuals in non-employment positions of trust, such as persons having access to vulnerable populations, client residences, significant organizational assets, or sensitive information;

Explanation

We believe that this authority and process should be extended to checks of persons placed in non-employment positions of trust. Not all positions that may warrant a background check will involve an employment relationship. Examples include volunteers for entities providing services to children, the elderly, and disabled persons. Also, businesses may have contractors whom they place in positions that have access to client residences, significant organizational assets, or sensitive information. A criminal history check on such individuals may be just as important as checking employees for purposes of security risk assessments, and in some cases may be more important depending on the individual's access to vulnerable persons or assets.[73]

The access allowed for such checks of volunteers under the NCPA/VCA has not resulted in any substantial use of that authority by the states. The process suggested in these recommendations addresses many of the issues identified by the states as the reasons for their lack of participation in NCPA checks, including providing authority, under certain conditions, to disseminate the record to qualified employers and entities for suitability screening by the organizations themselves.[74]

(C) any person or entity when the Attorney General determines such access promotes public safety or national security; and

Explanation

While access by all employers and by entities placing persons in positions of trust will cover most of the possible interest in access to criminal history records for non-criminal justice suitability screening done by non- governmental entities, there may be other contexts where access for such screening may be justified. In order to avoid having to seek new legislation to provide such additional access authority, the Attorney General should be given the authority to specify additional persons or entities with authority for access when he determines such access promotes public safety or national security.

(D) consumer reporting agencies or other third parties that:

(i) are acting on behalf of one of the above authorized users of FBI- maintained criminal history record information;

Explanation

The PROTECT Act's requirement for the Attorney General to conduct a "feasibility study for a system of background checks for employers and volunteers" requires consideration, among other things, of "[t]he extent to which private companies are currently performing background checks and the possibility of using private companies in the future to perform any of the background check process, including, but not limited to, the capture and transmission of fingerprints and fitness determinations."[75] Upon review of the existing private sector infrastructure for performing background checks, we have concluded that employers and other entities and persons authorized access under this new authority should be able to use the services of third party background check or screening companies in performing these background checks. Not all enrolled employers or entities will want, or be able, to meet the conditions that will be necessary for them to receive the criminal history record results directly and may want to hire a third party to conduct the screening of criminal history received under this authority on their behalf. It may be that only a relatively small percentage of employers that are big enough to have their own security departments will want to obtain direct access to the records without involving a third party. In addition, as noted below, the FBI and state repositories may need to limit the number of employers with direct access to a manageable number through minimum threshold limits, which means that the services of consumer reporting agencies will need to be used to create a means of access. As noted above, employers may also want a consumer reporting agency or background screening company to supplement the checks of FBI and state repository data with public record or credit information obtained from other sources, such as commercial databases or direct checks of courthouse records. Consumer reporting agencies also perform the record screening requirements, discussed in the Screening Recommendations below, under applicable state and federal laws.

Authorizing consumer reporting agency access will utilize the existing private sector infrastructure for conducting background checks on consumers, as regulated by the FCRA and applicable state consumer reporting laws. This will also allow authorized users to work with third parties who can perform suitability screening on behalf of an employer or organization based upon the user's criteria. The National Center for Missing and Exploited Children (NCMEC) is now performing this function for entities that qualify for participation in the PROTECT Act's Child Safety Pilot Program. Thus, subject to the conditions specified below, we recommend that consumer reporting agencies and other third parties that are acting on behalf of authorized users also be granted access to FBI-maintained criminal history records.

(ii) meet data security standards established by the Attorney General, including being certified through a public or private program, approved by the Attorney General, as being trained in applicable federal and state consumer reporting laws and in Attorney General standards relating to the secure handling of criminal history record information; and

Explanation

We are concerned that, although consumer reporting agencies are subject to the requirements of the FCRA, there is no direct regulation of consumer reporting agencies to ensure compliance with the FCRA requirements. The Federal Trade Commission (FTC) has jurisdiction over the enforcement of the FCRA, but FTC enforcement actions for rule violations relating to criminal history information are rare. Nor does the consumer reporting industry currently have an accreditation process for industry members to demonstrate that they are recognized providers of service that meet certain standards. Consumer reporting agencies can act on behalf of multiple employers, do so for profit, and could have access to FBI-maintained criminal history records of large numbers of individuals under this authority. As a result, we recommend that, as a precondition to access, consumer reporting agencies be required to meet data security and handling standards established by the Attorney General, including being certified by a public or private program, approved by the Attorney General, as being trained in applicable federal and state consumer reporting laws and in Attorney General standards relating to the secure handling of criminal history record information. The Attorney General should establish standards applicable to the certification in consultation with the consumer reporting industry, the Compact Council,[76] and other interested parties or entities.

Making such certification a precondition to access to FBI-maintained criminal history information under this new authority – in addition to the enrollment agreements relating to security and privacy procedures required of all authorized users under Privacy Protection Recommendation #1 – would further ensure the integrity of handling of such information by credit reporting agencies. It may also serve to elevate the industry's compliance with FCRA rules regarding criminal history record information, as most consumer reporting agencies will no doubt want to be certified so they can have authority to access fingerprint-based criminal history information under this authority when providing screening services to customers.

(iii) are prohibited, with limited exceptions, from aggregating the criminal history information obtained through these fingerprint-based checks for resale.

Explanation

In general, we do not think that consumer reporting agencies should use this authority to do fingerprint-based background checks as a means of gathering additional criminal history record information that they can resell in their consumer reports. In no case should they aggregate and re-disseminate a "no record" response, since that information would be stale in any subsequent re- disseminations. However, consumers may want to consent to retention of the information by a consumer reporting agency that is, for example, providing long-term credentialing services to individuals, or where the information is used to correct an otherwise inaccurate record. Congress should define the appropriate exceptions to the general rule of non-aggregation for resale.

Access to Criminal History Records Recommendation #2

(2) To allow the development of FBI system capacity to handle the increased number of background check requests under this new authority, whether handled through a participating state or directly through the FBI, the Attorney General should be

allowed to prioritize access by specifying classes of employers or entities with initial access authority:

(A) giving first priority to critical infrastructure industries, regulated industries and professions, and the placement of persons in positions of trust working with vulnerable populations;

(B) allowing the expansion of access, at the Attorney General's discretion and only as system capacity allows, to all employers or entities that meet the conditions of access; and

(C) allowing the FBI to manage access under the new authority, limiting access when necessary to avoid a reduction in the level of service available for criminal justice, national security, and other governmental uses of IAFIS;.

Explanation

Because it will be difficult to predict the demand that the FBI will face for checks that it processes under this new authority, the Attorney General should be given the authority to prioritize access by specifying particular industries first, until available resources permit the building of system capacity that can service all employers meeting the conditions of access. First priority should be given to critical infrastructure industries, regulated industries and professions, entities placing persons in positions of trust working with vulnerable populations, and other checks that the Attorney General determines would promote public safety or national security. The FBI should be allowed to manage access under this authority, limiting access when necessary to avoid a reduction in the level of service available for criminal justice, national security, and other governmental uses of the system.

If system capacity expands, the Attorney General should have the authority to expand access to allow requests by all employers and entities that meet the conditions of access. We emphasize, however, that the expansion of system capacity and the creation of necessary infrastructure that would allow all- employer access is at best likely to be many years away because the FBI is currently undertaking higher priority information technology projects that relate to its core criminal justice and national security/counterterrorism missions – including the general upgrade of FBI criminal history information systems known as Next Generation Identification (NGI) System (the full implementation of which is currently estimated to take through 2010), working with DHS on the IDENT/IAFIS "interoperability" initiative (a Congressional and Administration priority to improve information sharing between the FBI's and DHS's fingerprint files), and the implementation of Homeland Security Presidential Directive (HSPD)-12 (an Administration priority for identification cards). The FBI estimates that based upon legislation enacted or proposed to improve national security and/or public safety, civil fingerprint submissions could increase to 26 million annually over the next several years. While most of the functions contemplated for implementing this new authority could be outsourced by the FBI where cost- effective and funded by a fee, any costs necessary to expand capacity to cover all-employer access that can not be covered by a fee would be competing with limited information technology resources that will first be directed to higher priority projects.

We nevertheless believe that the Attorney General should be given the authority to expand access to all employers, depending on demand and system capacity, rather than limiting access by statute to only certain classes of employers. Doing so will avoid the shortcoming of the current approach of selective legal authority which would require the enactment of new legislation to authorize the Attorney General to expand access to additional employers when and if system capacity does become available.

At the same time, it should be noted that if Congress's goal is to create a means by which all qualified private employers can obtain a national fingerprint check of criminal history information, reaching that goal may not necessarily be possible by relying exclusively on the FBI to service all private sector needs for the information at the same time the FBI is focusing available resources on its core criminal justice and national security missions. Congress may therefore wish to seek further input on whether other possible solutions exist for meeting the goal of all-employer access to such information. Such solutions may include relying more directly on the use of private sector resources to establish connectivity to state or federal government-held, fingerprint-based criminal history records in a way that does not require significant new government resources, similar to the way the American Bankers Association creates such connectivity on a more limited scale for the banking industry today. The privacy and civil liberties issues discussed in our subsequent recommendations, as well as issues of governance (e.g,. information control by the agencies that own the data), accountability, and information security would have to be addressed in deciding how to create such alternative solutions and whether they are feasible. For example, we would have serious reservations about allowing the creation of a private sector repository of FBI-maintained fingerprint images. However, the fact that the FBI is currently the only source of nationwide fingerprint-based criminal history data, should not preclude consideration of possible alternatives for private sector access to such information. At the same time, consideration of alternative possibilities for servicing all employers should not delay the creation of authority to allow the FBI to begin doing the checks that it may be able to handle in the relatively near term for prioritized employers, such as critical infrastructure industries and those dealing with vulnerable populations.

Access to Criminal History Records Recommendation #3

(3) States should continue to be able to authorize background checks using FBI-maintained criminal history records for specific categories of employment or licensing pursuant to Pub. L. 92-544.

Explanation

We believe that states should continue to be able to authorize criminal history checks under Pub. L. 92-544 when they wish to regulate certain areas of employment or subject certain activities to licensing. The new authority should not supplant these existing state authorities or limit the ability of states to specify record screening and suitability criteria in areas of employment and licensing that they affirmatively undertake to regulate. Similarly, Congress will continue to be able to require background screening under terms or conditions tailored to the areas that it seeks to regulate. At the same time, as the states and the FBI implement the process for access under this new authority, parts of that process may be adopted by state and federal agencies as the preferred means for processing Pub. L. 92-544 checks under state law or background screening authorized or required under federal law.

B. Process for Record Access Recommendations

Background

We have also recommended a process for record access by the employers and entities that qualify under the new authority. The process specifies the role that the states and their records should play; the national standards that should be followed for providing access by and a quick response to an employer; the circumstances under which an FBI-administered process should be available for access; the use of consumer reporting agencies to facilitate access; the process by which fingerprints must be collected and submitted; and the circumstances under which the criminal records can be disseminated directly to an authorized user. The process contemplates the use of state databases and infrastructure whenever possible. The process also limits the role of the federal and state repositories to that of record providers, leaving the suitability determinations to the users or their agents. This allows the repositories to continue to focus on their primary mission of maintaining and updating criminal history record information and efficiently providing that information to authorized users. We believe that the process must avoid federal or state agencies acting as clearinghouses that make employment or volunteer suitability determinations for unregulated private employers and entities. At the same time, private entities that choose to do so should be allowed to work with qualified third-parties who apply suitability criteria specified by such entities.

Explanations for these record access process recommendations follow:

Process for Record Access Recommendation #1

(1) Access to records in the FBI repository should, when possible, be through states that agree to participate in processing these checks and should include a check of state records.

Explanation

Although the FBI maintains criminal history records submitted by all states and territories with criminal records on more than 48 million individuals, FBI criminal history records are not complete. Only 50 percent of arrest records in the III have final dispositions. State repositories are a more complete and accurate source of aggregated criminal history information within a particular state. The records maintained at the state level, for example, have a higher percentage of arrest records with final dispositions, ranging between 70 and 80 percent, than those available in the III. Moreover, until recently the FBI has not accepted criminal records relating to non-serious offenses. Thus, records of many non-serious, misdemeanor offenses are only maintained at the state repository. In addition, the FBI will not accept records from a state where the fingerprints do not meet its standards for inclusion in the III. States may also maintain sex offender records that do not qualify for entry into the National Sex Offender Registry file. These records are then only available through a check of the state repository. In addition, some states have already established an infrastructure for taking fingerprints and processing applicant checks under their Pub. L. 92-544 employment and licensing background check authorities. It makes sense to use this existing infrastructure where it is available and meets certain national standards, including live-scan capture in non-law enforcement settings. The added value of state databases and infrastructure strongly suggests that background checks for the newly authorized users of FBI-maintained criminal history records should, where possible, be processed through the state and include a check of state records.[77]

*(A) **In order to participate, states must meet standards specified by the Attorney General, within parameters set by statute, for the scope of access and the methods and time frames for providing access and responses for these checks.***

Explanation

We believe that states that opt in and agree to process these checks should be required to meet standards regarding the methods by which fingerprints are taken and the time frames for responding to these checks so that there is uniformity in this regard for all users among the states. Thus, users in one state should not be required to go to a police booking station, have their prints rolled by a police technician on paper cards, which are then mailed periodically to the FBI with responses being returned weeks later, while users in other states have their fingerprints taken through unobtrusive electronic capture machines at their employer's place of business or at non-law enforcement service centers with results being returned within minutes, hours, or only a few days. Some of the standards outlined below should be set in statute, while the Attorney General should be allowed to set additional standards.

In addition, as noted above in Access to Criminal History Records Recommendation #2, the Attorney General must be able to prioritize the scope of access, whether through a participating state or the FBI, in order to allow development of system capacity.

Process for Record Access Recommendation #2

*(2) **Access to FBI-maintained criminal history records should be available to employers and entities under this authority through a fee-funded, FBI-administered process when access is unavailable through the state level because the state has not opted to provide such access.***

Explanation

While we support the continued involvement of the states in the civil background check process, we recognize that due to a lack of resources or competing priorities, it is likely that some states will not be able to establish a process for background checks under this new authority. Therefore, some states may prefer to take either a limited role, or no role, in the performance of these checks. The FBI should establish a process for these checks in states that do not opt to participate, either because they lack the authority, the resources, or infrastructure (such as system capacity) to process such checks, or because the access they can offer is limited in scope or does not meet the national standards set for this system. The FBI process, and the improvements needed to make it work, should be paid for by user fees.

*(A) **In establishing a fee-funded, FBI-administered process for access to IAFIS records by employers and other authorized entities, the Attorney General should:***

*(i) **seek to create an efficient means by which the check will include a search, confirmed with fingerprints, of the criminal history records of as many state and federal criminal history records as possible, including records in the state where the check is being sought;***

Explanation

As noted above, the state record repositories have more complete criminal history records than those maintained at the FBI. Thus, even where a state does not participate in processing the checks, the FBI should endeavor to create a means by which the check through the FBI-administered process includes a search, confirmed with positive identification, of the records in the state where the check is being sought and as many other state repositories as possible. Doing so will help ensure records are not missed and reduce the screening efforts that may otherwise be necessary when the state check yields a disposition that is missing from an FBI record. As noted above, the records of states that are members of the National Fingerprint File (NFF) are now automatically part of an FBI check. Checking the records of non-NFF states will require other steps, such as centralizing at the FBI all of the records of states that are not part of the NFF (when those states agree to do so) or increasing the use of regional AFIS systems that centralize the fingerprint records of several states in a region.

(ii) establish a means by which state repositories and courts can be compensated, from fees charged to requestors, when appropriate for efforts that repositories and courts make in support of FBI-processed check requests; and

Explanation

The state repositories rely on the revenue from the fees they charge for non- criminal justice background checks. The money is used to manage the records maintained by the repository and to constantly upgrade the technology on which the repositories are heavily dependant for the improvement of record quality and service. If a large number of checks are processed under this new authority directly through the FBI, a means should be established for compensating the states for their efforts in supporting these FBI-processed checks. This support could come, for example, in the form of a search for a disposition missing from the FBI-held record or a search of the state records incorporated into the FBI-processed check. It could also come in the form of an NFF state responding directly to the user with a record that is now maintained at the state's repository instead of at the FBI. To ensure that state repositories have the funds necessary to operate their systems in conjunction with the FBI, a system for appropriate compensation for the use of their information and auxiliary support of the check process should be developed that relies on fees charged the requestor.

In addition, courts may need to utilize resources to track down missing dispositions for these checks. Without compensation, the courts may not be able to provide the services needed to provide complete information in response to a request.

(iii) establish a means by which improvements required to provide such access to employers and other entities will be paid for from a fee or other appropriate charge to the requestor.

Explanation

Non-criminal justice use of FBI-maintained criminal history information is currently funded by user fees and surcharges to help fund the automation of the record system pursuant to Pub. L. 101-515. The costs of improvements to provide this new access should also be paid for through fees and surcharges charged to the users benefitting from the access.

Process for Record Access Recommendation #3

> ***(3) State criminal history record repositories and the FBI should be authorized to disseminate FBI-maintained criminal history records directly to employers or entities authorized to request a criminal history background check, or consumer reporting agencies acting on their behalf, subject to screening and training requirements and other conditions for access and use of the information established by law and Attorney General regulations.***

Explanation

A major limitation in the background check scheme under Public Law 92-544 is the requirement that the records be disseminated only to a governmental agency that applies suitability criteria and provides the results of its fitness determination – qualified or not qualified – to the employer or entity involved. This makes sense when the state is affirmatively regulating employment in a particular area and a government agency is designated as responsible for reviewing the records and making suitability determinations according to specified criteria. This model does not necessarily make sense in industries where employment is not being regulated by the government. Requiring suitability screening by a government agency when there is no regulation generally has meant that the screening does not get done. This has been the true in the case of the NCPA/VCA. Notwithstanding the authority provided under those statutes, most states have not created means for the screening of employees or volunteers for entities providing services to children, the elderly, and disabled persons. According to a 2005 SEARCH survey, the primary obstacle cited by the states to setting up such programs is the limitation on their ability to disseminate the record to the qualified entities and allow the end user to make the suitability determination. In contrast, Florida's VECHS program has found a way to disseminate the record to the qualified entities under the NCPA/VCA by creating, under Florida law, a system of controls on the use of criminal history records by qualified entities. The Florida program has been very successful in enrolling qualified entities and allowing them to obtain fingerprint-based checks of employee and applicants.

It should be noted that the limitation on providing FBI-maintained records only to a government entity has not been applied to certain industries that Congress has authorized to request background checks directly from the FBI, such as the banking, securities, and nursing home industries. So there is precedent under federal law for allowing the dissemination of the records directly to an employer for use in employment suitability screening. It also should be noted that, according to a 2005 SEARCH survey, 33 states currently provide state criminal history record information to non- governmental entities.

Part of the reason for limiting dissemination to government agencies under Pub. L. 92-544 was to ensure the privacy and fair use of criminal history information, as well as to allow for effective government regulation of specified areas of employment and licensing. Employers and other private entities can, however, always obtain some, if not all, of the FBI-maintained information from other public and private sources and in ways that are not always reliable. Some commenters noted that private entities have been handling criminal history information for a long time and that companies are careful about safeguarding their personnel files. With appropriate conditions on the handling and use of the information, we believe allowing dissemination of FBI-maintained records to employers and other entities can not only provide more accurate and reliable information for use in the suitability screening, but also enhance individual protections for privacy and fair use of the information. We therefore recommend that the FBI and participating states be authorized to disseminate FBI-maintained criminal history information to employers and other authorized entities, subject to the access, training, and use requirements specified below.

(A) Access through the state and FBI-administered process should be facilitated through:
- ***(i) consumer reporting agencies meeting requirements specified by the Attorney General under Access to Criminal History Records Recommendations #1(D)(ii) and (iii); or***
- ***(ii) direct access by employers that meet criteria established by the Attorney General or state repositories aimed at limiting direct access by employers to a manageable number, including requirements for meeting a minimum volume threshold of checks and for the electronic submission of fingerprints.***

Explanation

As discussed above, the existing private sector infrastructure for criminal history record checks using consumer reporting agencies should be used. Access through consumer reporting agencies should not be exclusive; the FBI and participating states, however, should be allowed to establish criteria, such as minimum threshold requirements and direct electronic submission of fingerprints, that limits the number of direct access employers that they will have to enroll and audit and for whom they will have to screen records to a manageable number. Enrolled consumer reporting agencies will be able to enroll employers and audit them for compliance with access requirements, as well as to provide the required training on the interpretation of criminal records to employers. The FBI and participating state repositories can, in turn, audit the enrolled consumer reporting agencies performing these functions. This will decentralize these responsibilities and make the administration of system requirements more feasible.

Process for Record Access Recommendation #4

(4) The submission of fingerprints should continue to be required for positively matching records in the FBI criminal history record repository to a record subject when a check is made for non-criminal justice purposes.

Explanation

The National Crime Prevention and Privacy Compact requires the submission of fingerprints for non-criminal justice checks of FBI-maintained criminal history records in the III. Fingerprints provide the significant benefits of positive identification described above, including significantly reducing the likelihood that a false positive or false negative match will occur. We do not see any reason to change the Compact's general fingerprint requirement.

(A) The fingerprint submissions for criminal history record checks under this new authority should:

(i) be collected exclusively through electronic, live-scan capture and transmission of an individual's fingerprints on systems that have been certified by the FBI and submitted in the FBI standard format; and

Explanation

Many states continue to use paper and ink for the collection of fingerprints for the checks processed under Pub. L. 92-544 authority. This requires a fingerprint technician to grasp each finger, roll the finger in ink, and then roll it on the fingerprint card. The paper fingerprinting process typically takes five minutes to complete. The fingerprint cards are then either (a) mailed to the FBI, which then electronically scans the card to process the search and mails back the results, or (b) electronically scanned by an agency and transmitted electronically to the FBI. Other states, in contrast, have taken full advantage of the latest live-scan technology, capturing and transmitting applicant fingerprints electronically for the state and federal searches.

Devices now available for the live-scanning of fingerprints are much more affordable than the early live-scan models, particularly now that the Compact Council and the FBI have authorized, as of June 2005, the use of flat, or "slapped," fingerprints for non-criminal justice searches against the III.[78] The electronic, live-scan capture of the fingerprints eliminates the delays inherent in processing paper prints, such as using the mail or taking the extra-step of scanning the card. Live-scan devices also have better quality control than paper prints, reducing the chance that the prints will be rejected for the search because of poor quality. Live-scan capture is also less obtrusive to the applicant, and less likely to make an applicant feel like they are involved with the criminal justice process. In addition, the use of live-scan devices and electronic transmission also enables a rapid response for the check request. For these reasons, we believe that fingerprints submitted for checks under this new authority must be processed exclusively through the use of electronic, live-scan technology. The live-scan systems must, of course, be certified by the FBI and should also confirm the quality of the fingerprints so that poor fingerprints can be rejected prior to submission.

(ii) use, when reasonably available, electronic fingerprint capture technology that is fast and unobtrusive.

Explanation

As discussed above, the Department of Justice, through the National Institute of Justice (NIJ) and in conjunction with the Department of Homeland Security, the Department of Defense, and the Department of State, is leading a research and development initiative for the development of a device for the fast capture, in less then 15 seconds, of 10 rolled-equivalent fingerprints. In September 2005, NIJ issued over $7 million in grants to four recipients who are taking various approaches to creating such a device. At the same time, to meet its decision to take 10 flat fingerprints for enrollment and screening of aliens entering and exiting the United States through the U.S. Visit program, the Department of Homeland Security, in conjunction with the FBI, NIJ, the Department of Defense Biometric Fusion Center, and the National Institute of Standards and Technology, jointly-published a request for information on September 30, 2005, inviting fingerprint scanner hardware and software vendors to meet a "Challenge to Industry" to develop in the near term faster, smaller, more mobile, 10-fingerprint slap capture devices.[79] It appears that several vendors are stepping up to produce a slap capture device, no larger than 6 inches x 6 inches x 6 inches and weighing no more than 5 pounds, that is capable of capturing 10 "slap" images within 15 seconds or less.

We believe that the faster and less obtrusive the fingerprint capture process, the better for both the applicant and those responsible for capturing the fingerprints. We therefore recommend that those capturing fingerprints for checks under this new authority be required to use, when reasonably available, capture technology that is fast and unobtrusive. We also believe that, to support the expanding use of fingerprints for criminal history background checks, Congress should consider a specific Department of Justice authorization for research and development funding for fingerprint fast-capture development efforts.

Process for Record Access Recommendation #5

> ***(5) A participating state or the FBI should be required to respond to an enrolled employer, entity, or consumer reporting agency within three business days of the submission of the fingerprints supporting the request for the criminal history record check.***

Explanation

In October 2003, the FBI CJIS Division conducted a survey of the state repositories to determine the average time to process a civil fingerprint submission from the date of capture to the date of submission to the FBI. The survey revealed that the processing time ranged from 1 day to 42 days. Long response times would be clearly unacceptable, however, for users of this new authority. A point made by many submitting comments to the Department on this report is that criminal history checks of the FBI or state repositories that take a long time to return results will be both useless to the employer and unfair to an applicant. According to those engaged in the background screening industry, employers typically want screening results back within three business days. Results that take longer may cause them to pass over an applicant where the hiring need is time-sensitive.

The end-to-end electronic submission of fingerprints results in significantly better response times than partially electronic submissions or manual submissions. The FBI has a time frame of responding to civil checks submitted electronically within 24 hours and, frequently responds to such checks in 2 hours or less. The check of the state databases should be similarly quick. Based on FBI experience with current civil fingerprint checks, approximately 90 percent of the checks return a "no record" response. Additional time may be necessary for the screening when the search returns a record, such as where research is necessary to find missing dispositions.

We, therefore, think that a time frame should be established for responding to these checks within three business days of the receipt of the fingerprints by the participating state or the FBI. This parallels the time period the FBI is given for responding to federal firearms licensees requesting background checks on gun buyers through the NICS under the Brady Act. We also note that the feasibility of this time frame has been borne out by the experience of Florida's VECHS program, which returns results to participating entities within two hours when fingerprints are submitted electronically.

C. Privacy Protection Recommendations

Background

The access and use of FBI-maintained criminal history record information has been traditionally limited and controlled in large measure to protect the privacy of the individuals to whom the records pertain. Although generally considered to be a public record,[80] in many contexts, a criminal history record can have a stigmatizing affect on an individual. For that reason, dissemination of such records maintained in the national repository maintained by the FBI has been subject to careful control.[81] Consent of the individual for disclosure of FBI criminal history records to third parties for authorized non-criminal justice purposes has always been required, as have agreements by record recipients and authorized end-users concerning use-and-challenge requirements and procedures to be observed for securing the information.[82]

The FCRA established requirements governing the activities of consumer reporting agencies in reporting information on consumers, including public record information such as criminal history information, to third parties for purposes such as establishing the consumer's eligibility for credit or employment. Consumer reporting agencies regularly engage in providing such information on consumers to employers for a fee. Many of the requirements of the FCRA are for the protection of the privacy of the consumer, including requirements for the consumer reporting agency or employer to provide notice of the consumer's rights under the FCRA, written consent, and the opportunity to challenge the accuracy of records before an employer takes adverse action, such as the denial of employment, based on information in the record.

Employers who obtain criminal history record information about an applicant on their own, without the use of a consumer reporting agency, such as directly from the courts or other public agencies that make such information available to the public, are not subject to the FCRA requirements relating to notice, consent, and use of the information. Presumably, this is based on the fact that any member of the public can obtain and use such public record information about an individual directly from the public agency that originates the record without the record subject's knowledge or consent. Public access to criminal history records held by state record repositories has also expanded significantly. As noted above, a 2005 SEARCH survey found that 33 states currently provide state criminal history information to non-governmental entities. Employers obtaining records from these sources are, nonetheless, subject to the federal and state anti-discrimination laws, discussed above, regulating the use of criminal history information in employment decisions.

While government agencies are not and should not be considered consumer reporting agencies, the FBI has traditionally required consent to release criminal history records about an individual for employment and licensing purposes and has generally, with a few exceptions, been restricted in disseminating FBI-maintained records to government agencies. If the access to FBI- maintained records is broadened to all employers and authority is provided to disseminate the records directly to an employer, authorized entity, or a consumer reporting agency acting on their behalf, we believe that procedural protections parallel to, or in some cases exceeding, those currently found in the FCRA, should be provided to individuals subject to fingerprint-based criminal history checks under this new authority. Our privacy protection recommendations, as explained below, reflect this view.

Privacy Protection Recommendation #1

(1) Authorized employers and consumer reporting agencies seeking access should be required to enroll under the program and enter into agreements concerning conditions and requirements for access to FBI-maintained criminal history record information, including:

Explanation

The FBI has traditionally required users of their information to enroll as authorized recipients and enter into agreements concerning the conditions and requirements governing access and use of the information. As noted above, Florida has successfully implemented this enrollment approach to dissemination to private qualified entities under the NCPA/VCA though its VECHS program. We believe that enrollment and agreement requirements should be imposed on users qualifying for access under this new authority.

(A) certifying that the information obtained from the repository will be used solely for purposes of determining an individual's suitability for employment or placement in a position of trust, or another authorized purpose; and

Explanation

Upon enrollment, the user must certify that the records will be used solely for the authorized purposes.

(B) agreeing to:

(i) follow procedures established by the Attorney General to ensure data security and the privacy of the records obtained pursuant to this authority; and

Explanation

The user must agree to maintain the privacy of the information, such as limiting its use by only those who need to know the information in the employment or placement decision and have been trained to read and interpret such records, and to observe procedures to prevent the unauthorized disclosure of the information to third parties. The Attorney General, in consultation with the Compact Council, should prescribe the security and privacy procedures with which the user must comply in order to have access to the records under this authority.

(ii) maintain relevant records and be subject to audits by the FBI or another entity from which it receives criminal history records, e.g., an enrolled consumer reporting agency or a participating state repository, for compliance with record handling requirements.

Explanation

Audits must be done of employer/end-user compliance with the requirements to which they agree. Authorized users must also agree to maintain relevant records to facilitate such audits. The audits of end-users can be done by an enrolled consumer reporting agency, the FBI, or a participating state repository. A consumer reporting agency will be audited by the repository by which it is enrolled, whether it is the FBI or a state repository. The FBI should also have the authority to audit any authorized user.

Privacy Protection Recommendation #2

> ***(2) The limitation on the use of FBI-maintained criminal history information obtained under this authority exclusively for employment or placement suitability should be expressed in the law creating the authority.***

Explanation

The limitation on using the information obtained through fingerprint checks under this authority should be explicitly expressed in the law and not simply a matter of agreement. This will allow for the imposition of criminal penalties for the knowing unauthorized use of the information, as recommended below.

Privacy Protection Recommendation #3

> ***(3) The Attorney General should establish standards for adequate identification and verification:***
> ***(A) of employers and consumer reporting agencies seeking to enroll as qualified to request background checks pursuant to the new authority; and***
> ***(B) of individuals subject to the background check.***

Explanation

The FBI and participating state repositories must take steps to ensure they have adequately identified and verified that the employer or entity being enrolled is in fact qualified to request checks under the new authority. This is essential to prevent fraud and abuse by those who would seek access for unauthorized purposes. Best practices for identity verification of both the enrolled entity and the individual being checked should be used at every level of the background check process. These procedures should also be established by the Attorney General. The Compact Council currently is drafting standards for personal identification verification and the chain of custody of fingerprints. Best practices currently in use by private industry should also be used as guidelines to build in precautions to avoid identity theft.

Privacy Protection Recommendation #4

> ***(4) Privacy protection requirements should be made applicable to enrolled employers and entities obtaining under the new authority FBI-maintained criminal history information from a record repository, including:***
> ***(A) on a document that consists solely of a consent and notice document and that satisfies the requirements of the Privacy Act:***

Explanation

To better ensure informed consent, the FCRA requires that the notice providing an explanation of the consumer's rights and obtaining his or her consent to the consumer report be on a document that consists solely of a consent and notice document. This prevents the information from being buried in the fine print of a long application form. We believe that a similar procedure should be followed under this new authority. Since the information sought is protected by the Privacy Act, the consent form will need to be reviewed and approved by appropriate components of the Department of Justice, including its Office of Privacy and Civil Liberties, to ensure that it satisfies Privacy Act requirements.

(i) obtaining written consent by the individual to the fingerprint-based criminal history record check of the applicable government record repositories; and

Explanation

The consent should be in writing and should clearly explain that the record search being made is based on fingerprints, which the individual is consenting to provide.

(ii) providing notice to the individual of the following:

(a) the scope of the databases that will be searched based on the request;

Explanation

The individual should have notice of all of the databases that will or may be searched as part of the check. The notice should also explain which databases are being searched on the basis of name and other identifiers, as opposed to fingerprints. For example, the notice should state whether the check will include a check certain name-based files in the FBI's NCIC, such as the Wanted Persons File and the Domestic Violence Protection Order File, and the actions that will be taken if there is a hit on a record in one of those files. Currently, the FBI checks such files when conducting a civil check and provides notice of a hit and who requested the check to the originating agency.

(b) his or her rights relating to confidential access to and the opportunity to review and challenge a criminal history record returned by a fingerprint check before it is provided to the enrolled employer or entity or, if not so reviewed, before the employer takes any adverse action based on the information in the record; and

Explanation

Information about the right to challenge the accuracy of a record must be provided to the individual. As discussed below, criminal history records returned from a background check may contain inaccurate information, records which should have been expunged, or missing dispositions. This requirement will permit the individual to correct his or her record before it is seen by an employer or before an adverse action is taken.

(c) the fact that information in the record returned from the check may only be re-disseminated by the user in accordance with requirements specified by the Attorney General;

Explanation

Re-dissemination of the record by the user should be done only in accordance with conditions set by the Attorney General. The conditions may include requirements such as the individual's separate written consent, limiting re- disseminations to employment or contractor suitability purposes, the need to refresh old check results, and maintaining records of re-disseminations that are available to the individual upon request. This required notification will help ensure that both the individual and the enrolled user are aware of this restriction.

(B) the right of the individual to review and challenge the accuracy of a criminal history record produced by the repository search:
(i) before the record is provided to the enrolled employer or entity; or

Explanation

Under section 613 of the FCRA, a consumer reporting agency reporting a public record is required to either notify the consumer of the record being reported to the user or maintain strict procedures to ensure that the information is current and up to date, which for criminal history records means "the current public record status of the item at the time the report is reported."

While the FBI and participating state record repositories will make a reasonable effort to obtain missing dispositions, there is no practicable way for record repositories to do confirmatory searches at courthouses ensuring accuracy and completeness of every record before it is provided to an authorized user. Even where there is a record of conviction, the FBI and the participating state cannot be sure that a subsequent expungement or sealing order has been made part of the repository's record. Yet, simply providing the individual notice that a record (which he may, for example, know was later expunged) is being reported to the user does not in our view provide adequate privacy protection, particularly since the user may, notwithstanding disclaimers to the contrary, erroneously view the fingerprint-based record from a government repository as always current and reliable.

We therefore believe that the only way to allow an individual an effective chance to correct an inaccurate or incomplete repository record before it has an adverse effect on an employment opportunity is to provide the individual an opportunity to see the record before it is provided to the user.

This additional protection for the individual is less important when a government agency makes a "disqualified" determination based on statutory suitability criteria, since the agency can change the determination to "qualified" without the employer ever seeing the mistaken record. We think it is more important, however, in private employment contexts where the employer sees the inaccurate or incomplete record. In the latter situation, there is the risk that the employer will still be influenced by the record in his employment decision and find another ostensible reason not to hire the individual, even if a mistake in the record is corrected before the adverse action is taken.

Existing technology, such as Internet hotlinks that allow an individual to view and approve information before it is sent to the user, should be able to build in this protection. Individuals should be given the option of electing to review the results of the check only if there is a "hit" and a record is returned. This will enable an individual to forgo seeing a "no record" response before it goes to the employer. At the same time, it will allow the individual to see and correct a record if it is incomplete or inaccurate in some important respect, such as an arrest record missing a disposition or a conviction record that does not reflect a later expungement. Consideration should be given, however, to providing a time limit for an individual to exercise the option to review the results, so the user's application process is not unduly delayed to the detriment of both the employer and the applicant.

This requirement, which goes beyond the current requirements under the FCRA, also ensures that the individual's consent is fully informed. An applicant can provide written consent to the release of information about themselves by a repository to a third party, but, without first seeing the information, has no way of knowing what information he or she is agreeing or consenting to have released.

(ii) before adverse action is taken, if the individual has not availed him- or herself of the right to see the record before it is provided to the employer.

Explanation

If an individual does not take advantage of his or her opportunity to see the record before it is provided to the employer under this authority, then we believe the FCRA protection of the right to see the record before adverse action is taken by the user should be available to persons subject to a criminal history check under this authority.

Privacy Protection Recommendation #5

(5) Participating state repositories and the FBI should establish a process by which prospective applicants with enrolled employers or entities can obtain fingerprint check results about themselves once during any twelve-month period, allowing for review and correction in advance of application, but in a way that prevents passing such information on to employers or others as official record check results.

Explanation

We also believe it is important to allow individuals intending to apply with an enrolled employer or entity to see their record in advance of making the application. This would allow the individual to correct any errors outside the application process. It may also allow the individual to decide not to go forward with the application and unnecessarily permit the record to be disseminated to the employer if he realizes that his record would disqualify him for the job.

There currently is a process by which individuals can obtain copies of their FBI-maintained criminal history records and challenge the accuracy and completeness of the information. *See* Attorney General Order 556-73, 38 Fed. Reg. 32773, 32806 (November 28, 1973). Individuals can also obtain criminal history information about themselves maintained by the FBI through the Privacy Act. We believe that a process, more streamlined than these existing avenues of access, should be made available to persons intending to apply with enrolled employers or entities to obtain information about their records at least once during any twelve-month period. This parallels the right of consumers under the FCRA to request copies of their credit report from consumer reporting agencies once during any twelve month period.

Consumers can get copies of their credit report under this FCRA authority for no charge. Because the cost of processing a fingerprint check is significantly higher than producing a name-based credit report, however, we do not recommend that such checks be free.

It is also important that the information on the record is provided to the person in a way that prevents employers from abusing this process as an unauthorized way to obtain record check results.

Privacy Protection Recommendation #6

> ***(6) Participating state repositories and the FBI should establish a streamlined, automated appeal process for applicants seeking to challenge a record's accuracy, without requiring a separate set of fingerprints and an additional fingerprint fee, and ensure that appeal information is provided to applicants when reviewing their records during the check process.***

Explanation

The FBI and the states have processes for appeals challenging the accuracy of their records. We believe that participating states and the FBI should be required to streamline and automate the appeal process for individuals subject to checks under this new authority. If an appeal takes an excessive amount of time to process, the individual may lose the employment opportunity when an employer cannot wait to fill the position. Delays can also disadvantage employers who have to wait for the completion of an appeal before completing consideration of an application. We also do not think that the employee or applicant should be required to submit a separate set of fingerprints and be required to pay an additional fingerprint fee if the appeal can reasonably be pursued without doing so.

Information about the appeal process should be provided to individuals whenever they are provided an opportunity to review their records during the check process.

Privacy Protection Recommendation #7

> ***(7) Limits should be established governing the use, retention, and deletion of fingerprint submissions under this new authority:***
> ***(A) collected by enrolled users, or third party consumer reporting agencies acting on their behalf; and***

Explanation

Since some of these newly authorized users and their agents will be obtaining fingerprints of large numbers of individuals for the first time, we believe that rules governing the use, retention, and deletion of the fingerprints should be established in the law governing this new authority. Of particular concern are any attempts to use these checks to create large, private biometric databases without the consent of the individuals to whom the information pertains. Individuals subject to fingerprint checks should be assured that their biometric information will be protected and used only in ways consistent with their consent and privacy rights under federal and state law. The limits on fingerprint retention and use should take into account business practices relating to the necessary recordkeeping functions of users and consumer reporting agencies in connection with the background check process. There may also be circumstances under which it is reasonable to retain the fingerprint with the individual's consent, such as when the person is challenging a record's accuracy or when credentialing services are being offered. We think Congress should seek additional input from users and consumer reporting agencies before establishing these limits in the law.

(B) received by the FBI or a participating state repository, and channelers acting on their behalf.

Explanation

The law should also address the use, retention, and deletion of fingerprints submitted under this authority to the FBI and participating states and to the channelers or outside contractors they may use in implementing the new system. The public is likely to have significant privacy concerns about the government's retention and use of the large number of fingerprints submitted under this new background check authority. Among the issues to be considered in establishing these limits are (1) when the fingerprints must be deleted, *e.g*, after a reasonable amount of time to allow necessary use in connection with the background checks, including audits and appeals; (2) the circumstances under which the fingerprints may be retained (*e.g.*, at the request of the user and with consent of the individual) for the purpose of providing updates on the individual's criminal history record (the so-called "rap-back," which notifies an entity of an individual's arrest for a relevant offense after the original check is completed – a process under development at the FBI through its Next Generation Identification (NGI) System initiative, but already offered by some state repositories), or at the request of the individual to allow additional checks by other entities with the consent of the individual using one fingerprint without the need to recollect all 10 fingerprints; (3) whether fingerprint submissions from applicants for certain types of employment, *e.g.*, particularly sensitive critical infrastructure jobs, should be retained regardless of consent; and (4) the circumstances under which the fingerprints could be used in comparisons to latent fingerprints obtained from crime scenes.

The FBI currently retains the fingerprints of federal government employees, military personnel, applicants for immigration and naturalization benefits, and individuals who have requested that their fingerprints be retained for humanitarian purposes. The FBI does not retain fingerprints submitted by a state when the state requests that the fingerprints not be retained. Forensic fingerprints from crime scenes can be searched by the FBI Laboratory Division against the civil fingerprints retained by the FBI CJIS Division. Civil fingerprint submissions are not currently checked against the FBI's Unsolved Latent File, but the FBI plans to establish the capability of doing so as part of its NGI initiative.

D. Screening Standards Recommendations

Background

State record repositories currently screen criminal history information in civil checks before it is provided to the government entity that is performing the suitability determination under a Public Law 92-544 state statute. The state repositories, for example, make a reasonable effort to search for dispositions that are missing from arrest records. In addition, they remove records that may not be used for licensing and employment purposes under state law. Examples include sealed or expunged records, records of deferred adjudications where charges where dismissed, and certain conviction and arrest information. The screening gives effect to state laws that limit the use of specified criminal history records by employers in employment decisions. Those laws express a determination by state legislatures that certain types of offenses or records should not be a barrier to employment.

Under the National Crime Prevention and Privacy Compact, states conducting non-criminal justice background checks using FBI-maintained criminal history records originating in other states are required to apply the screening criteria of the state receiving the record, even if the screening criteria are different in the state from which the record originates. The Compact provides that the FBI must screen the records it disseminates based on any applicable federal law. Part of the goal of the Compact was to create a uniform screening rule that removed the pre-existing uncertainty regarding which state's record dissemination rule applied and thereby better facilitate the sharing of criminal history records for non-criminal justice purposes.

The FBI does not screen civil applicant records when it responds to a request for a civil fingerprint check. When the check request is channeled through a state repository, the FBI provides the full record to the state repository, which then screens the record under its screening standards. Nor does the FBI screen the record when it responds to an entity with authority under federal law to request the check, such as a federally insured banking institution. The FBI provides the full record to the bank, since there are no screening requirements in the federal law authorizing the check. The only time the FBI currently screens records and searches for dispositions is when it is responsible for a program that makes determinations of whether a person is disqualified from certain activities. The FBI is currently responsible for two such programs: (1) background checks on prospective firearms purchasers under the Brady Handgun Violence Prevention Act and (2) background checks on persons seeking access to select agents and toxins under the Public Health Security and Bioterrorism Preparedness and Response Act of 2002.

Consumer reporting agencies are also subject to specific screening requirements under the FCRA and the state consumer reporting and anti-discrimination laws discussed above. The FCRA generally limits the reporting of arrests over seven years old, unless the applicant's annual salary is expected to be $75,000 or more. There is no FCRA limit on reporting conviction information. In addition, many states provide more stringent screening requirements on consumer reporting agencies, some restricting the reporting of any criminal information older than seven years, some with lower salary limits for the seven year reporting rule, some prohibiting the reporting of certain types of misdemeanor offenses, and others creating exceptions to the non-reporting requirements for certain occupations, such as those who work directly with children or the elderly. These limitations are aimed at reducing the barriers to employment for persons with a criminal history in a way that is consistent with public safety.[83] They are imposed even though an employer may be able to obtain the criminal record directly from a primary source such as a courthouse. We think this is true principally because the consumer reporting agencies aggregating criminal history information in commercial databases have made access to the information much easier than through direct courthouse searches.

The FBI and participating repositories should make a reasonable effort to find missing arrest dispositions before responding to a consumer reporting agency or a direct access employer. Records provided to employers under this authority through consumer reporting agencies will be screened under applicable federal and state consumer reporting and equal employment opportunity laws. We believe that before producing records to a direct access employer under this new authority, the FBI or a participating state repository should screen the records according to the same limitations. The legal restrictions on the reporting by consumer reporting agencies are an expression of federal and state policy to limit the dissemination by those who assemble and provide reports on public record information for profit of certain types of criminal history information in order to ease the reentry of ex-offenders. They also provide a limit on how long certain derogatory information can easily follow an individual for particular purposes. Because broader access to fingerprint searches of FBI and states repository databases will also make obtaining criminal history information much easier for end users, thereby increasing the risk of reentry barriers, we believe that the FBI and participating state repositories should observe the same restrictions that consumer reporting agencies are required to observe in providing the records to a user. Congress and the state legislatures may change those restrictions from time-to-time based on the balance they wish to strike between promoting privacy and reentry and allowing the free flow of information to users making risk assessments to promote public safety.

These screening functions will be performed by consumer reporting agencies that facilitate access to fingerprint checks of criminal records under this authority because they are already subject to these restrictions under the law. It makes no sense to allow the repositories giving employers direct access to the records under this authority to ignore these restrictions when employers obtaining the fingerprint-based records through consumer reporting agencies will have the records screened. The screening functions for direct access employers could be outsourced by the FBI and state repositories to channeling agents that make up part of the infrastructure for collecting the fingerprints and disseminating the records. *See* Supporting Infrastructure Recommendation #2.

We also believe it is important to recognize that the criminal history records produced by the FBI and state record repositories are not always easily understood by persons unfamiliar with a "rap sheet." For example, state statutes and charge levels (misdemeanor or felony), vary from state to state and can confuse untrained employers when making fitness determinations. We, therefore, believe that records disseminated to users under this authority should identify the offense level. In addition, training and assistance in the reading of "rap sheets" should be provided by the enrolling entity (*e.g.*, a consumer reporting agency or an outsourced agent acting on behalf of a participating state repository or the FBI) and paid for through its fees. Such training and assistance will help ensure that the records provided are appropriately and accurately interpreted by users.

Additional explanations of our record screening recommendations follow:

Screening Standards Recommendation #1

(1) "No record" responses may be reported directly by a repository to an enrolled employer or entity or an enrolled third party consumer reporting agency acting on their behalf.

Explanation

When a fingerprint search by the FBI or a participating state does not "hit" on a record, then a "no record" response should be reported directly to the enrolled employer or entity or an enrolled consumer reporting agency acting on their behalf. The average hit rate for fingerprints experienced by the FBI, ranges between approximately 8 and 12 percent, depending on the population being checked. Thus, between 88 and 92 percent of the checks will return quickly, potentially within just minutes, a "no record" response.

Screening Standards Recommendation #2

(2) Searches that result in a "hit" on a record should be screened by the enrolled consumer reporting agency or, in the case of direct access employers, by the participating state repository or the FBI before the record is reported to an enrolled employer or entity.

(A) Such screening should include:

(i) a reasonable effort by the participating state repository or the FBI to find missing dispositions of arrest records before disseminating the record to an enrolled consumer reporting agency or a direct access employer or entity; and

Explanation

Participating state repositories and the FBI should be required to make a reasonable effort to find missing dispositions. If a disposition is not obtained within three business days, however, they should be able to able to report the record. Under the privacy procedures recommended above, the individual will have an opportunity to see the incomplete record before it is reported to the employer and assist in updating the record through the streamlined appeal process. In addition, consumer reporting agencies that are facilitating the checks may be able to find a disposition that the repositories could not locate within three business days. While an appeal in the case of a record missing a disposition may delay completion of the check and application, we think this process appropriately allocates the burden of updating the record with the missing disposition between the entity reporting the information and the individual who has direct knowledge of the disposition. The applicant could also decide to allow the record to be disclosed to the employer without the disposition and provide the disposition information himself directly to the employer. If the disposition is found after the expiration of three business days, the reporting entity should be able to report the disposition to the user, so long as the individual is provided the same opportunity to see and correct the information as provided in the initial response.

The FBI's experience in administering NICS checks on prospective gun buyers provides some insight into the success it has had in obtaining missing disposition information within the three business days it has to complete the check under the Brady Act before a gun dealer is allowed to transfer a firearm. The FBI NICS is able to find missing arrest dispositions within three business days in approximately 65 percent of all transactions that are delayed because of a missing disposition. This leaves approximately 2 percent of all NICS transactions processed by the FBI missing a disposition at the end three business days.[84]

(ii) screening in accordance with FCRA and applicable state law requirements in the state of employment that limit the dissemination to or use by employers of criminal history record information.

Explanation

As discussed above, to provide consistency with the access that will be facilitated through consumer reporting agencies and to respect the federal and state laws aimed at easing the barriers to reentry by ex-offenders by limiting the use and dissemination of certain criminal history records to employers or other users, the FBI and states repositories should observe these screening requirements before disseminating a record to a direct access employer. Congress or the states may add to or change these limits from time to time, and the screening under this process should apply those limits, whatever they may be.

A clear choice of law provision should also be included with respect to state statutes, paralleling the Compact's record screening rule that the law of the receiving state applies. Here, the law of the state of employment should be applied in the screening. (*See also* Additional Recommendation # 2(A)(iv)).

(B) Congress should consider providing that the screening requirements under the FCRA should not apply to the dissemination of records under this authority:

(i) of a record from the state of employment if the record can be disseminated by the state repository under applicable state law;

Explanation

If the law of the employing state allows access to a record from the state's repository by any person, we do not think that FCRA limits should apply to dissemination of such records under this authority, since the employer or entity would be able to separately apply for and receive such records from the state repository under the applicable state authority. Frequently, employers work around such limits on record access by doing available on-line checks of state records. The control over the dissemination of the criminal history records of the state of employment should be left to the laws of that state and the employer should not be forced to seek an available record separately from the record request made under this authority.

(ii) of a record when the law of the state of record origin would allow public access to the record and the law of the state of employment allows use of the record by employers for employment suitability determinations; and

Explanation

The same reality of alternative access applies when an employer can go to another state and obtain access to an individual's records and the record is allowed to be used by an employer in employment suitability decisions in the state of employment. Congress should consider whether to create an exception to the FCRA arrest record limits in these circumstances to respect the applicable state public record access laws and acknowledge the fact of the employer's ready alternative access to the record.

(iii) of records relating to violent or sexual offenses to employers or entities that provide care, as that term is defined in section 5 of the National Child Protection Act, for children, the elderly, or individuals with disabilities.

Explanation

We think that records relating to violent or sexual offenses should not be screened under FCRA or state consumer reporting law limits when the enrolled employer or entity is covered by the NCPA/VCA. The criteria established by the National Center for Missing and Exploited Children does not impose such limits in the suitability criteria it is applying under the PROTECT Act pilot. We believe older arrest and conviction records for violent or sexual offenses should be available to employers providing services to these vulnerable populations, even when the records are disseminated down to the employer.

Screening Standards Recommendation #3

(3) Records disseminated to a user under this new authority by a consumer reporting agency, the FBI, or a participating state repository should identify whether an offense is a felony, a misdemeanor, or some lesser violation under the law of the charging jurisdiction.

Explanation

In most instances an FBI or state criminal record only provides a citation to a criminal code section or its title when identifying the basis for a conviction or arrest charge, without identifying whether the offense is considered a felony, a misdemeanor, or some lesser charge under the law of the relevant jurisdiction. While employers can, through research, ascertain on their own the level of seriousness of the offense, we are concerned that either they may not do so or may assume the worst until they do. For that reason, we recommend that before screened records are disseminated, the entity disseminating the record to the user, whether a consumer reporting agency, the FBI, or a participating state repository, identify the level of seriousness of the offense based on the law of the charging jurisdiction.

Screening Standards Recommendation #4

(4) Except as noted below, the screened record may be disseminated to an enrolled employer or entity by consumer reporting agencies, a participating state repository, or the FBI:

(A) when as part of the enrollment process, the employer presents a certificate that it has received training, through a public or private program (including programs administered by consumer reporting agencies enrolling employers) recognized by the Attorney General in the reading and interpretation of FBI-maintained criminal history record information;

Explanation

FBI "rap sheets" are not always readily understood by persons who are unfamiliar with them. As a result, we believe that if an enrolled employer or entity elects to receive criminal history records directly from a repository, as opposed to having it screened through a third party background screening firm subject to consumer reporting laws (and therefore more likely to understand rap sheets because interpreting such information is their business), then they should be certified as having received training in reading and interpreting criminal history record information. The training certificates can be issued by public or private programs that have been recognized by the Attorney General. The cost of the training should be paid for by the employer or entity seeking to enroll.

(B) however, only enrolled consumer reporting agencies should disseminate the screened record to the user when the law of the state of employment requires that before the record is reported to an employer by a third party, the record must be confirmed as complete and up-to-date as reflected in the current status of the record at the agency from which it originates.

Explanation

Certain states, such as California,[85] have laws requiring that a record be confirmed as complete and up to date before it is reported to a user by a consumer reporting agency. As noted above, the FBI and participating state repositories cannot reasonably perform such confirmatory checks at county or federal courthouses. Although the FBI and participating state repositories cannot and should not be considered consumer reporting agencies, we believe that the disseminations under this authority should respect these state law requirements, which are intended to put the burden on the record provider, rather than the consumer, in confirming the accuracy of the record before it goes to a user. Therefore, employers in such states will not be able to directly receive the record from the participating state or the FBI. Instead, they will have to obtain the record through an enrolled consumer reporting agency which will perform the confirmatory search under the applicable state law.

Screening Standards Recommendation #5

(5) All disseminations of records to users under this authority should include an appropriate disclaimer that the response may not necessarily contain all possible criminal record information about the individual, either because it has not been entered in the repository database or because the responses have been screened in accordance with the above limitations on dissemination.

Explanation

The FBI and state repositories do not have all records that may exist at courts or criminal justice agencies in the United States. As noted above, law enforcement does not take fingerprints for a significant number of criminal charges, particularly misdemeanors. In addition, some fingerprint-based records may not be submitted by law enforcement agencies to the state repositories or forwarded by the repositories to the FBI. Final dispositions may also be missing from a record. Therefore, disseminations of records under this authority should contain a disclaimer to the user noting these and other applicable limitations on the completeness of the records reported. The disclaimer should also note the record screening rules that have been applied to the dissemination so that the user knows that certain information may not be included under these limits on record dissemination.

Screening Standards Recommendation #6

(6) In reporting information to an enrolled employer or entity, an enrolled consumer reporting agency should clearly distinguish the fingerprint-based criminal history information from other information reported.

Explanation

Because of the substantial distinction between checks based on name-based and fingerprint-based records and to better enable users to understand and judge the information they are receiving, we believe that consumer reporting agencies should be required to clearly distinguish the information received under this authority from the records they obtain from name-based checks of other information sources.

Screening Standards Recommendation #7

(7) The enrolling entity (e.g., a consumer reporting agency or an outsourced agent acting on behalf of a participating state repository or the FBI) should be required to establish a toll- free number and a web-site, paid for by the fees charged by the enrolling entity, that enrolled users can use for assistance in interpreting screened records.

Explanation

To support users receiving records under this new authority, we believe that enrolling entities should establish a toll-free number and a web-site to which users can turn for assistance in interpreting the fingerprint-based records that they receive. The cost of funding this service, including the necessary personnel, should be included in the fee charged for the check by the enrolling entity.

E. Suitability Criteria Recommendations

Background

Employers and entities placing persons in positions of trust, motivated by a desire to engage in safe hiring and avoid negligent hiring claims, reasonably wish to perform due diligence criminal history screening of prospective employees or volunteers. This interest does not necessarily mean that they will not hire or place anyone with a criminal history, rather it means that they want to make informed decisions about the risk of hiring or placing persons with criminal histories in particular positions. An uninformed choice can result in harm to the employer, other employees, or the public. On the other hand, a non-individualized, categorical screening approach of not hiring any person with a criminal history can have the effect of creating a class of unemployable ex-offenders, along with the recidivism that would inevitably result. Thus, the use of suitability criteria, whether general or specific, has been considered important in the screening process to guide the determination of the relevance of criminal history to the duties or responsibilities of the position. The lack of such guidance can result in the unfair denial of employment to or placement of an individual whose criminal history is not related to the position in question.

It was suggested that employers give advance notice of suitability criteria specifying particular disqualifying offenses, thereby giving the individual a chance to opt-out of applying for the position and the criminal history check if they have a disqualifying criminal history. This, it was argued, would help protect the individual's privacy by sparing the individual from consenting to disclosure of personal information to the employer and also spare the employer the cost and effort of processing an application by an individual with a disqualifying background.[86] Some employers may believe, however, that competitors may seek to take competitive advantage of publicly disclosed criminal history suitability criteria or that undue litigation may result from such required disclosures.

We also received comments from representatives of labor expressing concern that employers might use suitability criteria specifying particular disqualifying offenses as a pretext for taking an adverse action against an employee that is motivated by other reasons, such as retaliation against labor organizing activities. Others expressed concern that disqualifying criminal history criteria might result in the discharge of successful employees notwithstanding an excellent record of service in the job and without the opportunity to seek a waiver from the disqualification.

As discussed above, a number of states have tried to balance the interests here with laws governing the use of criminal history information by employers.[87] The laws provide guidance to employers on how to consider the relevance of criminal history when an applicant is otherwise qualified for the position. In addition, the EEOC has determined that policies that exclude individuals from employment solely on the basis of their arrest or conviction records may violate Title VII of the Civil Rights Act of 1964, which prohibits employment discrimination based on race, color, religion, sex, or national origin. To assist employers in compliance with Title VII, the EEOC has provided policy guidance to employers on the general job-relatedness factors that should be considered in determining the relevance of convictions and arrests in hiring decisions.[88] In addition, the EEOC has provided guidance to employers that specifies that no consideration should be given to arrest records that did not result in a conviction unless additional inquiry about the arrest context is made and an opportunity is given for the individual to explain.[89]

As noted above, large employers with human resource departments, such as those participating in the Labor Policy Association and applying its Background Check Protocol,[90] are likely to be aware of the EEOC general job-relatedness factors for determining relevancy of an individual's criminal history to employment suitability. Many other employers, however, may be unaware of these legal requirements and, as a result, there is a risk that some employers may take a "no tolerance" approach when screening applicants for criminal histories. Access under this new authority should therefore include an acknowledgment by users of their responsibilities under applicable equal employment opportunity laws.

The challenge here is to balance the competing interests in a way that follows applicable laws and encourages the hiring of qualified people with criminal histories, while allowing the responsible use of criminal history information in risk assessments intended to promote public safety in employment or placement decisions. Our suitability criteria recommendations are intended to account for the applicable legal requirements and the related interests. Explanations for our recommendations follow.

Suitability Criteria Recommendation #1

(1) Enrolled users seeking access to criminal history information under this new authority should certify that the information obtained will not be used in violation of any applicable federal or state equal employment opportunity law or regulation.

Explanation

Under these equal employment opportunity laws, employers are responsible for applying general job-relatedness factors when determining the relevancy of a criminal history record, obtained from any source, to an individual's employment suitability. The FCRA requires this certification by users obtaining consumer reports from consumer reporting agencies. We believe that it is also appropriately required of an authorized user before obtaining criminal history records under this authority.

Suitability Criteria Recommendation #2

> ***(2) Congress should consider whether guidance should be provided to employers on appropriate time limits that should be observed when specifying disqualifying offenses and on allowing an individual the opportunity to seek a waiver from the disqualification.***

Explanation

It is neither possible nor advisable to attempt to develop specific suitability criteria for all positions that might be subject to a criminal history check. Even so, some statutes provide specific guidance on the time limits that should be observed in using convictions to disqualify a person from particular employment. For example, the Maritime Transportation Security Act of 2002 (Pub. L. 107-295 (November 25, 2002)) requires that DHS issue regulations prohibiting an individual from entering certain secure areas unless that person possesses a transportation security card. 46 U.S.C. § 70105. An individual's conviction of certain felonies generally cannot be used to disqualify the individual from receiving a card if, at the time of issuance, it has been either more than seven years since conviction or five years since release from custody. (Such an individual, however, still may be denied access if DHS finds that the individual otherwise poses a terrorism security risk to the U.S.). 46 U.S.C. § 70105(c). In addition, the Private Security Officer Employment Authorization Act of 2004, which was enacted as section 6402 of the Intelligence Reform and Terrorism Prevention Act of 2004, established federal guidelines that could be used by states that do not have their own standards for employment of private security guards. The Act provides that states doing such checks notify employers where an applicant has been: (1) convicted of a felony, (2) convicted within the previous ten years of a lesser offense involving dishonesty or false statement or the use or attempted use of physical force; or (3) charged with a felony during the previous 365 days for which there has been no resolution. The Act does not compel an adverse employment determination if such information is returned by the check. While applying such across-the-board time limits would not be advisable for all employment decisions, it may be that general time limits on disqualifying criteria could be used to guide employers, if exceptions to the time limits were allowed when an employer determines it is warranted by the responsibilities of the position or other time periods are prescribed by law or set by the employer's industry.

In addition, to enable individual consideration of risk, Congress may wish to consider providing guidance on allowing an individual to seek a waiver from a disqualification. A waiver process was incorporated, for example, into the provision requiring DHS to issue transportation security cards.[91] The Transportation Security Administration has also established a waiver process under its regulations governing background checks on truck drivers seeking hazardous materials endorsements on their commercial drivers licenses.[92]

F. Supporting Infrastructure Recommendations

Background

The lack of an integrated nationwide infrastructure for capturing and transmitting fingerprints for non-criminal justice purposes is a major impediment to implementing programs for conducting fingerprint-based background checks. The majority of the nation's current infrastructure for collection of fingerprints for non-criminal justice checks is based in state and local law enforcement agencies. The reason for this is that law enforcement agencies are the primary source of fingerprint submissions to record repositories when they collect fingerprints for arrests. Law enforcement agencies are also convenient to access because they are in every county. At the same time, many law enforcement agencies do not believe that the capture and submission of high volumes of fingerprints for civil employment and licensing purposes is related to their law enforcement mission. Certain states, such as California, New Jersey, and Tennessee, have therefore established alternative points of fingerprint collection for civil purposes at places other than law enforcement agencies and in some cases involving the use of private entities or contractors. Some federal agencies have also created fingerprint collection centers for background check programs that they are implementing under federal law, such as the Department of Homeland Security's programs for airport workers and aliens seeking immigration and naturalization benefits.

We believe that new, fast, electronic, live-scan technology that is expected to become available in the near term will enable the movement of fingerprint collection for civil checks out of law enforcement agencies and closer to the users of the information. The decentralization of fingerprint collection should make the collection of fingerprints much more feasible and convenient and less stigmatizing. It should also eliminate the burden on law enforcement agencies of taking civil applicant fingerprints.

In addition to a means of collecting fingerprints in support of the checks, the FBI and state repositories need to have the system capacity necessary to process the increased volume of non- criminal justice checks. The FBI CJIS Division's 2003 survey of the state repositories examined the states' system capacity for performing fingerprint-based background checks. Thirteen states indicated they were operating at or near full capacity and would need additional resources to process their projected volume of background checks. Other states have only marginal additional capacity. Only one state described its additional capacity as "significant." The FBI CJIS Division's capacity to process and store fingerprint submissions also will be severely challenged if the volume of non- criminal justice background checks are substantially increased. The IAFIS is currently capable of processing approximately 150,000 fingerprints a day, and the FBI has sufficient personnel to process approximately 100,000 fingerprints a day. The FBI is currently processing approximately 80,000 fingerprints a day. The FBI's Next Generation Identification System initiative will further increase capacity to meet projected processing requirements under existing authorities. None of these expansions, however, take into account the possible increase in demand for fingerprint processing resulting if the Attorney General should exercise this new authority. Therefore, the FBI and the states may need greater funding to increase their capacity to capture, store, maintain, and process additional background checks and to otherwise support the system's ability to handle the demand under this new authority. The program is currently fully fee-funded, and any new costs should be covered by the fees charged for the checks.

We also believe that the use of outsourcing, under the Compact Council's recently published outsourcing standards, will enable the FBI and participating state repositories to establish parts of the necessary infrastructure, including fingerprint capture, record screening, and record dissemination, covering the costs of doing so through the fee charged for the checks.

Supporting Infrastructure Recommendation #1

(1) The electronic, live-scan fingerprint submissions under this authority should be collected:

Explanation

As noted above in the Access to Records Recommendation #4(A), in order to meet the required response time and make the fingerprinting process as user-friendly as possible to the individual, the fingerprint submissions under this authority should be made exclusively through electronic, live-scan devices and should be as fast and unobtrusive as reasonably possible. The fingerprint fast-capture research and development initiatives currently being pursued by the Department of Justice and other federal agencies should result in the development of devices in the relatively near term that will meet this need.

(A) at the place of business of an enrolled employer or entity or an enrolled consumer reporting agency acting on their behalf, or through an authorized channeling agent; or

Explanation

A key goal in developing an infrastructure must be to decentralize the fingerprinting process as much as possible. One of the major limitations currently faced today is the lack of adequate fingerprint collection locations and the inconvenience of utilizing the available locations. The closer the process is moved to the employer, however, the easier it will be for the employer and the individual to participate, and the faster the associated response time will be. The FBI's initiative to designate channeling agents to act for the FBI in the collection and submission of fingerprints for non- criminal justice checks should have the effect of further decentralizing the civil fingerprinting process.[93]

(B) at service centers established by a participating state through a governmental agency or outsourcing, that are:

Explanation

As noted above, several states have already taken steps to establish service centers for the collection of civil prints. The fees charged cover the cost of establishing and running such centers. Outsourcing would allow the centers to be established more quickly than if they had to be run by government personnel and set up through the use of appropriated funds. In the alternative, participating states may elect to use already established fingerprinting centers or state agencies that meet the criteria below.

(i) at a location other than a law enforcement agency; and

Explanation

One of the major concerns with the present infrastructure in most states is that it is an infrastructure designed to deal with fingerprints collected for criminal justice purposes. As a result, the collection points are often located at police stations. Requiring employees to be fingerprinted at police stations creates an unnecessary stigma that would be eliminated if the fingerprints are collected at dedicated non-law enforcement service centers. In addition, moving the collection outside of law enforcement agencies will reduce the adverse impact on those agencies and the likelihood that collecting fingerprints for non-criminal justice purposes will distract them from their primary law enforcement responsibilities.

(ii) at least as convenient to access as places where state identification documents, such as driver's licences, are obtained.

Explanation

The state divisions of motor vehicles are a good example of non-law enforcement facilities that interact with large segments of the population. As such, they provide a good model of the minimum accessibility that will be necessary in order to make fingerprint collection for non-criminal justice purposes more feasible.

Supporting Infrastructure Recommendation #2

(2) An appropriate number of channeling agents should be established to receive the fingerprints from the large number of service centers and enrolled employers and consumer reporting agencies that will be collecting fingerprints.

Explanation

The use of channeling agents will be necessary as a means of funneling the fingerprints to either the participating state repositories or the FBI. The Compact Council's outsourcing rule makes possible the use of channelers for the processing of civil applicant checks. An appropriate number of channeling agents must be established in order to prevent a bottleneck from occurring in the fingerprint submission process and to enable the rapid response that will be the goal of the system. The FBI has already taken a step in this direction with a request for proposal for channeling agents for non- criminal justice fingerprint submissions (*see supra* discussion accompanying notes 27 and 28). Consistent with current practice, the cost the service provided by the channeling agent will have to be added to the cost of the check. The channelers can also perform other functions such as record screening and record dissemination. These functions, unlike the ABA channeling model described above, involve the handling of the records. The outsourcing standards should, however, provide adequate privacy and security controls over the channelers' management of the records.

Supporting Infrastructure Recommendation #3

(3) Additional capacity at both the FBI and state repositories must be developed to enable the processing of these newly authorized checks.

Explanation

The volume of background checks conducted by the FBI and the state repositories is likely to increase substantially if the process discussed in this report is implemented. Given the Attorney General's ability to prioritize employers and other entities provided access to fingerprint checks directly through the FBI, as discussed in Criminal History Records Recommendation #2, the FBI should have the needed flexibility to ramp up its capacity to meet the demand for fingerprint checks, when and if the resources to do so become available. User fees should be used to develop this additional system capacity. The FBI's current efforts at developing a concept of operations for its Next Generation Identification System could incorporate detailed estimates on capacity requirements and other infrastructure needs that may be necessary to handle the new demand for civil background checks that are requested under this authority. The participating states will also have to determine their capacity needs for implementing this program and are likely to require funding for expansion of their AFIS capacity to accommodate this new demand for fingerprint checks. As noted above, most of the state AFIS systems are running at or near full operating capacity. Some states may need to outsource some or all of the infrastructure necessary to process this new demand for civil checks. A means will need to be developed for the funding of these additional capacity requirements through user fees.

G. Fee Recommendations

Background

The FBI fee for civil fingerprint checks is currently is $22 to $24, depending on the method the fingerprints are submitted – although volunteer organizations under the NCPA/VCA currently are charged a reduced fee of $16 or $18, depending on the method of payment. The fee is used to cover the cost of processing the check, including the cost of supporting the operations of CJIS in collecting, maintaining, and disseminating criminal history record information. The FBI fee includes a $6 surcharge that the FBI is allowed to collect under Pub. L. 101-515 for "the automation of fingerprint identification and criminal justice information services and associated costs." The money for the surcharge typically covers the cost of updating the automation technology used by CJIS. The FBI is currently conducting a study of the fee it charges which will provide more current information about the FBI costs for conducting fingerprint checks.

In October 2003, the FBI CJIS Division conducted a survey of state and local agencies to determine the fees charged for performing fingerprint-based non-criminal justice background checks. The survey revealed that there is wide variability in the state fees, with the fees ranging from $5 to $75. The average state fee for performing a fingerprint-based non-criminal justice background check was $20. Some states charge lesser fees or waive the fee for performing background checks on applicants for volunteer positions.

In November 2004, SEARCH conducted a survey of state fees for performing background checks, including the fees for supporting criminal justice services. The purpose of the study was to determine the various services the states provide and the fees charged for those services. The SEARCH survey revealed that the fees vary from state to state based on the type of search conducted, the level of processing, the services provided, and the method for establishing the fee. The survey also revealed that many states use the fees or a portion of the fees collected for performing background checks to operate and maintain their repositories.

Based on the above, it is clear that changes in the current state fee mechanism are needed, if wide variability in the fees charged by the states is to be minimized.

FEE Recommendation #1

1. ***A new business model should be developed to streamline the processing and funding of federal and state non-criminal justice criminal history background checks with the goal of:***
   (A) reducing the costs of the checks;

Explanation

The use of fingerprint-based criminal history checks for non-criminal justice purposes will be limited as long as employers and volunteer organizations view the fee as being too high. The fee charged is based on cost recovery. As the volume of checks increase, however, the FBI and the state repositories may be able to reduce the amount of the applicable fee if a new business model is developed for funding the cost to state repositories of processing the checks. The use of "lights out" processing, where automated record identifications are made without the involvement of an examiner's review if a high enough degree of confidence can be achieved in the automated match, may also provide a means of reducing the cost of the checks. Given the opportunities provided an individual to see and correct mistaken record matches provided under the Privacy Recommendations, automated identifications may be a justifiable cost reducing measure if the likelihood of an incorrect match is low enough. Many states currently do "lights out" processing for their civil checks. One state indicates that it provides a "lights out" response (meaning no review of the match by a fingerprint examiner) in 70 percent of civil checks, and expects that percentage to increase significantly with further improvements in the matching algorithm. The FBI is reviewing the use of "lights out" processing as part of its Next Generation Identification System initiative.

(B) establishing greater consistency in the state fees charged for such checks;

Explanation

As discussed above, there is a great variability in the fees charged by the states. This variability in cost is due in part to different funding models in the states. For example, in some states, the fees collected for civil fingerprint checks go directly to their general funds instead of allowing the state repositories to retain the fees to support their operations. The state appropriations to these repositories, in turn, may not fully reflect the fees that were collected, leaving the repository's needs for improved automation less than fully funded. In addition, some states provide different levels of service which may increase the cost of civil background checks, such as a "rap-back" service. The minimization of the differences in the fee charged by participating states should be a goal here, however, in order to reduce disparate costs for this service experienced by employers in different states. One possible option to consider may be to require that in order for a state to participate, it must allow its state repository to retain the fees charged under this authority, rather than taking the fees into the state's general fund.

(C) states receive appropriate compensation for the support they give to checks processed by the FBI in circumstances where the state does not charge a fee because it is not handling the check; and

Explanation

Even though a background check may be run through the FBI, the background check may require a state to review its records or otherwise support the check. However, because the FBI is handling the process, the state does not receive any compensation for its efforts. As noted above in Process for Record Access Recommendation #2(A)(ii), a process will need to be developed by which the state repositories can be appropriately compensated for their efforts supporting this background check program through the fees charged the requestors.

(D) ensuring that all state repositories have the funding necessary to support the technology required for improved data quality and efficient processing of check requests.

Explanation

The changes to the fee structure through this new authority may also be able to help fund state repositories' needs for technology refreshment and record quality improvements to the extent that some portion of the compensation is required to be earmarked for those purposes. The FBI does something similar to this through a surcharge that it is authorized under Pub. L. 101-515 to charge in connection with civil fingerprint checks.

Fee Recommendation #2

2. The question of who should bear the cost of checks under this new authority should generally be decided between the employer and the individual, although Congress may wish to consider requiring that the cost of fingerprint checks for lower paying jobs be borne by the employer.

Explanation

The employer is most often in the best position to pay the background check fee – particularly when the position in question is low paying. Fingerprint checks are also more costly than name checks. Allowing the cost to be passed on to the applicant, directly or indirectly, can raise barriers to employment to lower income applicants. At the same time, it may not be fair to compel the employer to pay for a criminal history record check that appropriately returns a record that an applicant failed to disclose on his or her application. Some applicants, knowing they have disqualifying records, may submit a false application, hoping that the record may not be discovered by the check. We think the decision of who bears the cost of a fingerprint check should be left to the employer and the individual. According to comments received from the professional background screening industry, most employment background checks are paid for by the employer. However, Congress may wish to consider whether is should require that the cost of the checks for lower paying jobs must be borne by the employer.

H. Enforcement Recommendations Background

We believe that there is insufficient authority under current law to deter and punish the unauthorized access and use of FBI-maintained criminal history record information. If the authority for access is to be broadened, adequate enforcement mechanisms are needed to deter and punish misuse of the information. The penalties should cover both intentional and negligent conduct and provide for criminal, civil, and administrative sanctions. The penalties should also be made uniformly applicable to all misuse of FBI-maintained criminal history record information, not just misuse by persons gaining access under this authority.

Enforcement Recommendation #1

(1) Penalties should be established for the unauthorized access to or misuse of records of government record repositories under this new authority, including:

(A) Criminal penalties for persons who knowingly:

(i) obtain criminal history record information through this authority under false pretenses; or

(ii) use criminal history record information obtained through this authority for a purpose not authorized under this authority; and

Explanation

Criminal history record information is generally considered personal and can have a stigmatizing affect on an individual. As a result, individuals are rightly concerned that such information not be misused. Without adequate sanctions for misconduct, including criminal penalties, individuals cannot be assured that their interests will be protected. Although the private organizations and employers will have enrolled and agreed to follow certain privacy and security procedures, these guarantees must be backed by criminal penalties.[94] An example that could be followed here is the criminal penalty provision in Pub. L. 105-277, which provides for background checks on employees of nursing homes and provides for a fine in accordance with Title 18, United States Code, imprisonment for not more than 2 years, or both, for the knowing unauthorized use of information obtained under that law.

The FCRA also provides criminal penalties for any person who knowingly and willfully obtains information on a consumer from a consumer reporting agency under false pretenses[95] and for any officer or employee of a consumer reporting agency who knowingly and willfully provides information on an individual from the agency's files to a person not authorized to receive the information.[96] The penalty for either offense is a fine or imprisonment for not more than two years, or both.

(B) Civil penalties, including monetary penalties and discontinued access, for violations of required security and privacy procedures resulting in the disclosure of information obtained from the repositories to unauthorized persons.

Explanation

Although criminal penalties will be necessary, not all violations warrant such a response. In some circumstances, the unauthorized disclosures of criminal history records that result from a failure to follow required procedures can best be addressed by the imposition of civil penalties or through the discontinuance of access to the background check process.

Enforcement Recommendation #2

> ***(2) The Attorney General should be authorized to establish an administrative process, to be administered by the FBI and participating state repositories, for sanctions, including termination of access, against enrolled employers, entities, and consumer reporting agencies for violations of requirements regarding access to, the use of, and the security of the information, including failure to observe required procedural rights of applicants.***

Explanation

It may be both difficult and unnecessary to pursue in court all alleged violations of the requirements relating to the access to and privacy and security of the information. The Attorney General should, therefore, be allowed to establish a simplified administrative process that the FBI and participating state repositories can use for determining violations of applicable requirements discovered through audits or complaints. Sanctioning such conduct by administratively terminating access will provide an additional avenue for redress.

I. Record Improvement Recommendations

Background

It is hard to overstate the importance of or reliance placed upon the criminal history record information maintained by the states and the FBI for the myriad uses of the information for criminal justice, homeland security, and non-criminal justice purposes. Much progress has been made, particularly through the funding provided to the states through the NCHIP awards, in improving the national record system in terms of automation and record completeness. Direct NCHIP awards to the states in the 10 years since the program started in 1995 total over $438 million. We believe, however, that the federal commitment to improving these record systems now needs to be rethought and reinvigorated.

Much more needs to be done to achieve uniformity in the improvement of record quality and completeness. The NCHIP program was created in large part to enable the National Instant Criminal Background Checks System (NICS), established under the Brady Act, to work efficiency in completing background checks for gun purchasers. While approximately 92 percent of NICS checks are completed while a dealer is still on the telephone, there are still a significant number of firearms transfers that are made where a potentially disqualifying record is missing a disposition that cannot be found by the NICS within the three business days allowed for completing the check. In many states older records are yet to be automated. The improvements that have been made in record quality throughout the states are uneven, as demonstrated in the findings of BJS through the Record Quality Index (RQI) it uses to evaluate the progress made by states repositories.

Notwithstanding this continuing need for record improvement, the NCHIP program over the last several years has been funded at smaller and smaller fractions of the amount requested in the President's budget each year. NCHIP Budget requests averaged approximately $60 million dollars for FY 2006-2006, while the direct appropriations were $40 million in FY 2003, $30 million in FY 2004, $25 million in FY 2005, and $10 million for FY 2006. At the same time, the purposes for which the money is to be used have increased, such as participation by the states in the national sex offender registry and the creation of files for sharing information, including civil protection orders on domestic violence.

We believe that improving the national criminal history record system is more important than ever, particularly if this new process is created for broadened access to FBI-maintained criminal history records for non-criminal justice purposes. To achieve uniformity in improvements across the nation, we also believe that it is time to rethink NCHIP's approach of allowing states to spend the money as they think necessary within broadly defined program goals. We believe that federal funds should now be more directly targeted at reaching specific goals for uniform record completeness and accuracy nationwide. Those goals should be set through national standards and enforced through an accreditation process to which states receiving the funds must submit. With this in mind, we make the following recommendations:

Record Improvement Recommendation #1

(1) There should be a renewed federal effort to improve the accuracy, completeness, and integration of the national criminal history records system.

Explanation

Complete, accurate, and accessible criminal history records are an essential tool for a variety of criminal justice and non-criminal justice functions including:

- identifying persons prohibited from certain occupations, professional certifications, firearms ownership and possession, or who may volunteer to work with certain populations (children, elderly, disabled);
- enabling decision-makers in the justice system to make better- informed decisions for case processing and for sentencing and correctional management (pretrial release, persistent or career criminal charging, sentencing guidelines applications, and inmate classification);
- assisting law enforcement investigators in evaluating potential arrest and charging decisions;
- use in certain national security matters, offender post-release tracking, immigration regulation, or other purposes which may involve tracking offenders from one jurisdiction to the next; and
- providing a source of information on wanted persons, persons in violation of community supervision requirements, or persons in a special legal status such as those under protection orders or who are registered sex offenders.

At the present time, the principal means for sharing records across jurisdictions is the FBI's III system and the NCIC. Among the estimated 75 million criminal history records in the U.S., about 50 million are accessible through III. Critically, many III records are missing final court disposition information. Effort needs to be directed to automating the one-third of all records which are in a manual format and to ensuring that the records are complete in terms of court dispositions.

In addition, much more can be done to improve the completeness of the state contributed records in national files in the FBI's NCIC that provide information to promote public safety, including the protection order file, the National Sex Offender Registry file, and the convicted persons on supervised release file.

In addition to the need to improve records coverage and accessibility, there is a substantial need to improve the quality of records and ensure continuous monitoring of gaps in quality that may adversely affect the variety of uses for records. While BJS's RQI evidences substantial improvement in record quality over the last decade, major gaps within states still remain in reporting disposition information following arrest transactions and the timeliness of posting transactions to records.

Record Improvement Recommendation #2

> ***(2) Federal funds should be targeted at reaching national standards established by the Attorney General relating to prompt disposition reporting and record completeness, including declinations to prosecute and expungement and sealing orders, so that there is uniformity in improvements by repositories nationwide.***

Explanation

To date, research on record quality and completeness, as measured by BJS's RQI, has demonstrated enormous variation from state-to-state in the completeness and utility of criminal records for providing a fully accurate transaction history. While Department of Justice regulations require that "[d]ispositions should be submitted by criminal justice agencies within 120 days after the disposition has occurred," the requirement is not phrased as a mandate. In addition, little is systematically known about potential uses of other databases to enhance the criminal record – DNA records, incident-based records, or other criminally-relevant databases.

We believe that any financial support to the states should be restricted to applications that will meet national standards that are established by the Attorney General concerning the content of records systems and the mechanisms by which such records can be merged and shared among the law enforcement/criminal justice community. Disposition reporting, including expungement and sealing orders and declinations by prosecutors, should be given the highest priority. Accomplishing this will require developing electronic connections between the record repositories and, not just law enforcement agencies where the arrest record is created, but also local law enforcement agencies, prosecutors' offices, and courts, where each step in the arrest's disposition is taken through finalization. Creating these electronic connections should also allow for much prompter and automated updating of the dispositions, perhaps allowing for updating at the repository on the same day the disposition is entered by the responsible agency. For the last four years modest additional funding has been requested in the President's Budget to support creating such connections for disposition reporting, but has not been appropriated.

Finally, we note that the Department received several comments suggesting that limits should be placed on the retention of arrest information without a disposition. We strongly disagree with this suggestion, believing that the response to the missing disposition should be to determine what disposition was made of an arrest, and not to destroy, or decline to report, the record of the arrest.

Record Improvement Recommendation #3

(3) Accelerate the standardization of rap sheets to make them more readily understood by non-criminal justice purpose users.

Explanation

BJS has worked with the states and FBI to produce a format and standards for transmission of a uniform rap sheet among states. The format relies on the Global Justice XML Data Dictionary. The format has been adopted by the FBI and a few states. The model provides for commonly defined and coded offense categories and transaction codes for recording dispositions and handling of all arrest transactions as fully cycled events. In addition to ensuring that shared criminal history record information is standard in look and format, it is important that consumers of this information understand and appreciate the criminal justice processes and terminology the records encompass. Because these standards are voluntary, the adoption and implementation of the standard rap sheet has been very limited to date. We believe that the adoption of the standardized rap sheet should be made a priority. We recommend that available state and federal funding be targeted at the uniform adoption of the standardized rap sheet by all states within the nextthree years. All users of criminal history record information, particularly non-criminal justice users, will benefit by the uniform adoption of this standard.

Record Improvement Recommendation #4

(4) Congress should consider requiring state repositories to establish procedures meeting national standards to remedy the adverse affects on individuals who are wrongly associated with criminal records because they are victims of identity theft.

Explanation

A national focus group on identify theft victimization as it relates to criminal history records was recently convened by SEARCH with the support of BJS. The focus group concluded that identity mistakes relating to criminal history records created about persons using a stolen identity can have very serious adverse consequences to the victim of the identity theft.

More needs to be known on how some of the suggested solutions might adversely affect the effectiveness of law enforcement. For example, although deleting stolen identification information from criminal history records could be an effective remedy for identity theft victims, this approach might hinder law enforcement. Sealing or flagging the information might be more acceptable for law enforcement officials, but might not be as effective in preventing repeated victimizations. Identity theft passports (a document identifying a person as having been wrongly associated with a criminal record) and passwords (a password maintained by repositories that an individual can use to demonstrate to law enforcement that they have been wrongly associated with a criminal record) may be effective in preventing inappropriate detentions and arrests following law enforcement stops of identity theft victims, but they may be less useful in preventing victimizations in connection with applications for employment or housing.

For these reasons, the focus group agreed that a survey aimed at state-by-state information gathering and analysis was required and should consider the following questions, among others:

- What procedures do law enforcement agencies employ at booking to try to establish the true identities of arrested persons? Are there better procedures that might help prevent the use of aliases?
- What procedures and remedies are in effect in law enforcement agencies and the state repositories to help prevent identity theft victimization and to help victims deal with the ensuing problems? How have these remedies worked?
- To what extent is law enforcement effectiveness adversely affected by the expunction from criminal history records of stolen identity information when it is detected? Are there adverse effects of sealing or flagging?
- Can the record-review and correction procedures in effect at the federal level and in all of the states be used to help alleviate the problems of identity theft and identity mistakes?

With Congressional direction to address the problem of identity theft in criminal history record information, and federal funding where appropriate, we believe that these questions can be answered and nationwide solutions can be implemented.

Record Improvement Recommendation #5

(5) Establish a national accreditation process for criminal history record repositories, much the same way that crime laboratories are accredited, to better ensure data quality by measuring repository performance against national standards.

Explanation

Voluntary standards for improving the quality of criminal history records were developed by the FBI in conjunction with BJS and published in the Federal Register in 1991. Surveys of the states' criminal history record operations conducted on behalf of BJS continue to indicate wide variability among the states in the data quality improvement activities they carry out. It is time for the 14-year-old standards to be re-evaluated, especially in light of new technological capacities and the expectations of the current users of criminal history records. Moreover, incorporating revised standards into an accreditation process, as opposed to leaving them as strictly voluntary, would better ensure uniformity in their application among the states. Accreditation could be based on an assessment carried out by the FBI in conjunction with BJS. Incentives for compliance with the national accreditation standards relating to federal grant funds could also be implemented.

Record Improvement Recommendation #6

(6) Seek to integrate the repository systems in ways that will efficiently allow a single fingerprint check to return all information on an individual maintained by all

states rather than the current process for obtaining such complete information of requiring separate fingerprint checks of 50 smoke-stacked record systems.

Explanation

It is generally acknowledged that the state repository criminal history records are more complete than the records held at the FBI. This is the reason for the Department's consistent support of incorporating a state check whenever possible into checks of FBI-maintained criminal history records. Up to now, however, this has meant a separate fingerprint check of the state of employment or licensing. Checks of the data in the remaining states and territories would require separate fingerprint checks of each record system. Yet, the technical hurdles that at one time made a consolidated national fingerprint inquiry a practical impossibility are largely gone. The use of automated fingerprint identification, live-scan and card-scan technology to capture fingerprint images, identify criminal history records and transmit these data to/from repositories is increasingly widespread. While the NFF will help to solve this limitation, it does not appear to be a complete solution, since many states may never become NFF members and even the NFF process will not report a state record if the first set of fingerprints on an offender has not been sent to the FBI. We recommend that a national effort be made to identify and resolve legal issues, policy concerns, and resources needed to enable a consolidated check of all repository records.

Record Improvement Recommendation #7

(7) ***Develop a realistic assessment of the cost to achieve these record improvement goals.***

Explanation

In order to guide budget requests and funding decisions, it is vitally important that an assessment of the costs of achieving these record improvement goals be carried out. This assessment must consider not only the initial federal and state outlays required, but also the extent to which fee revenues can be used to defray ongoing costs associated with record improvement activities.

Record Improvement Recommendation #8

(8) Develop a comprehensive ongoing data collection and research program by BJS that includes:

- ***(A) study of the extent of automation and accessibility of state and FBI criminal records;***
- ***(B) data collection documenting the accuracy, completeness, and timeliness of state and FBI criminal history records;***
- ***(C) assessment of the completeness and timeliness of local agency criminal records submissions to state and federal databases;***
- ***(D) trends in state and national records quality indices; and***
- ***(E) monitoring statistical trends in public and private criminal background checks in terms of the types of records examined, the number and results of checks done, costs, timeliness of responses, and other relevant factors.***

Explanation

The information suggested for data development and research in this recommendation is crucial to guiding decisions that need to be made regarding record improvements and to measuring outcomes of record improvement efforts, as well as understanding the non-criminal justice uses that are being made of the information.

J. Additional Recommendations

Background

In addition to our recommendations for creating a consolidated authority and standardized process for providing responsible and accountable access to FBI-maintained criminal history records for non-criminal justice purposes, we believe Congress should consider the additional steps discussed below:

Additional Recommendation #1

(1) Congress should consider whether employers that have suitability determinations made by a governmental agency under Pub. L. 92-544 should also have the option of seeking the records under this authority.

Explanation

Private employers who are having checks performed under Pub. L. 92-544 may wish to see the records even though a suitability review is being done by a governmental agency. If they meet the conditions for access that non-92-544 employers must meet under this new authority, it makes sense to also give them the option of seeing the records.

Additional Recommendation #2

(2) Congress should consider steps that would improve and create additional consumer protections relating to name checks of criminal history records used for employment purposes, such as:

(A) Amending the FCRA to:

(i) require a consumer reporting agency, before reporting name-based criminal history information along with fingerprint-based information to:

(a) confirm the accuracy and completeness of criminal history records obtained solely through a name-based search; or

(b) disclose the name-based information to the individual along with the fingerprint information and allow the individual to challenge the accuracy of the information before it is reported to the user.

Explanation

Consumer reporting agencies have the option under section 613 of the FCRA of simply notifying a consumer that a public record has been reported to the user, in lieu of having strict procedures to confirm the record's completeness and accuracy. In light of the additional procedural protections regarding the dissemination of fingerprint-based criminal history records recommended in this report, Congress should consider whether name-based criminal history information reported along with fingerprint-based information must be confirmed to be complete and accurate or disclosed to the consumer before being reported by a consumer reporting agency.

(ii) as an alternative to subparagraph (i), require a consumer reporting agency,whenever it is reporting criminal history information, to provide the consumer the opportunity to see and challenge the accuracy of the information before it is reported to the user;

Explanation

To provide greater consistency in the opportunities consumers have to verify and challenge the accuracy of criminal history information before it is provided to users, Congress may want to consider imposing the requirement of giving consumers the pre-reporting opportunity to see the information in all reports of criminal records by consumer reporting agencies, regardless of whether it is name-based or fingerprint-based.

(iii) require notice to an individual by an employer prior to adverse action based on name-based criminal history information obtained from public or non-FCRA sources;

Explanation

Some employers are now able to obtain name-based criminal history information from public sources or non-FCRA sources, with or without the knowledge of the individual, such as name searches of state repository records or commercial databases on the internet that are aggregated for non-FCRA purposes. Because such information is not from a consumer reporting agency, the employer has no obligation to provide pre-adverse action notice to the individual. As a result, even though there are significant risks of inaccuracy of such name-based data, the individual may never know that the employer is taking adverse action based on the information, whether accurate or not. In order to provide more consistency in the rules regarding the use of criminal history records in employment decisions, Congress may wish to consider whether employers obtaining criminal history record information from non-FCRA sources should be made subject to FCRA adverse action rules, including requiring pre-adverse action notice and an opportunity to correct inaccuracies in the information.

(iv) establishing a choice of law provision providing that, where there is a conflict between the law of the state where a record originates and the law of the state of the employment, the consumer reporting laws of the state of employment should apply to reports made by consumer reporting agencies; and

Explanation

In order to avoid confusion about the reporting of criminal history information by a consumer reporting agency that may be obtained from sources other than a check under this authority, the same choice of law rule used for record screening under the Compact and suggested under this new authority (i.e., the state of employment) could be applied to consumer reporting agencies making consumer reports under the FCRA containing criminal history information.

(v) if adopted, provide for the exceptions discussed in Screening StandardsRecommendation # 2(B); and

Explanation

The FCRA currently restricts the dissemination by consumer reporting agencies of arrest records more than seven years old for certain types of positions. In order to provide consistency, if the exceptions to this restriction discussed in Screening Standards Recommendation #2(B) are adopted for records obtained under this authority, they should be made generally applicable to consumer reports under the FCRA.

(B) establishing national standards for courts to confidentially maintain personal identifiers in criminal case dockets and to allow access to those identifiers for authorized purposes, such as record confirmations in connection with criminal history background checks sought with the written consent of the defendant.

Explanation

Federal and state courts have recently been adopting rules limiting the inclusion of personal identifying information about case parties, such as their date of birth and Social Security Number, in case dockets. The intent of these rules is to prevent the use of the information for identity theft. A possible unforseen downstream consequence of this, however, is that background screeners attempting to confirm the currency of a record may not be able to confirm a match of an individual with the court records. As noted above, such confirmations are an important part of background screening. We therefore recommend that Congress consider whether it should set national standards for state and federal courts to maintain basic personal identifying information about criminal case parties, and provide limited access to that information for authorized purposes, such as criminal history background check confirmations being done with the written consent of the individual.

CONCLUSION

We have attempted with these recommendations to provide a way forward in establishing a system and process that allows broader private sector access to FBI-maintained criminal history information. The recommendations seek to address the legitimate interest in reliable information for criminal screening needs, while at the same time protecting the privacy interests of the individual being checked. We also try to account for the individual and social interests in ensuring the fair use of the information in order to both prevent unlawful discrimination in employment and minimize any adverse impact that increased access could have on the successful reentry of ex-offenders into society.

Finally, we note again that while we relied on the public comments on the congressionally- defined factors in preparing this report, we did not seek public comment on the report's recommendations. We, therefore, do not think of this report as the final word but rather as our effort to contribute to the public debate on these questions. We fully expect that

Congress will want to receive additional input from the public as it considers possible solutions. We will continue to answer questions and provide whatever support is necessary as Congress considers how to address these very important issues.

APPENDIX 1. FEDERAL STATUTES AUTHORIZING FINGERPRINT CHECKS FOR NON-CRIMINAL JUSTICE PURPOSES

1. 28 U.S.C. § 534 (2002) Note (federally chartered or insured banking industry and, if authorized by a state statute approved by the United States Attorney General (approval authority has been delegated to the FBI), state and local employment and licensing).
2. 42 U.S.C. § 5119a (1998) (relating to providing care to children, the elderly, or disabled persons).
3. 28 U.S.C. § 534 (2002) (relating to the parimutuel wagering industry (horse/dog racing)).
4. 7 U.S.C. §§ 12a and 21(b)(4)(E) (2000), (commodity futures trading industry).
5. 42 U.S.C. § 2169 (2005) (nuclear utilization facilities (power plants)).
6. 15 U.S.C. § 78q(f)(2) (2004) (securities industry).
7. 49 U.S.C. §§ 44935-44936(2003) (aviation industry).
8. 49 U.S.C. § 44939 (2003) (relating to flight school training).
9. 28 U.S.C. § 534 (2002) Note (nursing and home health care industry).
10. 49 U.S.C. § 5103a (2005) (relating to issuance and renewal of HAZMAT-endorsed commercial driver license).
11. 5 U.S.C. § 9101 (2000) (relating to federal government national security background checks).
12. 25 U.S.C. §§ 3205 and 3207 (2000) (relating to Indian child care).
13. 42 U.S.C. § 13041(1991) (relating to federal agencies and facilities contracted by federal agencies to provide child care).
14. 42 U.S.C. §§ 1437d(q) (1999) (relating to public housing and section 8 housing).
15. 25 U.S.C. § 4138 (1999) (relating to Indian housing).
16. 25 U.S.C. § 2701 (1988) (relating to Indian gaming).
17. 42 U.S.C. § 13726 (2000) (relating to private companies transporting state or local violent prisoners).
18. 8 U.S.C. § 1105 (2001) (relating to visa issuance or admission to the United States).
19. Executive Order 10450, 18 Fed. Reg. 2489 (Apr. 27, 1953) (follows 5 U.S.C. § 7311 (1966)) (relating to applicants for federal employment).
20. Pub. L. No. 107-188 § 201 and 212 (2002), 116 Stat. 594 (2002 (relating to handling of biological agents or toxins).
21. 46 U.S.C. §§ 70101 Note, 70105, and 70112 (2002) (relating to seaport facility and vessel security).
22. Pub. L. No. 108-458 § 6402 (2004) (relating to private security officer employment).

APPENDIX 2. FBI CRIMINAL HISTORY RECORD CHECKS FOR NON-CRIMINAL JUSTICE PURPOSES

New legislative initiatives introduced since September 11, 2001 have contributed to an increase in the number of requests for criminal history record checks. Prior to FY 2001, the FBI processed an average of less than 7 million non-criminal justice requests per year. The FBI processed in excess of 9 million non-criminal justice fingerprint cards in FY 2005. Approximately 3.7 million fingerprint submissions were received from federal agencies, while approximately 5.9 million fingerprint cards were received from non-federal entities in FY 2005. The FBI also produces identification records in response to written requests by subjects as authorized by Department Order 556-73. The following chart represents the total workload by type of non-criminal justice receipt.

Fiscal Year	Fingerprint Submissions Received			Name Searches Received Federal
	Federal	Non-Federal	Department Order	
2001	3,007,018	3,793,807	70,045	546,900
2002	3,511,996	4,886,782	89,073	434,611
2003	3,001,586	4,893,226	97,338	504,842
2004	3,270,108	5,104,686	118,587	325,681
2005	3,680,975	5,950,347	143,749	353,883

Entities responsible for the payment of FBI user fees for non-criminal justice criminal history record checks vary by contributor. Both federal and non-federal entities have programs where the contributing agencies are responsible for the payment. There are also federal and non-federal pass through programs where the individual fingerprinted is responsible for the payment. The following charts reflect the current non-federal and federal fee structure.

CURRENT NON-FEDERAL USER FEE STRUCTURE	
Base fee $16 Surcharge $ 6 Handling $ 2 $24	*NON-FEDERAL DIRECT PAYMENT AGENCIES (A check with each card)* Non-federal, non-criminal justice, non-law enforcement applicant fingerprint cards. $6 surcharge defrays cost for automation of fingerprint identification services. $2 handling covers processing direct payments for each transaction.

CURRENT FEDERAL USER FEE STRUCTURE	
Base fee $16 Handling $ 2 $18	*NON-FEDERAL DIRECT PAYMENT AGENCIES (A check with each card)* Non-federal, non-criminal justice, non-law enforcement applicant fingerprint cards. This fee relates to the submissions of individuals applying to provide care to children, the elderly, or disabled persons as defined in the National Child Protection Act of 1993. $2 handling covers processing direct payments for each transaction. (Boys and Girls Club of America, PROTECT Act)

(Continued)

Base fee $16 Surcharge $ 6 $22	*NON-FEDERAL BILLING AGENCIES (FBI bills contributor each month)* Non-federal, non-criminal justice, non-law enforcement applicant fingerprint cards. $6 surcharge defrays cost for automation of fingerprint identification services.
Base fee $16 $16	*NON-FEDERAL BILLING AGENCIES VOLUNTEER RATE* Non-federal, non-criminal justice, non-law enforcement applicant fingerprint cards. This fee relates to the submissions of individuals applying to provide care to children, the elderly, or disabled persons as defined in the National Child Protection Act of 1993.
$18	*FINGERPRINT SEARCH* Non-criminal justice, non-law enforcement applicant fingerprint cards. Submission: Paper Fingerprint Card Search: Name Search & Full Fingerprint Card Search Response: Paper or Electronic
$16	*FINGERPRINT SEARCH* Non-criminal justice, non-law enforcement applicant fingerprint cards. Submission: Electronic Fingerprints Search: Name Search & Full Fingerprint Search Response: Paper or Electronic
$6	*MANUAL NAME SEARCH* Submission: Paper Search: Auto/manual indices check Response: Paper
$4	*MRD NAME SEARCH W/FINGERPRINT CARD FOR FILING* Submission: MRD Search: Auto/manual indices check Response: MRD/paper
$2	*MRD NAME SEARCH* Submission: MRD Search: Auto/manual indices check Response: MRD/paper
No Charge	Resubmission of previously rejected submission (only 1st resubmission is no charge). Both federal and non-federal

APPENDIX 3. USAGE OF DIFFERENT TERMS AND DEFINITIONS REGARDING CRIMINAL HISTORY INFORMATION

These definitions are from the CJIS Security Policy, 28 CFR §20.3, and the National Crime Prevention and Privacy Compact (Compact):

Access means the opportunity to make use of an automated information system resource. The ability to have contact with a terminal from which a transaction may be initiated. (CJIS Security Policy)

Act means the Omnibus Crime Control and Safe Streets Act, 42 U.S.C. 3701, *et seq.,* as amended. (28 CFR §20.3)

Administration of Criminal Justice means performance of any of the following activities: detection, apprehension, detention, pretrial release, post-trial release, prosecution, adjudication, correctional supervision, or rehabilitation of accused persons or criminal offenders. The administration of criminal justice shall include criminal identification activities and the collection, storage, and dissemination of criminal history record information. (28 CFR §20.3)

Attorney General means the Attorney General of the United States. (Compact)

Audit means the independent examination of records and activities to ensure compliance with established controls, policy, and operational procedures, and to recommend any indicated changes in controls, policy, or procedures. (CJIS Security Policy)

Audit Logging means the process of gathering and saving information in a written or automated electronic form to record the session initiation and termination messages, logins and failed login attempts, logout, file access or other various activities to include all forms of access violations such as attempts to access data beyond the level of authorized access. (CJIS Security Policy)

Audit Trail means a chronological record of system activities that is sufficient to enable the reconstruction, review, and examination of the sequence of environments and activities surrounding or leading to an operation, a procedure, or an event in a transaction from its inception to final results. This includes user login, file access, other various activities, and whether any actual or attempted security violations occurred, legitimate and unauthorized. (CJIS Security Policy)

Authorized Access means the ability to perform an authorized transaction from a CJIS terminal device or having access to CJIS data that is routinely prohibited by organizational policy or law by satisfying the appropriate background checks, clearance and training. (CJIS Security Policy)

Authorized User means an individual who has been appropriately vetted, holds a current certification, and has been authorized to access CJIS Data. (CJIS Security Policy)

Background Check means a check of all appropriate information sources to include a state of residency and national 10-print fingerprint-based record check. (CJIS Security Policy)

CJIS Data means data considered to be criminal justice in nature, including images, files, records, and intelligence information. FBI CJIS data is information derived from state or federal CJIS systems. (CJIS Security Policy)

CJIS Network means a telecommunications infrastructure dedicated to law enforcement users only. The usage of such a network by noncriminal justice entities dictates that it be considered a sensitive but unclassified non-secure network. (CJIS Security Policy)

CJIS Systems means the computer network infrastructure dedicated to criminal justice uses that facilitates interfaces with the national CJIS Division systems. (CJIS Security Policy)

CJIS Systems Agency (CSA) means a duly authorized state, federal, international, tribal, or territorial criminal justice agency on the CJIS network providing statewide (or equivalent) service to its criminal justice users with respect to the CJIS data from various systems managed by the FBI CJIS Division. There shall be only one CSA per state or territory. In federal agencies, the CSA may be the interface or switch to other federal agencies connecting to the FBI CJIS systems. (CJIS Security Policy)

CJIS Systems Officer (CSO) means an individual located within the CJIS Systems Agency responsible for the administration of the CJIS network for the CJIS Systems Agency. (CJIS Security Policy)

Compact means the National Crime Prevention and Privacy Compact set forth in section 14616 of this title. (Compact)

Compact Officer means -- (Compact)

(1) with respect to the federal government, an official so designated by the Director of the FBI; and
(2) with respect to a Party State, the chief administrator of the state's criminal history record repository or a designee of the chief administrator who is a regular full-time employee of the repository.

Confidential Information means information maintained by state agencies that is exempt from disclosure under the provisions of the Public Records Act or other applicable state or federal laws. The controlling factor for confidential information is dissemination. Criminal History Record Information (CHRI) is protected by federal legislation. (CJIS Security Policy)

Confidentiality means the property that sensitive information is not disclosed to unauthorized individuals, entities, or processes. (CJIS Security Policy)

Control Terminal Agency means a duly authorized state, foreign, or international criminal justice agency with direct access to the National Crime Information Center telecommunications network providing statewide (or equivalent) service to its criminal justice users with respect to the various systems managed by the FBI CJIS Division. (28 CFR §20.3)

Control Terminal Officer (CTO) -- Per a change in bylaws, CTO is now referred to as a CJIS Systems Officer. See definition for a CJIS Systems Officer. (CJIS Security Policy)

Council means the Compact Council established under Article VI of the Compact. (Compact)

Criminal History Record Information means information collected by criminal justice agencies on individuals consisting of identifiable descriptions and notations of arrests, detentions, indictments, informations, or other formal criminal charges, and any disposition arising therefrom, including acquittal, sentencing, correctional supervision, and release. The term does not include identification information such as fingerprint records if such information does not indicate the individual's involvement with the criminal justice system. (28 CFR §20.3)

Criminal History Record Information System means a system including the equipment, facilities, procedures, agreements, and organizations thereof for the collection, processing, preservation, or dissemination of criminal history record information. (28 CFR §20.3)

Criminal History Record Repository means the state agency designated by the governor or other appropriate executive official or the legislature to perform centralized recordkeeping functions for criminal history records and services in the state. (28 CFR §20.3 and Compact)

Criminal History Records means – (Compact)

(1) information collected by criminal justice agencies on individuals consisting of identifiable descriptions and notations of arrests, detentions, indictments, or other formal criminal charges, and any disposition arising therefrom, including acquittal, sentencing, correctional supervision, or release; and

(2) does not include identification information such as fingerprint records if such information does not indicate involvement of the individual with the criminal justice system.

Criminal Justice means activities relating to the detection, apprehension, detention, pretrial release, post-trial release, prosecution, adjudication, correctional supervision, or rehabilitation of accused persons or criminal offenders. The administration of criminal justice includes criminal identification activities and the collection, storage, and dissemination of criminal history records. (Compact)

Criminal Justice Agency means: (28 CFR §20.3 and Compact)

(1) Courts; and
(2) A governmental agency or any subunit thereof that performs the administration of criminal justice pursuant to a statute or executive order, and that allocates a substantial part of its annual budget to the administration of criminal justice. State and federal Inspector General Offices are included.

Criminal Justice Network means a telecommunication infrastructure dedicated to the use by criminal justice entities exchanging criminal justice data. (CJIS Security Policy)

Criminal Justice Purposes -- See Administration of Criminal Justice. (CJIS Security Policy)

Criminal Justice Services means services provided by the FBI to criminal justice agencies in response to a request for information about a particular individual or as an update to information previously provided for criminal justice purposes. (Compact)

Criterion Offense means any felony or misdemeanor offense not included on the list of nonserious offenses published periodically by the FBI. (Compact)

Degaussing means a method for purging operational and non-operational magnetic data storage media and is an alternative to physical destruction of magnetic data storage media. Approved degaussing equipment must have a minimum field strength of 1500 Gauss at the degaussing platform. Field strength is measured with a gauss meter. (CJIS Security Policy)

Direct Access means having the authority to access systems managed by the FBI CJIS Division, whether by manual or automated methods, not requiring the assistance of or intervention by any other party or agency. (28 CFR §20.3)

Disposition means information disclosing that criminal proceedings have been concluded and the nature of the termination, including information disclosing that the police have elected not to refer a matter to a prosecutor or that a prosecutor has elected not to commence criminal proceedings; or disclosing that proceedings have been indefinitely postponed and the reason for such postponement. Dispositions shall include, but shall not be limited to, acquittal, acquittal by reason of insanity, acquittal by reason of mental incompetence, case continued without finding, charge dismissed, charge dismissed due to insanity, charge dismissed due to mental incompetency, charge still pending due to insanity, charge still pending due to mental incompetence, guilty plea, nolle prosequi, no paper, nolo contendere plea, convicted, youthful offender determination, deceased, deferred disposition, dismissed-civil action, found insane, found mentally incompetent, pardoned, probation before conviction, sentence commuted, adjudication withheld, mistrial-defendant discharged, executive clemency, placed on probation, paroled, or released from correctional supervision. (28 CFR §20.3)

Executive Order means an order of the President of the United States or the Chief Executive of a state that has the force of law and that is published in a manner permitting regular public access. (28 CFR §20.3)

FBI means the Federal Bureau of Investigation. (Compact)

FBI CJIS Data means information derived from the national CJIS Division systems. (CJIS Security Policy)

Federal Service Coordinator means a non-Control Terminal Agency that has a direct telecommunications line to the National Crime Information Center network. (28 CFR §20.3). Per a change in bylaws, FSC Agencies are now referred to as CJIS Systems Agencies. See definition for a CJIS Systems Agency. (CJIS Security Policy)

Fingerprint Identification Records System or "FIRS" means the following FBI records: Criminal fingerprints and/or related criminal justice information submitted by authorized agencies having criminal justice responsibilities; civil fingerprints submitted by federal agencies and civil fingerprints submitted by persons desiring to have their fingerprints placed on record for personal identification purposes; identification records, sometimes referred to as "rap sheets," which are compilations of criminal history record information pertaining to individuals who have criminal fingerprints maintained in the FIRS; and a name index pertaining to all individuals whose fingerprints are maintained in the FIRS. See the FIRS Privacy Act System Notice periodically published in the Federal Register for further details. (28 CFR §20.3)

Interface Agency means any entity at federal, state, international, tribal or local levels which has a direct or indirect communications link to the FBI CJIS Division's systems. (CJIS Security Policy)

Internet means a global system interconnecting computers and computer networks. The computers and networks are owned separately by a host of organizations, government agencies, companies, and colleges. The Internet is the present "information super highway." (CJIS Security Policy)

Internet Access means access to CJIS systems or CJIS data which requires data to be transmitted over the Internet. (CJIS Security Policy)

Interstate Identification Index System or "III System" means the cooperative federal-state system for the exchange of criminal history records, and includes the National Identification Index, the National Fingerprint File, and, to the extent of their participation in such system, the criminal history record repositories of the states and the FBI. (28 CFR §20.3 and Compact)

Local Agency Security Officer (LASO) means the security point-of-contact (POC) for local agencies that have access to a CTA criminal justice network. This POC could also be the Terminal Agency Coordinator (TAC). (CJIS Security Policy)

Local Area Network means a data communications network spanning a limited geographical area -- a few miles at most. It provides communication between computers and peripherals at relatively high data rates and relatively low error rates. (CJIS Security Policy)

Logging means the process of storing information about events that occurred on the firewall, host system, or network. This process creates audit logs. (CJIS Security Policy)

National Crime Information Center or "NCIC" means the computerized information system, which includes telecommunications lines and any message switching facilities that are authorized by law, regulation, or policy approved by the Attorney General of the United States to link local, state, tribal, federal, foreign, and international criminal justice agencies for the purpose of exchanging NCIC related information. The NCIC includes, but is not limited to, information in the III System. See the NCIC Privacy Act System Notice periodically published in the Federal Register for further details. (28 CFR §20.3)

National Fingerprint File or "NFF" means a database of fingerprints, or other uniquely personal identifying information, relating to an arrested or charged individual maintained by the FBI to provide positive identification of record subjects indexed in the III System. (28 CFR §20.3 and Compact)

National Identification Index or "NII" means an index maintained by the FBI consisting of names, identifying numbers, and other descriptive information relating to record subjects about whom there are criminal history records in the III System. (28 CFR §20.3 and Compact)

National Indices means the National Identification Index and the National Fingerprint File. (Compact)

Nonconviction Data means arrest information without disposition if an interval of one year has elapsed from the date of arrest and no active prosecution of the charge is pending; information disclosing that the police have elected not to refer a matter to a prosecutor, that a prosecutor has elected not to commence criminal proceedings, or that proceedings have been indefinitely postponed; and information that there has been an acquittal or a dismissal. (28 CFR §20.3)

Nonparty State means a state that has not ratified this Compact. (Compact)

Noncriminal Justice Agency means a governmental agency or any subunit thereof that provides services primarily for purposes other than the administration of criminal justice. (CJIS Security Policy)

Noncriminal Justice Purposes means uses of criminal history records for purposes authorized by federal or state law other than purposes relating to criminal justice activities, including employment suitability, licensing determinations, immigration and naturalization matters, and national security clearances. (Compact)

Party State means a state that has ratified the Compact. (Compact)

Positive Identification means a determination, based upon a comparison of fingerprints or other equally reliable biometric identification techniques, that the subject of a record search is the same person as the subject of a criminal history record or records indexed in the III System. Identifications based solely upon a comparison of subjects' names or other nonunique identification characteristics or numbers, or combinations thereof, shall not constitute positive identification. (Compact)

Remote Access means any access to the CTA network through a non-CTA controlled network, device, or medium. (CJIS Security Policy)

Residual CJIS Data means CJIS data left in storage (hard drive) after processing operations are complete, but before degaussing or rewriting has taken place. Any data left in a file from previous CJIS transactions that is not purged or encrypted is susceptible to unauthorized access, as in the case of also having Internet access from CJIS terminals or workstations. (CJIS Security Policy)

Sealed Record Information means -- (Compact)

(1) with respect to adults, that portion of a record that is–
   (A) not available for criminal justice uses;

(B) not supported by fingerprints or other accepted means of positive identification; or

(C) subject to restrictions on dissemination for noncriminal justice purposes pursuant to a court order related to a particular subject or pursuant to a federal or state statute that requires action on a sealing petition filed by a particular record subject; and

(2) with respect to juveniles, whatever each state determines is a sealed record under its own law and procedure.

Secondary Dissemination means the re-dissemination of FBI CJIS data or records from an authorized agency that has direct access to the data to another authorized agency. (CJIS Security Policy)

State means any state of the United States, the District of Columbia, the Commonwealth of Puerto Rico, and any territory or possession of the United States. (28 CFR §20.3)

Terminal Agency Coordinator (TAC) -- generally, means the primary point of contact at the local level which serves as liaison between the CJIS Systems Officer and the local agencies that have access to a CSA criminal justice network. The responsibilities afforded to the TAC may vary from state to state. (CJIS Security Policy)

Definitions applicable to the Compact Council's Security and Management Control Outsourcing Standards are published in the *Federal Register*, dated December 16, 2004.

End Notes

[1] We note input on these issues was also provided through a report of a SEARCH task force on criminal history background check issues provided to the Department in October 2005 and published on the SE ARC H we bsite on May 1, 2006. The SEARCH task force effort was undertaken with funding from the Bureau of Justice Statistics, and its report is available at http://www.search.org/events/news/ criminalrecord2006.asp.

[2] Vermont and Maine are the two states that are not yet participating in the III due to technology limitations. Vermont expects to have the technology necessary to meet minimum III standards in 2006, and Maine continues to work with CJIS to take the step s necessary to achieve all of the required III standards . Additional jurisdictions that are not yet participating in the III include American Samoa, the District of Columbia, Guam, the Mariana Islands, Puerto Rico, and the Virgin Islands.

[3] *See infra* note 7.

[4] The eight states currently participating in the NFF are New Jersey, Florida, North Carolina, Oregon, Kansas, Oklahoma, Colorado, and Montana.

[5] Section 103 of Pub. L. 103-159.

[6] *See* 28 CFR 20.3 (b).

[7] *See* The National Crime Prevention and Privacy Compact, Pub. L. 105-251, Art. I (18), 42 U.S.C. 14616. We note that another category of use made of the III under the Attorney General's authority under 28 U.S.C. 534 are checks for national security purposes, such as the checks made by the FBI and other law enforcement agencies for counterterrorism and related purposes. Whether such checks are subject to the Compact is determined by the Attorney General on a case-by-case basis.

[8] Pub. L. 103-209 (42 U.S.C. 5119a).

[9] Pub. L. 105-251.

[10] The authority to provide information to federally insured or chartered banking institutions is also part of Public Law 92-544.

[11] 5 U.S.C. 552a.

[12] 5 U.S.C. 552.

[13] Appendix A provides a breakd own of these checks Fiscal Years 2001-2005 by federal and non-federal users and shows with the fees charged by the FBI for fingerprint-based civil checks.

[14] *See supra* note 5.

[15] The current Compact-member states include Maine, New Hampshire, Connecticut, New Jersey, Maryland , North Carolina, South Carolina, Georgia, Hawaii, Florida , Tennessee , Ohio, Minnesota, Iowa, Missouri, Arkansas, Kansas, Oklahoma, Montana, Wyoming, Colorado, Idaho, Arizona, Alaska, Oregon, Nevada, and West Virginia.

[16] The three states and one territory with pending legislation to ratify the Compact include New York, Kentucky, Washington, and Puerto Rico.

[17] The 10 jurisdictions that are MOU signatories include North Dakota, South Dakota, Nebraska, New Mexico, Illinois, Mississippi, Vermont, Kentucky, Hawaii, Guam, and American Samoa.

[18] The 16 jurisdictions with no known current action include California, Utah, Texas, Wisconsin, Louisiana, Michigan, Indiana, Alabama, Virginia, Rhode Island, Delaware, Massachusetts, Puerto Rico, Virgin Islands, Northern Mariana Islands, and the District of Columbia.

[19] The 15 Council members are appointed by the Attorney General, and include appointments of 9 Compact officers from Party States based up on the recommendations of the Compact Officers of all Compact Party States, two a t-large members from federal agencies and one FBI employee nominated by the Director of the FBI, two a t-large members from state agencies nominated by the Council Chairman, and one member from the FBI CJIS Division's Advisory Policy Board (APB) nominate d by the A PB. The Council is administratively supported by the F BI and h olds public meetings twice a year .

[20] National Task Force to the U.S. Attorney General, Interstate Identification Index Na me Check Efficacy, NCJ-17935 (July 1999) , available at http://www.search.org/files/pdf/III_Name_Check.pdf. Also, in testimony to Congress in May 2000, the FBI shared the results of an analysis of the 6.9 million fingerprints submitted for employment and licensing purposes in Fiscal Year 1997 . Accor ding to the FB I, 8.7 percent or just over 600,000 of the prints produce d "hits;" an d 11.7 percent of the "hits," or 70,2 00 civil finger print cards , reflected names different than those listed in the applicants' criminal history records. These individuals would have been missed entirely by name-only background checks. *See Hearing on H.R. 3410, Volunteer Organization Safety Act of 1999, Before the House Judiciary Comm., Subcommittee on Crime, 106th Cong.* (May 18, 200 0) (Testimony of Mr. David Loesch, Assistant Director in Charge of the Criminal Justice Information Services Division of the Federal Bureau of Investigation), *available at* http://judicia ry.house.gov/lega cy/loes0518 .htm.

[21] The Compact Council published a rule that allows for the delayed submission of fingerprints following a name check of the III specific ally authorize d by the Council for non-criminal justice checks when there are exigent circumstances involving a risk to health and safety, such as in cases of the emergency placement of children with individuals when fingerprint checks are not feasible before the placement must be mad e. *See* 28 CFR 901.3.

[22] The pilot was extended to 60 months by section 1197 of the Violence Against Women and Department of Justice Reauthorization Act of 2005, Pub. L. 109-162.

[23] This feasibility study has not been completed due to the necessary start-up times for the PROTECT Act Pilot Programs, the limited participation in the pilots, and the duplicate requirements of this report. The factors required to be considered in the PRO TE CT Act feasibility study are very similar to the factors ad dressed in this report. Moreover, much of the data gathered during the preparation of the feasibility study has been used as a foundation for this report. Therefore, this report is intended to be responsive to the reporting obligations under the PRO TEC T Ac t in that it recommends a national system for criminal history record access that can apply not only to volunteers working with vulnerable populations, but also to employers generally.

[24] The California Department of Justice has developed a list of Applicant Live-Scan Fingerprint Services available to members of the public, including locations, hours of operation, and collection fees, available at: http://ag.ca.gov/fin gerprints/p ublications /contact.h tm

[25] As noted above, Vermont is one of two remaining states that is still working toward participating in the III.

[26] *See* "Outsourcing of Noncriminal Justice Administrative Functions," National Crime Prevention and Privacy Compact Council, 70 Fed. Reg. 74200 (Dec. 15, 2005), and "Security and Management Control Outsourcing Standard," National Crime Prevention and Privacy Compact Council, 70 Fed. Reg. 74373 (Dec. 15, 2005).

[27] *See* Federal Business Opportunities, June 21, 2005, Department of Justice, Federal Bureau of Investigation, Information Technology Contracts Unit, "R – Outsourcing Request for Information," Solicitation Number 06212005, available at: www.f edbizop ps.gov.

[28] *See* Federal Business Opportunities, June 21, 2006, Department of Justice, Federal Bureau of Investigation, Information Technology Contracts Unit/PPMS, "R – Channeling for NonCriminal Justice Fingerprint Submissions," Solicitation Number RFQ 06212 005, available at: www.f edbizop ps.gov. See also, "Notice of Intent To Publish a Request for Proposal for the Section of Channelers," Federal Bureau of Investigation, Department of Justice, 71 Fed. Reg. 28,38828,389 (May 16, 2006).

[29] *See* 49 CFR 1572.13(f).

[30] Presolicitation Notice, 7 0 – 10 Print Scanner Requirement Workshop, Federal Business Opportunities (September 30, 2005), available at :http://www .fedbiz opps.gov/spg/DHS%2DD R/OCPO/USV ISIT/Reference%2DNumber% 2DUSV% 2D5M% 2D03/Synops isP.html

[31] Fla. Stat. ch. 943.0542 (1999).

[32] The VECHS fee for performing a background check is $47 for each employee or $36 for each volunteer. The fee includes the FBI's fee for performing the national criminal history background check.

[33] *See* the discussion of negligent hiring and retention doctrines in the *Report of the National Task Force on the Commercial Sale of Criminal Justice Record Information*, SEARCH, the National Consortium for Justice In formation and Statistics, 65-68 (Dec . 2005), http://www.search.org/files/pdf/RNTFCSCJRI.pdf.

[34] In 2002, the Bureau of Justice Statistics published the results of a major study on recidivism, which tracked prisoners discharged in 15 States (representing two-thirds of all prisoners released in 1994). The study included findings that 67 percent of former inmates released from State prisons in 1994 committed at least one serious new crime within the following three years; within three years, 52 percent of the 272,111 released prisoners were back in prison either because of a new crime or because that had violated their par ole conditions; and the released offenders had accumulated 4 .1 million arrest charges before their most recent imprisonment and another 774,000 charge s within three years of release . Report of the Bureau of Justice Statistics, Two-Thirds of Former State Prisoners Rearrested for Serious New Crimes (June 2, 2002), available at www.oj p.usdoj.gov/bj s/abstrac t/rpr94.htm .

[35] Some of the state web sites that sell criminal history information include:
Colorado: www.C birecordchec k.com
Florida: www.fdle.state.fl.us/criminalhistory
Kansa s: www.accesskansas.org/kbi/criminalhistory
Michigan: http://mi-mall.michigan.gov/ichat
Pennsylvania: https://epatch.state.pa.us
South Carolina: http://www.sled.state.sc.us
Tennessee : www.tb i.state.tn.us/Info% 20Systems %20Div/T ORIS/TORIS.h tm
Tex as: http://records.txdps.state.tx.us
Virginia: www.vsp .state.va.us/ncji/cjisncji.htm
Washington: http://www .wa.gov/wsp /crime/c rimhist.htm
Wisconsin: www.doj.state.wi.us/dles/cib/crimback.asp

[36] *The Role of FCRA in Employee Background Checks and the Collection of Medical Information: Before the Subcommittee on Financial Institutions and Consumer Credit of the Committee on Financial Services*, 108th Cong. 82, Serial No. 108–38 (June 17, 2003) (Prepared Statement of Harold Morgan, Senior Vice President, Human Resources, Bally Total Fitness Corporation, on Behalf of LPA, The HR Policy Association).

[37] *Id.* at 90.

[38] *Private Security Officer Employment Authorization Act of 2003, Before the Subcommittee on Crime, Terrorism, and Home land Security of the Committee of the Judiciary, House of Representatives*, 108th Cong., Serial No. 108-89 (March 30, 2004) (Prepared Statement of Mr. Don Walker, Chairman, Pinkerton Security, Executive Member, America n Society of Industrial Security, Board of Directors, National Association of Security Guard Companies).

[39] *Private Security Officer Employment Authorization Act of 2003, Before the Subcommittee on Crime, Terrorism, and Homeland Security of the Committee of the Judiciary, House of Representatives*, 108th Cong., Serial No. 108-89 (March 30, 2004) (Prepared Statement of the Honorable Jeanine Pirro, District Attorney, Westchester County, NY).

[40] 15 U.S.C. § 1681 *et. seq.*

[41] 15 U.S.C. § 1681K (FCRA § 613).

[42] *See* SEARCH *Report of the National Task Force Report on the Commercial Sale of Criminal Justice Record Information*, *supra*, note 30, at 60-61.

[43] 15 U.S.C. 1681u.

[44] *Id.*

[45] *See* FTC Official Staff Commentary on the Fair Credit Re porting Act, 16 CFR 622.1

[46] The FCRA also includes certain specific preemption provisions that override any state law that differs from the federal provision, regardless of its consistency with the FCRA, depending upon when the State la w was enacted. *See, e.g.*,15 U.S.C. § 1681t(b)(1).

[47] CAL. CIV . CODE § 1786 .18(a)(7) (California); M ONT . CODE ANN . § 31-3- 112 (5) (Montana) ; NEV . REV . STAT . 5698C.150(2) (Nevada); N.M. STAT . ANN . § 56-3-6(a)(5) (New Mexico).

[48] CAL. CIV . CODE § 1786.18(a)(7) (California); N.M. STAT . ANN . § 56-3-6(a)(5) (New Mexico); N.Y. BUS. LAW § 380-j(a)(1) (New York).

[49] KAN . STAT . ANN . §§ 50-70 4(a)(5) & (b) (Kansa s); MD . CODE ANN . §§ 14-12 03(a) (5) & (b)(3) (Maryland); M ASS. GEN . LAWS 93 §§ 52(a)(5) & (b)(3) (Massachusetts); N.H. REV . STAT . ANN . §§ 359-B:5(I)(e) & 5(II)(c) (New Hampshire). New York sets the salary level at $25,000 (N.Y. GEN . LAWS §§ 380-j(f)(1)(v) & (j)(f)(1)(iii)), and Texas sets it at $75,000 (TEX . BUS. & COM . CODE ANN . §§ 20.05 (a)(4) & (b)(3)).

[50] *See, e.g.*, CAL. CIV . CODE § 1786.20(a)(2) (California); 20 ILL. COMP. STAT . ANN . 2635/7(A)(1) (Illinois); MINN . STAT . § 13C.0 3 (Minnesota); O KLA . STAT . TIT . 24 § 148 (Oklahoma). 402 CAL. CIVIL CODE § 1786.53.

[51] CAL. CIVIL CODE § 1786.53.

[52] A general discussion of the background and applications of the FIPs can be found in *Justice Information Privacy Guideline – Developing, Drafting and Assessing Privacy Policy for Justice Information Systems*, 22-25, (September 2002), National Criminal Justice Association, available at http://www.ncja.org/pdf/ privacyguideline.pdf. See also, the Federal Trade Commission discussion of the FIPs principals, available at http://www .ftc.gov/reports/p rivacy3/fairin fo.htm.

[53] *See, e.g., Privacy and Information Quality Policy Development for the Justice Decision Maker*, Global Justice Information Sharing Initiative, Bureau of Justice Assistance , Office of Justice Programs, U .S. Department of Justice, available at: http://it.ojp.gov/process_links.jsp?link_id=5052.

[54] 42 U.S.C. 2000e *et seq.*

[55] "Policy Statement on the Issue of Conviction Records Un der Title VII of the Civil Rights Act of 1964, as amended, 42 U.S.C. §§ 20003 *et seq.* (1982)," EEOC, Feb. 4, 1987 . See EEOC Compliance Manual, Vol. II, Appendix 604-A.

[56] "Policy Guidance on the Consideration of Arrest Records in Employment Decisions Under Title VII of the Civil Rights Act of 19 64, as amended, 42 U .S.C. §§ 2000e *et seq.* (1982) ," EEO C, Sept. 7, 1 990. *See* EEOC Compliance Manual, Vol. II, Sec. 604.

[57] Those states include Arizona (ARIZ . REV . STAT . § 13-904(E); Colorado (COLO . REV . STAT . § 24-5-101); Connecticut (CONN. GEN . STAT . § 46a-80 (c); Florida (FLA. STAT . § 120); Kentucky (KY . REV . STAT . § 335B); Louisiana (LA. REV . STAT . § 37:2950); Minnesota (MINN . STAT . § 364.03); New Mexico (N.M. STAT . §§ 28-2); and Washington.

[58] Those states include Hawaii (HAW . REV . STAT . § 378-1 et. seq.); Kansas (KAN . STAT . ANN . § 22-4710(f); New York (N.Y. EXEC . LAW § 296(15); N.Y. CORRECT. LAW §§ 750-54.; Pennsylvania (18 PA. CONS. STAT . §§ 9124-9125); and Wisconsin (WIS. STAT . § 111.335).

[59] See supra, note 36 at 9.

[60] Those states are: Alaska (ALASKA STAT . § 12.62.160(b)(8); Arkansas (ARK . CODE ANN .§ 12-1 2-1009(c)); California (CAL. LAB. CODE § 432.7(a)); Illinois (775 ILL. COMP. STAT . 5/2-103(A)); Massachusetts (MASS. GEN .LAWS ch. 151B § 4(9)(I)); Michigan — but for misdemeanor offenses only (MICH COMP. LAWS § 37.2205a(1)); Mississippi — if the arrest is more than a year old (MISS. CODE ANN . § 45-27-12(1)); Nebraska — if the arrest is more than a year old (NEB. REV . STAT . § 29-3523(1)); New York (N.Y. EXEC . LAW § 296(1 6)); North Dakota (N.D. CENT.CODE § 12-60-16.6)); and Rhode Island (R .I. GEN . LAWS § 28-5-7(7)).
For example, the California Labor Code, section 432.7, provides:

> 432.7(a). No employer, whether a public agency or private individual or corporation, shall ask an applicant for employment to disclose, through any written form or verbally, information concerning an arrest or detention that did not result in conviction, or information concerning a referral to, and participation in, any pretrial or posttrial diversion program, nor shall any employer seek from any source whatsoever, or utilize, as a factor in determining any condition of employment including hiring, promotion, termination, or any apprenticeship training program or any other training program leading to employment, any record of arrest or detention that did not result in conviction, or any record regarding a referral to, an d participation in, any pretrial or posttrial diversion program. As used in this section, a conviction shall include a plea, verdict, or finding of guilt regardless of whether sentence is imposed by the court. Nothing in this section shall prevent a n employer from asking a n employee or applicant for employment about an arrest for which the employee or applicant is out on bail or on his or her own recognizance pending trial.

CAL. LAB. CODE § 432.7(a) (1992). Section 433 of that Code provides that: "Any person violating this article is guilty of a misdemeanor."

[61] Those states are: Alaska (ALASKA DEPARTMENT OF LABOR AND WORKFORCE DEVELOPMENT, ALASKA EM PLOYER HANDBOOK 83) Arizona (ARIZONA CIVIL RIGHTS DIVISION 'S PRE-EMPLOYMENT GUIDe); Colorado (COLORADO CIVIL RIGHTS COMMISSION GUIDE TO PRE-EMPLOYMENT QUESTIONS); Kansas (KANSAS HUMAN RIGHTS COMMISSION'S GUIDANCE ON EQUAL EMPLOYMENT PRACTICES); Michigan (MICHIGAN CIVIL RIGHTS COMMISSION PRE-Employment Inquiry Guide); Nevada (NEVADA PRE-EMPLOYMENT INQUIRY GUIDE); New Jersey (NEW JERSEY GUIDE TO PRE-EMPLOYMENT INQUIRIES, NEW JERSEY DIVISION ON CIVIL RIGHTS); Ohio (A GUIDE FOR APPLICATION FORMS AND INTERVIEWS, OHIO CIVIL RIGHTS COMMISSION); South Dakota (SOUTH DAKOTA DIVISION OF HUMAN RIGHTS PRE-EMPLOYMENT INQUIRY GUIDE); Utah (Pre-Employment Inquiry Guide, UTAH ADMIN . Code R606-2-2); and West Virginia (WEST VIRGINIA BUREAU OF EMPLOYMENT PROGRAMS GUIDELINES FOR PRE-EMPLOYMENT INQUIRIES).

[62] Those states are: Idaho (IDAHO COMMISSION ON HUMAN RIGHTS, PRE-EMPLOYMENT INQUIRIES); Missouri (COMMISSION ON HUMAN RIGHTS, MISS OU RI DEPART MENT OF LABOR AND INDUST RIAL RELATIONS , PRE-EMPLOYMENT INQUIRIES); New Ham pshire (N .H. CODE ADM IN . R. HUM 405.03).

[63] District of Columbia (D.C. CODE ANN . § 2-1402 .66); Hawaii (HAW AII CIVIL RIGHTS COMMISSION , GUIDELINE FOR PRE-EMPLOYMENT INQUIRIES); and Ohio (A GUIDE FOR APPLICATION FORMS AND INTERVIEWS, OHIO CIVIL RIGHTS COMMISSION).

[64] HAW . REV . STAT . § 378-2.5(a)-(b).

[65] CAL. LAB. CODE § 432.8.

[66] MASS. GEN . LAWS ch. 151B § 4(9)(ii).

[67] Those states are: Missouri (COMMISSION ON HUMAN RIGHTS, MISSOURI DEPARTMENT OF LABOR AND INDUSTRIAL RELATIONS , PRE-EMPLOYMENT INQUIRIES); New Hampshire (N .H. Code Admin . R. Hum 405.03); New Jersey (NEW JERSEY GUIDE TO PRE-EMPLOYMENT INQUIRIES, NEW JERSEY DIVISION ON CIVIL RIGHTS); RHODE Island (R .I. Gen . lAWS § 28-5-7(7)); South Dakota (SOUTH DAKOTA DIVISION OF HUMAN RIGHTS PRE-EMPLOYMENT INQUIRY GUIDE); and Utah (Pre-Employment Inquiry Guide, Utah Admin . Code R606-2-2).

[68] THE ASSOCIATION OF SENIOR HUMAN RESOURCE EXECUTIVES, LPA BACKGROUND CHECK PROTOCOL (2003). Also cited and discussed in the *Report of the National Task Force on the Commercial Sale of Criminal Justice Record Information*, SEA RCH , the National Consortium for Justice Information and Statistics, 7 7-78 (D ec. 200 5), *supra*, note 33.

[69] Id.

[70] Id.

[71] President George W. Bush, Address Before a Joint Session of Congress on the State of the Union, 40 WEEKLY COMP. PRES. DOC . no. 4 at 94 (Jan. 20, 2 004), *available at* http://www.gpoaccess.gov/sou/index.html.

[72] The factors listed in section 6403 relate principally to questions regarding access to FBI-maintained criminal history information for employment suitability purposes, and, for that reason, we have focused our recommendations on that area of private sector access. We note, however, that criminal history background screening is also widely used by landlords for screening prospective tenants. The Department of Housing and Urban Development, for example, requires criminal background checks for certain public housing programs. *See* 66 Fed. Reg. 28776 (May 24, 2001). Broadening access to include private housing checks would involve issues similar to those addressed here concerning access for employment purposes. *See, e.g.,* the discussion in the SEARCH *Report of the National Task Force on the Commercial Sale of Criminal Justice Record Information*, at 20 and 68-69, *supra*, note 33.

[73] For example, at the request of the banking industry, the FBI recently issued a statement making it clear that the authority under Pub. L. 9 2-544 to con duct fingerprint checks to promote the security of federally chartered or insured banking institutions includes checks of employee s of other entities , such as bank subsidiaries, holding companies, or contractors who have a direct relationship with a banking institution affecting the security of the institution. *See* "FBI Checks on Employees of Banks and Related Entities," available at http://www.f bi.gov/hq/cjisd /banknotic econtrib torltr.htm

[74] As noted above, the process outlined in these recommendations also constitutes the Department's recommendation required under the PROTECT Act for how a national system could be created for performing background checks on volunteer s for entities providing service s to children , the elderly, and disabled per sons. *See* note 23, *supra.*

[75] PROTECT ACT, section 108(d)(1)(G).

[76] We expect that the Compact Council will be an appropriate and useful resource for the Attorney General to consult in establishing this and other requirements under this new authority. The Council is responsible for promulgating rules and procedures regarding the u se of III records for non-criminal justice purposes subject to the Comp act. The Council has already promulgated outsourcing standards for security and privacy that must be followed by private contractors engaged by authorized users that are outsourcing any portion of the functions they perform relating to the management and dissemination of criminal history record information from the III for non-criminal justice purposes.

[77] This conclusion is supported by da ta obtained as a result of the PROTECT Act pilot program. The PROTECT Act allows background checks to be conducted on individuals who work with certain volunteer organizations. As of August 28, 2005, the FBI had processed 12,718 background checks for volunteers, resulting in 1,024 identifications. Based on a review of 400 of the 1,024 criminal history records, it was determined that 63 percent of the volunteers had a criminal history record in the state of application and 8 percent had multiple state arrests, at least one of which was in the state of application. As a result, 71 per cent of the volunteers with criminal history records would have been identified at the state level.

[78] The National Fingerprint-Based Applicant Check Study, conducted through the cooperation of the FBI and the Ohio Bureau of Criminal Identification and Investigation, explored the feasibility of establishing a national, rapid, and positive background check system for authorized non-criminal justice purposes. The study specifically explored the feasibility of using 10-flat fingerprints to conduct civil applicant criminal history checks. The study was completed on December 31, 2003. Based on the results of the study, the Compact Council, in May 2004, formally accepted 10-flat fingerprints as another method for determining positive identification for exchanging criminal history record information for non-criminal justice purposes.

[79] *See* Federal Business Opportunities, *supra* note 30.

[80] *See, e.g., Paul v. Davis*, 424 U .S. 693 (1 976) (holding that there is no constitutional privacy right that pre vents a state from publicizing a record of an official act such as an arrest).

[81] *See, e.g., U.S. Dept. Of Justice v. Reporters Committee*, 489 U.S. 749 (1989) (holding that the personal privacy exemption of FOIA prohibited the disclosure of an FBI rap sheet to a third party without the consent of the record subject).

[82] *See, e.g.*, 28 CFR 50.12(b), which provides in relevant part:

Records obtained under this authority may be used solely for the purpose requested and cannot be disseminated outside the receiving departments, related agencies, or other authorized entities. Officials at the governmental institutions and other entities authorized to submit fingerprints and receive FBI identification re cords under this authority must notify the individuals fingerprinted that the fingerprints will be used to check the criminal history records of the FB I. The officials making the determination of suitability for licensing or employment shall provide the applicants the opportunity to complete, or challenge the accuracy of, the information contained in the FBI identification record. These officials also must advise the applicants that procedures for obtaining a change , correction , or updating of an FBI identification record are set forth in 28 CFR 16.34. Officials making such determinations should not deny the license or employment based on information in the record until the applicant has been afforded a reasonable time to correct or complete the record, or has decline d to do so. A statement incorporating these use-and -challenge requirements will be place d on all records disseminated under this program. This policy is intended to ensure that all relevant criminal record information is made available to provide for the public safety and, further , to protect the interests of the prospective employee/licensee who may be affected by the information or lack of information in an identification record.

[83] In introducing the House version of the original Fair Credit Reporting Act, Representative Gallagher noted that the bill prevented outmoded information , including criminal records , from being included in consumer reports, stating "I have long been concerned that one derogatory item could 'damn a person to the grave,' that an early mistake could haunt a man all throughout his adult life, and that redemption is in the process of being programmed out of American society." Cong. Rec ., 91st Cong., First Sess., p. 33785 (Statement of Representative Gallagher) (November 12, 1969).

[84] *See* National Instant Criminal Background Check Operational Report (NICS) – 2003-2004, 39-40 (January 2005), available at http://www .fbi.gov/hq/cjisd /nics/ops_r eport20 03-200 4/ops_re port200 3-2004 .pdf?file.

[85] *See* CAL. CIV . CODE § 1786 .28(b) (providing that a criminal conviction or other matters of public record can be reported for employment purposes if "it is complete and up to date," which is defined as checking the status of at the time the record is reported).

[86] See Recommendation 2.3 in the SEA RCH report on criminal history background screening, found at http://www. search.org/events/news/criminalrecord2006.asp

[87] *See supra* text accompanying notes 57 and 58.

[88] *See supra* text accompanying note 55.

[89] *See supra* note 56.

[90] *See, supra*, pages 49-50.

[91] *See* 46 U.S .C. § 701 05(c) (2), which provides :

(2) The Secretary shall prescribe regulations that establish a waiver process for issuing a transportation security card to an individual found to be otherwise ineligible for such a card under paragraph (1). In deciding to issue a card to such an individual, the Secretary shall - (A) give consideration to the circumstances of any disqualifying act or offense , restitution made by the individual, Federal and State mitigation remedies, and other factors from which it may be concluded that the individual does not pose a terrorism risk warranting denial of the card; and (B) issue a waiver to an individual without regard to whether that individual would otherwise be disqualified if the individual's employer establishes alternate security arrangements acceptable to the Secretary.

[92] See 49 CFR §§ 1572.7 and 1572.143.

[93] *See supra* text accompanying notes 27 and 28.

[94] We note that the Privacy Ac t provides that any person who knowingly and willfully requests and obtains any record concerning an individual from a federal agency under false pre tenses is guilty of a misdemeanor and subject to a fine of up to $5,00 0. *See* 5 U.S.C. 552a(i)(3). This provision would not, however, cover records disseminated under this authority by a participating state repository that is not subject to the federal Privacy Act, nor does it cover unauthorized disseminations of such information by persons other than agency officers or employees. In addition, since the fraudulent use of this authority could result in the inappropriate disclosure of criminal history record on many individuals, stronger penalties should be available.

[95] 15 U.S.C. § 1681q.

[96] 15 U.S.C.§ 1681r.

In: Criminal History Records and Background Checks
Editor: Brian Wilkins
ISBN: 978-1-63483-438-4

Chapter 2

CRIMINAL HISTORY RECORDS: ADDITIONAL ACTIONS COULD ENHANCE THE COMPLETENESS OF RECORDS USED FOR EMPLOYMENT-RELATED BACKGROUND CHECKS*

United States Government Accountability Office

ABBREVIATIONS

BJS	Bureau of Justice Statistics
CFPB	Consumer Financial Protection Bureau
CNCS	Corporation for National and Community Service
DOJ	Department of Justice
EEOC	Equal Employment Opportunity Commission
FBI	Federal Bureau of Investigation
FCRA	Fair Credit Reporting Act
FTC	Federal Trade Commission
NCHIP	National Criminal History Improvement Program
NCPA	National Child Protection Act
NGI	Next Generation Identification
OPM	Office of Personnel Management
PSOEAA	Private Security Officer Employment Authorization Act

WHY GAO DID THIS STUDY

Authorized employers use information from FBI criminal history record checks to assess a person's suitability for employment or to obtain a license. States create criminal records and

* This is an edited, reformatted and augmented version of a report, GAO-15-162, issued by the Government Accountability Office, dated February 2015.

the FBI facilitates access to these records by other states for nationwide checks. GAO was asked to assess efforts to address concerns about incomplete records, among other things.

This report addresses to what extent (1) states conduct FBI record checks for selected employment sectors and face any challenges; (2) states have improved the completeness of records, and remaining challenges that federal agencies can help mitigate; and (3) private companies conduct criminal record checks, the benefits those checks provide to employers, and any related challenges.

GAO analyzed laws and regulations used to conduct criminal record checks and assessed the completeness of records; conducted a nationwide survey, which generated responses from 47 states and the District of Columbia; and interviewed officials that manage checks from the FBI and 4 states (California, Florida, Idaho, and Washington). GAO selected states based on geographic location and other factors.

WHAT GAO RECOMMENDS

GAO recommends, among other things, that the FBI establish plans with time frames for completing the Disposition Task Force's remaining goals. The Department of Justice concurred with all of GAO's recommendations.

WHAT GAO FOUND

Most states that responded to GAO's nationwide survey reported conducting Federal Bureau of Investigation (FBI) criminal history record checks for individuals working with vulnerable populations—such as children and the elderly—and other employment sectors that GAO reviewed (see fig. below). States that did not conduct FBI record checks said this was because the state lacked a designated agency to review check results, among other challenges. In 2006, the Attorney General proposed that nongovernmental entities also serve in this role but noted that this would require considerations about securing data and protecting personal information.

States Conducting FBI Criminal Record Checks for Selected Employment Sectors

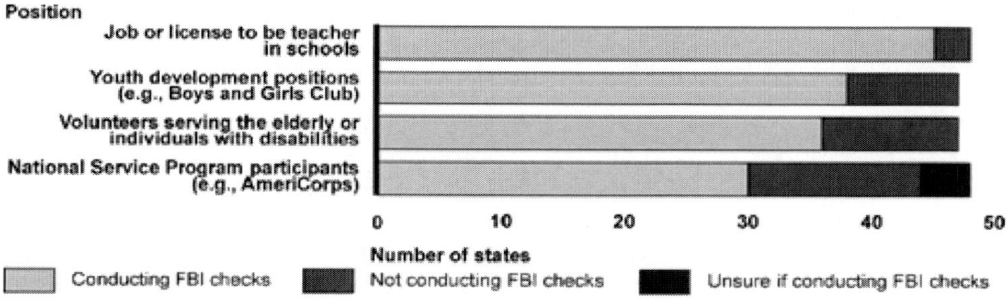

Source: GAO analysis of national survey of state and District of Columbia record repositories. | GAO-15-162.

States have improved the completeness of criminal history records used for FBI checks—more records now contain both the arrest and final disposition (e.g., a conviction)—but there are still gaps. Twenty states reported that more than 75 percent of their arrest records had dispositions in 2012, up from 16 states in 2006. Incomplete records can delay checks and affect applicants seeking employment. The Department of Justice has helped states improve the completeness of records through grant funding and other resources, but challenges remain. For example, the FBI's Advisory Policy Board—which includes representatives from federal, state, and local criminal justice agencies— created a Disposition Task Force in 2009 to address issues regarding disposition reporting, among other things. The task force has taken actions to better measure the completeness of state records and identify state requirements for reporting disposition information. However, the task force does not have plans with time frames for completing remaining goals, such as examining and recommending improvements in national standards for collecting and reporting disposition information.

According to stakeholders GAO contacted, the use of private companies to conduct criminal history record checks appears to be increasing because of employer demand and can provide benefits, such as faster response times. Federal agencies regulate these companies and have settled complaints, such as in cases where the wrong records were sent to employers. Private companies can face challenges in obtaining complete and accurate records, in part because not all states make their criminal record information accessible for private companies to search.

* * *

February 12, 2015

Congressional Requesters

From fiscal years 2009 through 2013, about 120 million criminal history record checks were conducted through the Federal Bureau of Investigation (FBI) for non-criminal-justice purposes. Employers can use information from these types of checks to screen job applicants, including those seeking positions working with children, the elderly, or other vulnerable populations. States primarily create and maintain criminal history records—which can include arrest and disposition information— and make these records available to the FBI to facilitate the interstate sharing of records for criminal and non-criminal-justice purposes. In general, disposition refers to the result or conclusion of criminal proceedings, such as charge dismissed, acquittal, adjudication withheld, probation, or conviction.[1] Authorized state agencies have direct access to FBI-maintained criminal history records to conduct non-criminal-justice record checks, and the results are automatically sent back to the requesting agency.

The primary vehicle for states to conduct FBI criminal history record checks for non-criminal-justice purposes is through provisions contained in the Departments of State, Justice, and Commerce, the Judiciary, and Related Agencies Appropriation Act, 1973 (hereinafter referred to as Public Law 92-544).[2] Pursuant to Public Law 92-544, the FBI is authorized to use funds for the exchange of identification records, including criminal history record information, with officials of state and local governments for purposes of employment and licensing if this is authorized by state statute and approved by the Attorney General. In general, government agencies that receive the results of FBI criminal record checks apply their own suitability criteria for employment or licensing or criteria established under state law. In addition, to expand access to FBI record checks for certain populations—such as individuals who provide services to children—federal laws have been enacted that authorize state governmental agencies to conduct FBI checks without requiring a separate state statute and approval from the Attorney General.

In June 2006, the Attorney General reported that the criminal history background check system was a patchwork of state and federal laws that had resulted in inconsistencies in access to FBI criminal record checks across states and industries.[3] Since then, Congress has raised questions about the extent to which FBI record checks are carried out across states, as well as the impact that incomplete records may have on employment or licensing decisions.[4]

Employers can also obtain background information on an applicant— including criminal record information—from private sector companies that compile and sell information that they may obtain directly from states or other sources. You asked that we assess the states' use of FBI record checks, the completeness of records, and the role of the private sector in conducting checks.[5] This report addresses the following questions:

- To what extent do states conduct FBI criminal history record checks for selected employment sectors and what challenges, if any, do they face in conducting these checks?
- To what extent have states made progress in improving the completeness of criminal history records and what challenges remain that federal agencies can help mitigate?
- To what extent do private companies conduct record checks, what benefits do they provide, how are they regulated, and what challenges do they face?

Regarding access to FBI record checks and state challenges, we assessed whether states had established laws or were using authorities under federal laws to conduct FBI checks for three employment sectors—those related to the National Child Protection Act of 1993,[6] which covers, among other things, individuals with responsibility for vulnerable populations;[7] the Edward M. Kennedy Serve America Act (Serve America Act),[8] which covers organizations that can serve vulnerable populations and receive funding under national service laws (e.g., AmeriCorps);[9] and the Private Security Officer Employment Authorization Act of 2004, which covers organizations that employ private security officers.[10] We selected these laws to represent a range of factors, including variation in whether the law requires or authorizes (permits) an FBI record check. In addition, we conducted a web-based survey of officials at agencies within all 50 states and the District of Columbia that maintain criminal history records (state repositories) to determine the extent to which states are conducting FBI checks for the employment sectors covered under the three federal laws and what challenges, if any, states face in doing so. We received a response rate of 94 percent—47 states and the District of Columbia— which we collectively refer to as states throughout this report. We also interviewed management officials from state repositories and courts that maintain criminal history information in 4 states—California, Florida, Idaho, and Washington—to determine the extent to which they conduct FBI checks, any challenges, and actions taken to address those challenges. We selected the 4 states based on geographic location and other factors. In addition, we analyzed federal regulations and procedures for conducting criminal record checks and interviewed FBI officials who manage the checks to determine any challenges in providing access. We also interviewed senior officials from the Compact Council—the primary state and federal body for setting policy around the interstate sharing of criminal history records for non-criminal-justice purposes.[11] Further, we interviewed management officials from the Corporation for National and Community Service—a federal agency that oversees service programs such as AmeriCorps and the Senior Corps and requires background checks for its participants and program employees—to determine whether challenges existed in obtaining information from FBI record checks. We also interviewed management officials from the National Center for Missing and Exploited Children—an organization that uses criminal history records provided by the FBI to determine suitability of its volunteers—to determine what challenges existed in its use of FBI criminal history records.

Regarding the progress states have made in improving the completeness of criminal history records and related challenges, we analyzed data that states provided to the Department of Justice (DOJ) via a survey from 2006 through 2012 on the percentage of their arrest records that contained information on the disposition of those arrests.[12] We selected this time frame because 2006 was the year the Attorney General issued the criminal history background check report and 2012 was the year with the most current available survey data. To assess the reliability of the data, we analyzed the survey methodology, interviewed DOJ officials who conducted the surveys, and examined data for obvious errors. We determined that the data were sufficiently reliable for the purposes of this report. We also analyzed the results of the FBI's most recent round of triennial state audits, which include assessing the completeness of state records and use of the records for non-criminal-justice purposes.[13] As of January 2014, the FBI had finalized 44 state audits that the bureau conducted from 2011 through 2013. Further, we interviewed management officials who maintain criminal history records in the 4 states we contacted to determine challenges they face in maintaining complete records and related initiatives to improve record completeness. We also interviewed officials from the FBI and DOJ's Bureau of Justice Statistics (BJS) who have key roles in providing access to FBI record checks and providing assistance to states in maintaining complete records. Further, we interviewed officials from the Office of Personnel Management (OPM) who collect disposition information as part of OPM background investigations.

Regarding the role of the private sector in conducting employment-related criminal record checks, we reviewed relevant sections of the Fair Credit Reporting Act[14] and Title VII of the Civil Rights Act of 1964[15] that related to private background screening companies' use of criminal history records. We also analyzed a 2005 national task force report on the commercial sale of criminal justice record information[16] and a 2006 Attorney General's report on criminal history background checks.[17] We also interviewed senior officials from associations that represent background companies, such as the National Association of Professional Background Screeners and the Consumer Data Industry Association, to determine the role of private sector agencies in providing criminal history information to employers. Further, we interviewed senior officials from federal agencies that regulate these private sector entities—including the Federal Trade Commission, the Equal Employment Opportunity Commission, and the Consumer Financial Protection Bureau—to determine how the industry is regulated as well as the size and scope of the industry.

We conducted this performance audit from October 2013 to February 2015 in accordance with generally accepted government auditing standards. Those standards require that we plan and perform the audit to obtain sufficient, appropriate evidence to provide a reasonable basis for our findings and conclusions based on our audit objectives. We believe that the evidence obtained provides a reasonable basis for our findings and conclusions based on our audit objectives. Appendix I contains additional information on our scope and methodology.

BACKGROUND

Private, public, and nonprofit employers can use information from criminal history records for non-criminal-justice purposes, such as screening an individual's suitability for working with children, the elderly, or other vulnerable populations. States primarily create and maintain criminal history records, but the FBI facilitates the interstate sharing of these records for criminal and non-criminal-justice purposes. Specifically, state central record repositories collect criminal history information from law enforcement agencies, courts, and other agencies throughout the state and submit records to the FBI. For example, state repositories collect arrest records from local police departments and disposition records from prosecutors or courts.

The FBI maintains a fingerprint-based criminal history record repository called the Next Generation Identification (NGI) System (previously the Integrated Automated Fingerprint Identification System). The NGI System contains records from all states and territories, as well as from federal and some international criminal justice agencies. The FBI's Interstate Identification Index provides for the decentralized interstate exchange of criminal history record information for authorized criminal and noncriminal-justice purposes and functions as a part of the NGI System.[18] In general, states conduct FBI criminal history record checks by searching an applicant's fingerprints against records in the NGI System (see fig. 1).[19]

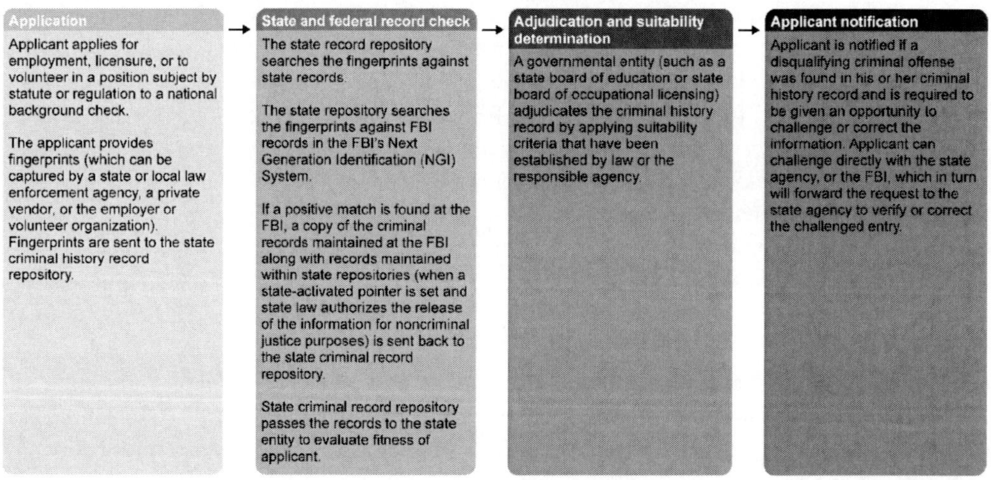

Source: GAO analysis of Department of Justice information. | GAO-15-162.

Figure 1. Example of a Process for Conducting a FBI Criminal History Record Check.

In general, the FBI provides the results of a FBI criminal history record check to a designated agency—such as a state department of health and human services or board of occupational licensing—through a criminal history summary. This summary—often referred to as a criminal history record, or rap sheet—includes the name of the agency that submitted the criminal record to the FBI; the date of the arrest; the arrest charge; and the disposition of the arrest, if known, to the FBI.

Federal laws that require or authorize states to conduct FBI criminal history record checks for non-criminal-justice purposes—including employment and licensing—cover a wide range of industries, such as those that serve vulnerable populations. These federal laws may authorize states to conduct FBI checks using just the authority of the federal law without requiring a related state statute.[20] This report primarily addresses the states' use of three federal laws, as shown in table 1.

Table 1. Description of Selected National Background Check Laws

Federal law	Population affected by law	Is criminal record check required or authorized?
The National Child Protection Act of 1993/Volunteers for Children Act[a]	Providers with responsibility for the safety and well-being of children, the elderly, or individuals with disabilities (also defined as "vulnerable populations"). Examples include applicants to work as teachers in schools, providers in health and day care centers serving vulnerable populations, counselors for youth development, and volunteers for the elderly.	Authorized
The Edward M. Kennedy Serve America Act[b]	Individuals who receive a living allowance, stipend, national service education award, or salary through a program receiving federal assistance under national service laws. Examples of programs include AmeriCorps and Senior Corps programs.	Required
The Private Security Officer Employment Authorization Act of 2004[c]	Employees or applicants for employment as private security officers. Examples include licensed security guards and unlicensed security employees.	Authorized

Source: GAO analysis of selected federal laws. | GAO-15-162

[a]Pub. L. No. 103-209, 107 Stat. 2490/Pub. L. No. 105-251, 112 Stat. 1885.

[b]Pub. L. No. 111-13, 123 Stat. 1460.

[c]Pub. L. No. 108-458, § 6402, 118 Stat. 3755.

In addition to federal laws, states may pass statutes that the Attorney General approves pursuant to Public Law 92-544 that require or authorize employers or organizations to request FBI criminal record checks for applicants seeking employment or licensing in their state. For example, states can require FBI checks for non-criminal-justice purposes in areas regulated by the state, such as civil servants and nursing home workers. States can also pass laws to implement federal laws, which can include, for example, additional provisions on the types of criminal activities that would disqualify an applicant from employment or licensing. All state laws related to Public Law 92-544 have to be approved by the Attorney General. According to FBI officials, as of 2014, states had passed a total of about 2,800 laws that require or authorize FBI criminal history record checks, which include checks for employment or licensing purposes.

DOJ, states, and others have emphasized the importance of having complete records when conducting FBI checks—records that contain the arrest charge and the disposition of the arrest (e.g., conviction or acquittal)—since incomplete records can lead to delays in completing checks and have adverse impacts on applicants. In 1995, DOJ established the National Criminal History Improvement Program (NCHIP) to enhance the quality, completeness, and accessibility of criminal history record information maintained by the states. All 50 states, the District of Columbia, and U.S. territories have received grant awards. The FBI also helps to ensure the integrity of state-level criminal record systems through periodic audits.

Employers can also obtain background information—including criminal record information—from private sector companies that compile and sell information that they may obtain from state courts or other public sources. These companies are classified as consumer reporting agencies under the Fair Credit Reporting Act (FCRA).[21] This act contains provisions that are intended to require these agencies to adopt reasonable procedures for using consumer credit, personnel, insurance, and other information in a manner that is fair and equitable to the consumer, with regard to the confidentiality, accuracy, relevancy, and proper utilization of such information.[22] At the federal level, the Federal Trade Commission (FTC) and the Consumer Financial Protection Bureau (CFPB) regulate private background companies and employers that conduct background checks that may contain criminal record information. In addition, the Equal Employment Opportunity Commission (EEOC) regulates and oversees employers' use of criminal record information provided by private background companies under Title VII of the Civil Rights Act of 1964.[23]

MOST STATES CONDUCT FBI RECORD CHECKS FOR SELECTED EMPLOYMENT SECTORS, BUT LACK OF STATE AGENCIES TO REVIEW CHECK RESULTS REMAINS A CHALLENGE

Most states that responded to our nationwide survey reported that they conduct FBI record checks for individuals working with vulnerable populations and other employment sectors we reviewed.[24] States not conducting such checks reported lacking designated state agencies to review the check results, among other challenges.[25] The Attorney General has proposed expanding FBI record checks to employers and other third parties, but also noted that any expansion should consider concerns about securing data and protecting personal information.

Most States Conduct FBI Checks for Individuals Working with Vulnerable Populations and Other Selected Employment Sectors, but Gaps Remain in Conducting Checks

Employment and Volunteer Positions with Vulnerable Populations

The National Child Protection Act (NCPA), as amended, authorizes states to have procedures that require qualified entities designated by the state to contact an authorized state agency to request an FBI criminal background check. This check is for the purpose of determining whether a person has been convicted of a crime that bears upon the person's fitness to have responsibility for the safety and well-being of children, the elderly, or individuals with disabilities.[26] Our survey results show that 45

of 48 respondents conduct FBI record checks for individuals seeking jobs or licenses to be teachers in schools—positions that are typically regulated by states.[27] The largest gap in FBI record checks was for volunteers serving the elderly or individuals with disabilities, where 36 of 47 respondents reported conducting such checks, but 11 of 47 respondents did not, as shown in figure 2.[28]

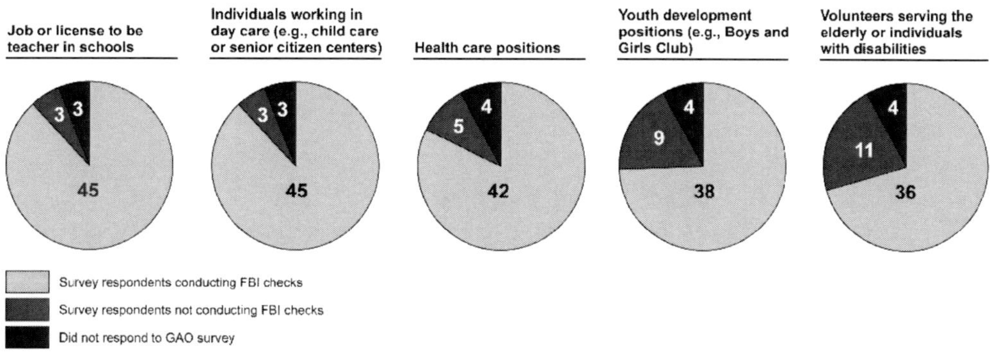

Source: GAO nationwide survey of criminal history repositories in 50 states and the District of Columbia. | GAO-15-162.

Figure 2. Number of Survey Respondents Conducting Federal Bureau of Investigation (FBI) Checks for Selected Employment and Volunteer Positions Covered under the National Child Protection Act.

The primary reasons states reported not conducting FBI criminal history record checks for employment or volunteer positions covered by the NCPA were the lack of a designated state agency to review the FBI record check results or the states did not have licensing or regulatory requirements to check volunteers. One survey respondent noted that, in some cases, state legislatures do not support expanding the availability of background checks to certain classes of employees, despite the existence of federal laws that seek to encourage such checks.

Recognizing concerns about the background check process available to volunteer organizations, the Prosecutorial Remedies and Other Tools to End the Exploitation of Children Today Act of 2003 established the Child Safety Pilot Program. The act required the Attorney General to establish an 18-month program that would provide for the FBI to conduct 100,000 criminal history record check requests from certain youth-serving organizations, such as the Boys and Girls Clubs of America.[29] Under the pilot, the FBI provided the results of a check to the National Center for Missing and Exploited Children—rather than through a state agency— which made suitability determinations and conveyed the decision to the organization that made the request.[30] According to officials from the national center, of the approximately 105,000 FBI checks that the organization conducted over the 8-year pilot, about 6,500 (6.2 percent) of all applicants had a criminal record that disqualified them from working with children.[31] Officials who represent volunteer organizations said that they plan to continue to pursue legislation in upcoming congressional sessions that would provide for certain youth-serving organizations to use information from FBI record checks to screen applicants.

Some states have also developed programs that allow volunteer organizations to obtain information from FBI criminal record checks. For example, according to officials from the Florida Department of Law Enforcement, Florida has established a program—which the FBI approved—that authorizes certain volunteer organizations to receive the results of FBI record checks from the department and determine an applicant's suitability for employment, rather than relying on a Florida agency to adjudicate the results on the organization's behalf. Senior officials from the Florida Department of Law Enforcement noted that the state requires volunteer organizations to sign a user agreement before gaining access to FBI-maintained criminal records, a requirement that is intended to help ensure that the organizations properly use and safeguard the records. The Florida officials also said that the department can audit these entities to ensure compliance with the agreement.

Individuals Serving in National Service Programs

In general, the Edward M. Kennedy Serve America Act requires, with limited exceptions, that entities conduct FBI criminal history checks for certain individuals working with vulnerable populations.[32] These individuals serve in positions that provide the individuals with a living allowance, stipend, national service educational award, or salary through a program receiving assistance under national service laws.[33] Among other things, these individuals can tutor children in reading, run after-school programs, provide health information to a vulnerable population, and conduct neighborhood watch programs. Our survey results show that 30 of 44 respondents conduct FBI record checks for national service program grant recipients and 14 of 44 respondents did not conduct such checks.[34]

Of the 14 respondents that did not conduct FBI checks, 12 reported not having procedures or agencies in place to review the results of checks for national service program grant recipients, 6 reported lacking sufficient resources to review check results, and 5 reported lacking a state licensing or regulatory need to conduct such checks.[35] According to a senior official from the Corporation for National and Community Service (CNCS)—the federal entity that administers programs established under national service laws—CNCS has received hundreds of requests from national service program grantees for an exemption from the FBI record check requirement and for approval to use an alternative screening procedure, such as the ability to use a substantially equivalent process. The officials noted that a subset of these requests are from organizations that seek an exemption to the FBI record check requirement because of the difficulties they have encountered in obtaining such checks.

According to CNCS officials, CNCS is authorized to receive FBI criminal history records and adjudicate applicants' criminal records on behalf of its national service program grantees. The officials noted, however, that CNCS opted not to develop a national, centralized mechanism for conducting state and national fingerprint-based criminal history record checks for national service program participants, in part to allow states to make their own suitability determinations. In October 2014, CNCS officials stated that in light of the challenges national service programs have faced in obtaining FBI record checks, CNCS is assessing the costs and benefits of acting as a national clearinghouse for such checks if no option is available in the organization's own state. CNCS expects to make a decision in 2015 regarding whether acting as a clearinghouse is feasible.

Private Security Officers

In general, the Private Security Officer Employment Authorization Act (PSOEAA) of 2004 and its associated regulations permit authorized employers to submit the fingerprints of an employee or applicant for employment as a private security officer to a state repository of a participating state for purposes of conducting an FBI criminal history record check.[36] Congress found that employment of private security officers in the United States was growing rapidly; private security officers function as an adjunct to, but not replacement for, public law enforcement by helping to reduce and prevent crime; and such officers protect individuals, property, and proprietary information. Private security officers provide protection to banks, hospitals, manufacturing facilities, nuclear power plants, airports, and schools, among other operations.[37]

Our survey results show that

- 37 of 43 respondents conduct FBI record checks for private licensed security officers, and
- 7 of 43 respondents conduct FBI record checks for private unlicensed security officers.[38]

The primary reasons why states reported not conducting FBI record checks for private security officers were because the states did not license or regulate security officers or because the states did not have a designated state agency to adjudicate the results of the checks. Under certain circumstances, PSOEAA regulations also generally permit authorized employers to submit the fingerprints to a state other than the state in which the employee or applicant would be working for purposes of an FBI criminal history record check.[39] The chair of the Compact Council informed us about 1 state (Minnesota) that was conducting FBI checks for employers located in other states. According to a senior official from Minnesota's Bureau of Criminal Apprehension, the bureau did not face any challenges in conducting such checks. The official noted, however, that only one employer had requested Minnesota's help and the employer asked Minnesota to conduct FBI checks for employees in 11 other states where the employer operated.

According to an executive-level official from the National Association of Security Companies—the nation's largest contract security trade association—requiring that a state agency be involved in conducting FBI checks is a barrier for employers. The official explained that for a state agency to set up an FBI background check program, the state may need legislative authority, appropriations, and employees with expertise in interpreting criminal records, among other things. The official added that PSOEAA and federal requirements only allow states to provide employers with a determination as to whether or not an applicant failed to meet the state's or PSOEAA's criteria that would disqualify an applicant from employment, and that the private security industry would like to see revisions to PSOEAA that would allow employers greater access to the actual information returned in a FBI record check. The official said that the association plans to propose legislative changes in future congressional sessions to address these and other barriers.

DOJ and Others Have Recommended Expanding Access to FBI Checks, but Concerns Remain about Securing Data and Protecting Personal Information

Recommendations for Expanding Access to FBI Record Checks

In 2005 and 2006, the Attorney General and others recommended expanding employer and third-party access to FBI criminal history record checks as a way to overcome barriers presented by the need for a state agency to adjudicate record check results. For example, according to a 2005 national task force report on criminal background checks, states faced challenges in conducting FBI record checks for employment purposes, which resulted in inconsistent use of records across the states.[40] The task force made recommendations to state and federal policymakers regarding access to records for non-criminal-justice purposes, which included removing the federal requirement that a public agency must receive record check results. Senior officials from SEARCH and the FBI, as well as a state official we met with who participated on the task force, said that they were not aware of any specific actions that either Congress or DOJ took related to expanding record access as a result of the recommendations. Our discussions with officials from organizations representing employers for the various employment sectors we reviewed indicate that the access issues identified in the 2005 report are still of concern to employers today.

Also, according to a 2006 Attorney General report, inconsistent national access to background checks was a challenge for employers and volunteer organizations.[41] The report proposed recommendations that would broaden and standardize the private sector's authority to access state-held and FBI-held criminal history record information. The report noted that criminal history information that the FBI and state record repositories maintain should be a source of information—as system capacity allows—that private employers are authorized to use to inquire if an applicant or employee has a criminal history. Senior DOJ officials, a former official from the Attorney General's office with direct knowledge of the report's history, and SEARCH officials who work with states on related policy issues were not aware of any specific actions on these recommendations.

Concerns Remain over Expanding Access

Senior officials from the FBI's Criminal Justice Information Services Division and officials from all 4 case study states raised some concerns that any attempt to expand access to FBI criminal records checks must consider. Specifically, FBI officials said that a primary concern is the extent to which nongovernmental entities would be able to adequately protect and store criminal history record information and the potential impacts on individual privacy rights if records were to be shared extensively beyond state agencies. The officials added that another concern is the potential resulting increase in the FBI's workload in auditing these entities' compliance with security policies regarding the storage, use, and dissemination of criminal record information. Senior officials from SEARCH and all 4 of our case study states noted that expanding access too broadly to nongovernmental entities could mean that state agencies could lose the fees collected for facilitating checks, thereby undermining the revenue streams that states use in turn to maintain and operate criminal history repositories.

The SEARCH and Attorney General reports discussed above noted similar concerns with expanding access, and proposed some potential solutions that could balance expanded access with data security and applicant privacy concerns. For example, SEARCH recommended steps to improve the completeness and accuracy of criminal history records and protection of applicant privacy rights, through allowing individuals to access and correct their records, among other things.[42] The task force also recommended expanding access only to organizations that appoint individuals to positions or responsibilities involving access to vulnerable populations, sensitive information, or as otherwise deemed necessary by the Attorney General for public safety or national security. In addition, to address concerns regarding information security, the Attorney General recommended that (1) criminal and civil penalties be established for those provided access under any new authority for the unauthorized use of criminal history information and (2) users of such information should enter into agreements that specify the requirements for access, including security of the information and notice to individuals concerning record access and correction and fair use of the information. Further, to address concerns about state fee revenues, the task force noted that any expansions in access should require authorized entities to go through state criminal history repositories for access—not directly to the FBI— unless states have specifically opted out of providing such access.

STATES HAVE IMPROVED THE COMPLETENESS OF CRIMINAL HISTORY RECORDS WITH DOJ'S ASSISTANCE, BUT CONTINUE TO FACE CHALLENGES

States Reported Progress in Providing Complete Records to the FBI, but Incomplete Records That Can Delay Criminal Record Checks and Affect Applicants Still Exist

According to BJS surveys of state criminal history information systems, from 2006 through 2012, states reported making progress in providing complete criminal history records to the FBI—records that include the arrest and the final disposition of the arrest.[43] For example, BJS surveys show that the number of states that reported providing more than 75 percent of their arrest records with final dispositions increased from 16 states in 2006 to 20 states in 2012, as shown in figure 3.[44]

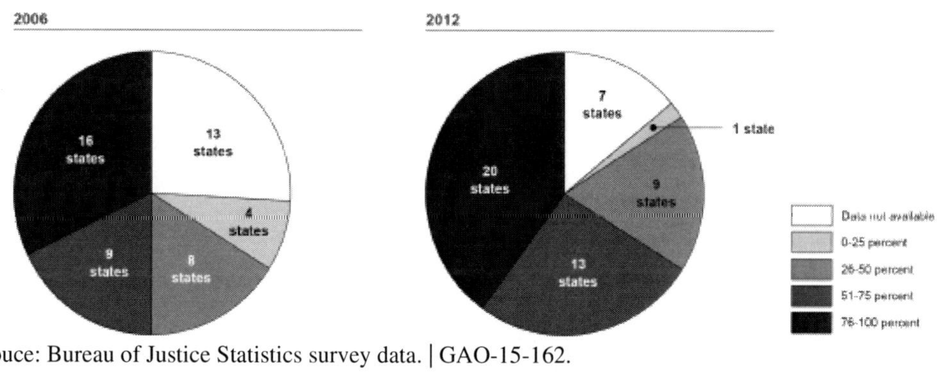

Souce: Bureau of Justice Statistics survey data. | GAO-15-162.

Figure 3. Percentages of Arrest Records with Final Dispositions per State, 2006 and 2012.

According to officials from BJS's Statistical Planning, Policy, and Operations Division and senior officials from our 4 case study states, factors that help states compile complete criminal records include the automation of criminal record information—such as devices that digitally record and electronically transmit fingerprint images from police departments to state agencies that maintain criminal history records—and improved coordination among local criminal justice entities. For example, according to a director in the Florida Department of Law Enforcement, the high level of coordination among officials on the Florida Criminal and Juvenile Justice Information Systems Council has helped increase the completeness of state records because the members collectively decided on the best use of federal grant funding to improve state record completeness.[45]

Nevertheless, in 2012, 10 states reported that 50 percent or less of their arrest records had final dispositions. FBI officials noted that it is not possible for states to have 100 percent complete records because it can take more than 1 year for criminal felony cases to conclude and disposition information to be entered into criminal record systems.

FBI officials also noted that the statement in the 2006 Attorney General's report on criminal history background checks that only 50 percent of arrest records in the FBI's Interstate Identification Index have final dispositions reflects a misunderstanding of how criminal history records are maintained. Rather, during an FBI criminal history record check, the FBI accesses certain records that states maintain that are not forwarded to the FBI. For example, some states forward arrest records to the FBI but not disposition information. For these states, during an FBI record check, the FBI reaches out to the state to obtain the arrest and disposition information from the state's records.

The impact of incomplete criminal history records on individuals seeking employment or licensing depends in part on whether a state's laws permit employers or licensing agencies to hire applicants contingent upon the completion of a criminal record check. According to senior repository officials from our 4 case study states, 2 states permit contingent hiring for certain positions and 2 do not. For example, a manager within the Idaho State Police's Bureau of Criminal Identification said that it could take months to obtain disposition information from other states, but that applicants are placed in certain jobs if they are supervised pending the results of the FBI record check. In contrast, a bureau chief within the California Department of Justice said that applicants cannot be hired or licensed until all aspects of the background check are completed, which includes following up on incomplete criminal records. A senior official from Washington's Department of Social and Health Services Background Check Central Unit said that incomplete records can lead to negative impacts on the applicant, since the applicant is responsible for obtaining missing information from courts. The official added that when employers have urgent hiring needs, they may choose another qualified applicant rather than wait for an individual to gather court records that are needed to complete the FBI record check.

According to a 2005 BJS report, complete records enable hiring entities to avoid delays due to the time needed to track down missing criminal record information.[46] Senior officials from central record repositories at all 4 of the states we visited noted that incomplete criminal records returned from an FBI record check can result in a variety of challenges when screening an individual's suitability for employment or licensing. For example, an official from 1 state said that because of limited staff and resources, criminal justice agencies in other states may not be responsive to requests for information on incomplete criminal records. The official noted that these agencies may also give a higher priority to addressing inquiries from law enforcement, further delaying responses to record inquiries for employment and licensing purposes. Repository officials from another state noted that it generally takes 1 or 2 days to finish an FBI criminal record check when no records are returned or the records are complete, but otherwise it can take up to several months, for example, to conduct the research needed to complete a record.

Further, officials from the four record repositories said that state privacy laws—which can restrict the information that agencies are allowed to disseminate for non-criminal-justice purposes—can affect a state's ability to obtain information. For example, officials in Washington State said that according to state law, they can disseminate a criminal record for noncriminal-justice purposes only if the record contains conviction information or arrest information that is less than 1 year old. Also, the officials said that it can be difficult to interpret whether records returned from another state would prohibit employment or licensing in the state where an individual is seeking employment, since state laws can define felonies and misdemeanors differently. The officials noted that these differences require following up with the state that generated the record, thus adding more time to the background check.

DOJ Helps States Improve Record Completeness, but States Continue to Face Challenges in Submitting Complete Records to the FBI

DOJ has several programs designed to help states improve the overall quality of criminal history records—including the completeness of records—and officials from our 4 case study states said that they generally found DOJ's assistance to be helpful. Our analysis of published reports and interviews with officials from our case study states, BJS, SEARCH, and the National Center for State Courts[47] indicate that state challenges in submitting complete records to the FBI are generally inherent to local jurisdictions, and states have used DOJ's assistance programs to help address these challenges.[48]

DOJ Efforts to Help States

DOJ provides a number of different resources to help states improve criminal record completeness, including grant funding, sharing best practices, task forces, and audits.

National Criminal History Improvement Program: DOJ assists states in improving the completeness, accuracy, and timeliness of criminal history records through the National Criminal History Improvement Program.[49] For fiscal years 2008 through 2012, DOJ targeted approximately $23 million in NCHIP grants to state record disposition improvement projects, such as updating records that only contain arrests to include disposition information and upgrading and automating criminal history record systems to capture data on dispositions from courts and prosecutors. Senior officials from all 4 of our case study states reported that NCHIP grants have helped improve the quality and completeness of their criminal history records. For fiscal years 2008 through 2012, NCHIP grant funds ranged from $6 million to $11 million and averaged approximately $9.5 million per year. Appropriations for NCHIP for fiscal year 2014 were at $46.5 million. This was primarily intended to support state efforts to increase the number of felony records and criminal-related mental health records available for firearm background checks through the National Instant Criminal Background Check System.[50] BJS officials who administer the NCHIP grants said that an increase in felony records available for firearm checks will also benefit non-criminal-justice checks because the FBI searches the Interstate Identification Index, which stores felony records for both types of checks.[51]

Best practices: DOJ has also worked to help states improve record completeness by sharing best practices through informational websites and reports, among other avenues. For example, under a DOJ grant, the National Center for State Courts is creating a web-based tool kit that brings together information from state pilot projects, focus groups, and other research reports to identify, among other things, best practices on how to overcome disposition reporting and coordination challenges among state and local criminal justice agencies.[52] Also, under DOJ's funding and direction, SEARCH is implementing the State Repository Records and Reporting Quality Assurance Program, which includes a voluntary self-assessment checklist for states as a way to disseminate best practices. According to a director at SEARCH, after a state completes the checklist, a SEARCH official provides on-site technical assistance to review the responses and recommend additional state follow-up actions. The official noted that, as of September 2014, SEARCH officials had provided on-site technical assistance in 20 states. The official said that the program will continue under BJS grant funding in order to provide on-site technical assistance to additional states, continue improving the checklist, and incorporate new standards that states need to meet in order to utilize the FBI's technology advancements related to criminal record information.

Disposition Task Force: The FBI's Advisory Policy Board formed the Disposition Task Force in 2009 to address issues related to the completeness, accuracy, and availability of criminal record dispositions from courts and prosecutors and develop a national strategy for improving the quality of disposition reporting.[53] The task force is composed of representatives from different components of state and local criminal justice systems—including state repositories, state courts, prosecutors, and Compact Council members—as well as federal criminal justice officials, such as from DOJ and OPM. According to an FBI official who helps facilitate task force meetings, the task force established an initial set of goals in 2009, but under new leadership in 2012 determined that these goals would not address the greatest disposition-reporting challenge—the lack of national disposition-reporting standards.[54] As a result, the FBI official noted that the task force decided to take a broader look at disposition-reporting issues, and evolved its initial goals into five broader goals and the foundation of a national strategy.[55]

According to FBI officials, as of September 2014, the task force had achieved one of its 2012 goals by refining the calculation that the task force would use to estimate the rate in which state and federal arrest records contained dispositions and reaching consensus on the definition of the term "disposition" to calculate the disposition rate. The officials noted that the task force had also taken steps to achieve two other goals by (1) reviewing the results of a National Center for State Courts national survey to identify existing federal and state requirements for collecting and reporting disposition information, and (2) identifying steps to develop and produce a guide on disposition best practices.

The task force, however, did not have a plan with time frames or milestones for either completing the best practices guide or achieving the remaining goals, which could also lead to a national strategy—an original 2009 objective for the task force. Our work indicates that the task force has not formulated such plans or set time frames and milestones in part because of the changes in leadership and goals in 2012. Nevertheless, after more than 5 years, the task force has not issued best practices or national standards for collecting and reporting disposition information or developed a national strategy, even though disposition reporting has been a long-standing challenge. Establishing plans with time frames and milestones could help hold the task force accountable for more progress in achieving the goals and the overall results of improved disposition reporting. Taking these steps would also be consistent with program management standards that call for specific goals and objectives to be conceptualized, defined, and documented in the planning process, along with the appropriate steps, time frames, and milestones needed to achieve those results.[56]

FBI audits of states: The FBI conducts a triennial audit of state criminal justice information systems to determine, among other things, whether (1) the records the state maintains contain all known arrest and disposition information and (2) the submission of criminal record information to the FBI has been "unduly" delayed. Federal regulations provide that states should submit dispositions to the Interstate Identification Index within 120 days after the disposition occurred.[57] To determine whether states are meeting these two requirements, FBI auditors review state-level processes and procedures and assess, among other things, if the state repository has a backlog of dispositions that it has not submitted to the FBI. The FBI found that from 2011 through 2013, 12 of the 44 states that it had audited were noncompliant with one or both of the requirements.[58]

For example, a 2012 FBI audit of 1 state found that the state was submitting dispositions to the FBI only twice a year. In response to noncompliant audit findings, states are required to submit a corrective action plan to the FBI describing how the state plans to come into compliance with audit requirements.

Challenges Faced by State Criminal Justice Agencies

In addition to the lack of national standards that govern the submission of dispositions from state criminal justice agencies and repositories to the FBI, our discussions with officials from our 4 case study states, BJS, SEARCH, and the National Center for State Courts—and our review of reports that these entities published—identified three challenges as most frequently cited as negatively affecting the completeness of state criminal records: (1) prosecutors not reporting final decisions in a case, (2) lack of official arrest records when law enforcement cites and then releases an individual, and (3) case numbers not transferring accurately among local agencies. DOJ's grant funding and other assistance programs have helped states address these challenges.

Prosecutors not reporting final case decisions: According to officials from DOJ and our case study states, one of the major contributors to arrest records not having final dispositions occurs when prosecutors decline to prosecute an individual but do not report this information to the state's central records repository.[59] Prosecutors may decline to prosecute an individual for a variety of reasons, such as insufficient evidence or the low severity of the offense. Prosecutors also have the authority to offer plea bargains, which reduce the seriousness of a charge in return for a guilty plea or other forms of cooperation with the prosecution. Prosecutors cited excessive workload and the lack of technology and human resources as reasons why they did not report declinations to prosecute, according to a 2005 BJS survey.[60] When not reported, other prosecutorial decisions that can lead to an arrest record without a disposition include decisions to consolidate a case into another case and to close a case that has become dormant because of insufficient evidence or witnesses, among other things.

Fingerprints not collected under cite-and-release practices: Incomplete criminal history records can also result from law enforcement officials citing and releasing individuals without formally arresting and fingerprinting them. This can result in state and local courts submitting dispositions to a state's central records repository without a corresponding arrest record because the individual was never fingerprinted. Typically, states allow citation and release for misdemeanor offenses, but according to the National Conference of State Legislatures, at least 2 states permit citation and release for some felonies.[61] Cite-andrelease policies can result in a significant number of incomplete criminal history records. For example, a senior official from 1 of our case study states said that cite-and-release arrests were one of the practices that contributed to approximately 1.6 million dispositions that are not linked to an arrest, which the state keeps in an independent data system and is working to match up with the corresponding arrest records.

According to the National Conference of State Legislatures, cite-andrelease arrests are a common practice for law enforcement agencies and are useful to these agencies. These arrests can lower jail populations and reduce costs by releasing arrestees who pose little risk to public safety. According to officials from our 4 case study states and a national focus group convened by the National Center for State Courts, mobile "live scan" devices that digitally record and electronically transmit fingerprint images or live scan devices in courtrooms could help improve the completeness of criminal history records. Courts can use such devices to immediately fingerprint individuals upon arrival in court for the citation hearing. However, a senior official from one of our case study states and a senior official from the National Center for State Courts said that local criminal justice agencies face significant barriers—such as the lack of resources and difficulty of integrating live scan devices into existing courtroom procedures.

Case numbers not transferring among local agencies: Senior officials in 3 of our 4 case study states said that they faced challenges in transferring unique case control numbers among local criminal justice agencies—such as law enforcement agencies, courts, prosecutors, and the state record repository. Law enforcement typically generates the case control number when an individual is arrested and fingerprinted, and some states use the number to associate all subsequent criminal history information from criminal justice entities with the original arrest event. According to the state officials, the process to transfer the case control number among local criminal justice entities may be manual and therefore prone to errors or occur inconsistently. For example, officials from 1 state said that certain local agencies that make arrests write case control numbers on a white board, and the numbers do not always get transferred to prosecutors and courts. A disposition-reporting focus group convened by the National Center for State Courts proposed that local and state governments develop policies that identify the case control number and specify that this number should be maintained in all criminal justice systems.[62]

DOJ's assistance programs—such as best practice dissemination programs and NCHIP grant funding—have helped states address challenges in providing complete criminal records. For example, sections of the Quality Assurance Program's checklist address state practices regarding prosecutors failing to report declinations to prosecute, cite-andrelease arrests, and the transfer of case numbers among local agencies. Further, the National Center for State Courts' web-based tool kit contains information on the impact that each of these challenges has on the completeness of criminal records as well as potential solutions to overcome these challenges. Additionally, states have used NCHIP grants to help overcome these challenges. For example, in fiscal year 2013, 1 state received NCHIP grant funds to implement the electronic transfer of prosecutorial case management information to the state's court system, and another state used

NCHIP grant funds to automate transferring the case control number from some prosecutors to the courts.

The FBI and OPM Have Not Yet Determined How the FBI Could Use Information Obtained during OPM Security Clearance Investigations to Help States Update Criminal Records

In June 2010, the Compact Council and the FBI's Advisory Policy Board approved the practice of having the FBI supply states with source documents that OPM personnel obtain during their investigations of applicants for federal employment and security clearances.[63] The information contained in these source documents, such as arrest dispositions, could help to enhance the completeness of state criminal history records. The agencies did not enter into a formal written agreement for this information-sharing arrangement, but it was discussed and recommended in Advisory Policy Board meeting minutes.

According to FBI and OPM officials, each week, OPM is to provide criminal justice-related information to the FBI, such as disposition information related to an applicant's arrest records. The FBI would then review the information and send any relevant information to state record repositories so that the states could decide whether to update their records. OPM began sending this information to the FBI in January 2011. According to OPM officials, OPM sends approximately 3,500 to 4,500 investigative records to the FBI each week, with each record representing state or local criminal record information obtained by an OPM investigator.[64]

According to officials from the FBI's Criminal Justice Information Services Division, the FBI has not been able to utilize any of the information that OPM has provided since 2011 because OPM has not provided the source documents uncovered during OPM's investigations, such as a copy of a court record. Instead, OPM provided the FBI with information derived from its final investigative reports, which can include the results of OPM investigators' phone or in-person conversations with court officials or other state criminal justice officials, among other things. According to OPM officials, OPM informed the FBI during briefings prior to when it started sending information to the FBI that OPM investigators generally do not collect source documents as part of their investigations and would not be able to do this on a routine basis. OPM officials noted that there may have been a misunderstanding with the FBI regarding the term "source" as to whether the FBI required an original court record.

In October 2014, senior FBI officials said that they had had recent discussions with OPM officials to determine what, if any, criminal record information that OPM collects could be provided to the FBI to meet the FBI's requirement for source documents. A senior OPM official noted that these discussions included an FBI request for OPM to change how it provided the disposition information to the FBI to better support sorting of the information. The official added that OPM's initial assessment of the FBI's request was that it is most likely feasible. Further, the official noted that OPM had been engaged in a dialog with the FBI regarding its request and was researching the possibilities as the FBI further defined what it needed from OPM. Prior GAO work has found that collaborative activities—such as the one between the FBI and OPM—benefit from agreeing upon decisions to achieve desired outcomes.[65] By clarifying what disposition information OPM will provide to the FBI and formally agreeing on how OPM will provide it, the FBI would be able to forward the information to states. This would allow each state to determine if the information can be used to update their criminal history records.

Many States Did Not Fully Comply with Federal Requirements to Inform Individuals of Rights to Correct or Complete Their Criminal History Records

FBI audits of the states' use of criminal history records conducted from 2011 through 2013 show that 44 states went through an audit within these 3 years, and 31 of the 44 states (about 70 percent) had at least one state agency that was out of compliance with federal regulations related to applicant notifications. Specifically, the agency did not provide all of the required notifications to a job or license applicant on the individual's rights to challenge and correct that person's criminal history records.[66]

According to FBI audit management officials, state agencies did not provide the required notifications primarily because the agencies were not aware that they had to do so. According to federal regulations:

Officials at governmental institutions and other entities that are authorized to submit fingerprints and receive FBI identification records, including criminal history records, must notify the individuals that their fingerprints will be used to check FBI criminal history records.

- Officials making the determination of suitability for employment or licensing must provide applicants the opportunity to complete or challenge the accuracy of information contained in the FBI records.
- Officials making suitability determinations must also advise applicants that procedures for obtaining a change, correction, or update to FBI identification records are set forth in 28 C.F.R. § 16.34.
- Officials making employment and licensing determinations should not deny employment or licenses based on information in the record until the applicant has been afforded a reasonable time to correct or complete the record, or has declined to do so.[67]
- On the basis of our analysis of FBI audit results, the two notifications that state agencies most frequently did not provide to applicants were (1) that the applicant's fingerprints would be used to check FBI criminal history records, and (2) the process for changing or updating FBI records. For each audit finding related to applicant notifications, the FBI is to make a recommendation to the state that addresses the finding. The state in turn is to respond in writing with a description of the state's plans to address the FBI's recommendation, including how the state will correct its practices to ensure compliance with the audit requirements. The Compact Council or FBI may also require the state to provide additional information or updates on the state's progress in addressing the FBI's recommendations.[68]

According Compact Council and FBI officials, the Compact Council and the FBI have educated states on the applicant notification requirements through different methods, including biannual Compact Council meetings, a communication notice from the FBI to states in 2010, and during the FBI's triennial audit of states. Additionally, from May through August 2012, the Compact Council disseminated documents to states that are affiliated with the Compact Council via e-mail and at FBI Advisory Policy Board meetings that, among other things, describe (1) applicant rights to challenge and correct their criminal records during a FBI record check, and (2) the states requirement to notify applicants of these rights.[69] The FBI also published the information from these documents on the FBI's website. FBI officials noted that these documents have been widely distributed to the states and are now provided as training tools during audits. Therefore, the FBI expects that audit findings regarding the provision of applicant notice may improve in the future.

Despite the FBI's audit process and the FBI's and Compact Council's efforts to educate states on the applicant notification requirements, FBI audit findings show that states generally do not provide all of the required applicant notifications. Specifically, the FBI finalized audits for 14 states after August 2012—when the Compact Council disseminated the documents to states—and 13 of the 14 states had at least one agency out of compliance with the federal notification requirements. Internal control standards note that an agency's management should ensure that audit findings are resolved, and that separate evaluations of control activities that are designed to ensure compliance with regulations can be useful to determine their effectiveness.[70] Taking additional action to identify the reasons why states continue to fail to comply with applicant notification requirements could help the FBI and Compact Council revise the methods they use to educate states and achieve compliance, thereby helping the FBI and states ensure that applicants are aware of their rights to challenge and correct their criminal history records.

PRIVATE COMPANY CRIMINAL RECORD CHECKS INCREASING; COMPANIES FACE CHALLENGES IN OBTAINING COMPLETE AND ACCURATE RECORDS

Number of Private Companies Conducting Criminal Record Background Checks Appears to Be Increasing because of Employer Demand

The exact number of private companies that conduct criminal record checks, the number of checks conducted each year, and the number of employers and industries requesting checks are generally unknown, but appear to be increasing. According to a 2005 SEARCH report on criminal background checks—the most recent report DOJ has funded on this issue—in addition to a few large industry players, there are hundreds, perhaps even thousands, of regional and local background check companies that conduct criminal record checks.[71] Management officials from the FTC, EEOC, and two industry associations we contacted said that they believed the industry is growing because of employer demand for such checks. For example, according to a senior official from the Consumer Data Industry Association—a trade association that represents private background screening companies and other companies that compile data on consumers—new companies that perform criminal records checks are regularly forming due in part to employers' increasing demand for background checks, as well as the availability of online criminal history records and publicly available databases of court records.

The 2005 SEARCH report also noted that private background check companies can offer benefits that government agencies are not always able to provide, including collecting and consolidating criminal justice information from multiple sources, achieving faster response times than state agencies, and creating reports that include non-criminal-justice information. For example, in addition to an applicant's criminal history record, private companies can search other sources of information to help employers assess an applicant's suitability for employment, including public records (e.g., real estate records, liens, and motor vehicle registrations) and nonpublic information related to an individual's credit history (mortgages, auto loans, and student loans). Information provided to us by a senior official from the Consumer Data Industry Association in September 2014 cited similar benefits that private background check companies can provide.[72]

Private Background Check Companies That Compile and Use Criminal Record Information Are Subject to Federal Regulation

At the federal level, the Federal Trade Commission and the Consumer Financial Protection Bureau are responsible for, among other things, enforcing provisions of the Fair Credit Reporting Act. FCRA provisions require consumer reporting agencies to maintain reasonable procedures designed to avoid violations of requirements relating to information that may not be contained in consumer reports, to limit furnishing consumer reports to the permissible statutory purposes, and to assure maximum possible accuracy of the information concerning the individual referenced in the report.[73] In addition, generally under FCRA, if an employer intends to take an adverse action on an employee or applicant based in whole or in part on a consumer report, the employer must first provide that person with a copy of the report and a description in writing of that person's rights under FCRA.[74]

According to senior FTC and CFPB officials, the agencies can take law enforcement action in connection with alleged FCRA violations through filing civil lawsuits in federal courts or through settlements with companies. In addition, the FCRA contains provisions that generally allow for a civil action to address certain FCRA violations to be brought in an appropriate United States district court or another court of appropriate jurisdiction within specified time frames.[75] FTC officials stated that the FCRA does not require private criminal background check companies to submit to federal audits or provide disclosure statements on their activities.

According to FTC officials, from fiscal years 2009 to 2014, the FTC settled 16 complaints against private background screening companies and employers for alleged FCRA violations involving information that private background check companies reported. Of the 16 complaints, 4 included allegations that related to the use of criminal record information in employment matters, such as not following reasonable procedures when providing information to employers or not providing proper notice to employees under FCRA provisions on how the information will be used. For example, in 1 complaint, the FTC alleged that a private background company failed to follow reasonable procedures to prevent the company from including the same criminal offense information in a consumer report multiple times, failed to follow reasonable procedures to prevent the company from providing obviously inaccurate consumer report information to employers, and in numerous cases provided the records of the wrong person to employers. The FTC alleged that these failures led to consumers being denied employment or other employment-related benefits. The private background company agreed to settle with the FTC by paying a civil penalty and is barred from continuing the practices that the FTC identified as violating the FCRA. [76]

CFPB also accepts complaints regarding consumer financial products and services within its jurisdiction. According to senior CFPB officials, the bureau forwards those complaints directly to the relevant companies for a response. The CFPB officials noted that they have not received many consumer complaints regarding the use of criminal history records in employment background checks. The officials said that consumers may not think to contact CFPB with such complaints because consumers may think that criminal background checks are outside of CFPB's jurisdiction since the complaints are not "financial" in nature, even though CFPB has had jurisdiction to enforce most FCRA provisions since 2011. As of October 2014, CFPB had not brought any FCRA enforcement actions against private companies related to the use of criminal history information in employment background checks.

In addition, the Equal Employment Opportunity Commission enforces Title VII of the Civil Rights Act of 1964, which makes it illegal to discriminate in employment against a job applicant or employee on the basis of race, color, religion, national origin, or sex. In general, there are two ways in which an employer's use of criminal history records may violate Title VII—disparate treatment and disparate impact. Under disparate treatment, an employer may face liability for discrimination if an employer treats criminal history information differently for different applicants or employees based on a Title VII-protected characteristic, such as race or national origin. Under disparate impact, if an employer's neutral employment practice (e.g., excluding any applicant from employment based on certain criminal conduct) disproportionately harms individuals based on race or national origin, the policy will violate the law if it is not job related and consistent with business necessity for the position in question. For example, in fiscal year 2012, a large employer agreed to pay a monetary penalty and make major policy changes to resolve an EEOC administrative charge. Specifically, under the company's former background check policy, the company did not hire job applicants for permanent jobs if the applicants had been (1) arrested and were pending prosecution but were never convicted of an offense, or (2) arrested or convicted of certain minor offenses. The EEOC investigation revealed that this policy operated to disproportionately deny permanent employment to African-Americans, and found reasonable cause to believe that the policy was discriminatory under Title VII of the Civil Rights Act of 1964.

In addition to enforcing the FCRA and Title VII of the Civil Rights Act of 1964, federal agencies have taken actions to help ensure industry compliance with, and consumer awareness of, employers' and private background companies' use of criminal history records. For example, according to senior EEOC officials, because of the increased ease of employers' access to criminal history record information, in 2012, EEOC updated its guidance on the use of criminal records in employment decisions.[77] The guidance provides information on how an employer may use criminal history information—such as conviction records—to make nondiscriminatory employment decisions and to ensure that the employer uses the information for legitimate job-related purposes. For example, the guidance states that the fact of an arrest does not establish that criminal conduct has occurred, and excluding an applicant based on an arrest, in itself, is not job related and consistent with business necessity. The guidance notes, however, that an employer may make an employment decision based on the conduct underlying an arrest if the conduct makes the applicant unfit for the position in question.

The guidance also suggests examples of best practices that employers may adopt on the use of criminal history information to make employment decisions. One example from the guidance suggests that employers develop a narrowly tailored written policy and procedure for screening applicants and employees for criminal conduct that (1) identifies essential job requirements and the actual circumstances under which an applicant would perform the jobs, and (2) determines the specific offenses that may demonstrate an individual is not fit for performing such jobs. In addition, EEOC and the FTC jointly published employer guidance on how to comply with federal requirements when an employer receives background check information from private background screening companies.[78] For example, the guidance states that if an employer is going to get criminal history and other background information from a company that is in the business of compiling such information, the employer must first get an applicant's or employee's written permission to do the check.

Private Companies Face Challenges in Obtaining Complete and Accurate Criminal Records

Officials from private background check companies, states we contacted, and DOJ identified challenges that private companies face in obtaining complete and accurate criminal history records. For example, the officials said that private companies do not always have access to complete commercial databases, which can result in companies providing employers with incomplete information. The 2006 Attorney General's report also noted that not all states make their criminal record information accessible for private companies to search. The report added that states and state agencies that do make their criminal history records accessible to the public may only periodically update these records, which may affect the information the private background companies access. Senior officials from the Washington State Patrol who maintain the state's criminal record repository said that the state provides a subscription service to private vendors for access to public records, but that the state updates the records only every few months.

Also, private companies generally conduct name-based checks (versus fingerprint-based checks), which can decrease the accuracy of the information that the check produces. According to the Attorney General's 2006 report, name-based checks can result in false positives—which can occur when a person with a common name is associated with another person's records—and false negatives, which can occur when a search misses a record because of errors in the record or in the information used to initiate the search. According to CFPB officials, private background check companies can use additional identifiers—such as date of birth— when conducting checks in order to help mitigate inaccurate search results. We have also reported that using personal identifying information in addition to an individual's name when conducting a check, such as the person's date of birth, can minimize false positives and false negatives.[79] The stakeholders we contacted did not have information on the extent to which private companies use additional identifiers when conducting checks.

Related to the accuracy of private company checks, senior officials from two private sector screening companies we interviewed raised concerns about FCRA's "contemporaneous notice" provision and its potentially negative effects on employees and applicants. In general, under FCRA, a consumer reporting agency that provides a consumer report for employment purposes that contains public record information and is likely to have an adverse effect on an individual's ability to obtain employment is required to either (1) notify the individual that is the subject of the report that the public record information is being reported and of the name and address of the person receiving the information or (2) maintain strict procedures designed to insure that the public record information reported is complete and up to date.[80] The officials explained that notification to an employee that a company is reporting public record information to the employer relieves the consumer reporting agency from ensuring that criminal record information provided to an employer is accurate. The officials did not have data or other information on how this provision has affected employees and applicants.

CONCLUSION

Employers' increasing use of criminal history record checks to determine applicants' suitability for employment, licensing, or volunteering underscores the need for accurate and complete criminal records— including the final disposition of any criminal charges—and assurances that applicants have an opportunity to challenge or correct potentially inaccurate records. DOJ components have taken a range of actions to help state and local agencies improve the accuracy and completeness of their criminal history records and address related challenges. However, the FBI Advisory Policy Board's Disposition Task Force has been in existence since 2009, but it has not issued best practices or national standards for collecting and reporting disposition information or developed a national strategy for improving the quality of disposition reporting, as intended. Establishing a plan with time frames and milestones could help the task force achieve its remaining goals and help improve disposition reporting.

In addition, for more than 3 years, the FBI has received but not used disposition information from OPM to potentially help states enhance the completeness of their criminal history records. It is important that the FBI and OPM clarify what disposition information that OPM collects will be provided to the FBI and formally agree on how OPM will provide it. This would enable the FBI to forward the information to states and allow each state to determine if the information can be used to update their criminal history records. Finally, although the FBI and the Compact Council have taken steps to educate states on the regulatory requirement that they notify applicants of their right to challenge and correct the information in their criminal history records, FBI audits of state and local agencies' use of criminal history records consistently show that states do not notify all applicants as required. Taking additional action to determine why states do not comply with this requirement could help the FBI and the Compact Council revise their educational programs and achieve compliance, thereby helping to ensure that applicants are aware of their rights to challenge and correct their criminal history records.

RECOMMENDATIONS FOR EXECUTIVE ACTION

We are making the following three recommendations:

- To improve disposition reporting that would help states update and complete criminal history records, we recommend that the Director of the FBI task the FBI Advisory Policy Board to establish a plan with time frames and milestones for achieving its Disposition Task Force's stated goals.
- To potentially help states enhance the completeness of their criminal history records, we recommend that the Director of the FBI and the Director of the Office of Personnel Management clarify what disposition information OPM will provide to the FBI and formally agree on how OPM will provide it. This would enable the FBI to forward the information to states and allow each state to determine if the information can be used to update their criminal history records.
- To better equip states to meet the regulatory requirement to notify individuals of their rights to challenge and update information in their criminal history records, and to ensure that audit findings are
- resolved, we recommend that the Director of the FBI—in coordination with the Compact Council—determine why states do not comply with the requirement to notify applicants and use this information to revise its state educational programs accordingly.

AGENCY COMMENTS AND OUR EVALUATION

We provided a draft of this report to DOJ and OPM for their review and comment.

DOJ concurred with all three recommendations in this report in an e-mail provided on January 13, 2015. In its written comments, OPM concurred with the one recommendation that was directed to the office. Specifically, the recommendation calls for the FBI and OPM to clarify what disposition information that OPM collects as part of its background investigations will be provided to the FBI and formally agree on how OPM will provide it. OPM noted that preliminary discussions between the FBI and OPM indicate that the disposition data in OPM's reports of investigations may be useful to the FBI in identifying records in its system that are lacking dispositions but that contain a disposition at the local level. OPM added that it has been researching internal technical strategies that will provide specific data fields to the FBI that can be formatted and sorted in a manner best suited to the FBI's needs. OPM noted, however, that the format in which OPM collects and maintains data is necessarily oriented toward fulfilling the agency's assigned mission. OPM added that it is not tasked with the authority to perform criminal justice record management functions for the FBI or criminal justice assistance functions for the states and localities.

DOJ and OPM also provided technical comments, which we incorporated in this report as appropriate.

David C. Maurer
Director, Homeland Security and Justice

APPENDIX I: OBJECTIVES, SCOPE, AND METHODOLOGY

This report addresses the following questions:

- To what extent do states conduct Federal Bureau of Investigation (FBI) criminal history record checks for selected employment sectors and what challenges, if any, do they face in conducting these checks?
- To what extent have states made progress in improving the completeness of criminal history records and what challenges remain that federal agencies can help mitigate?
- To what extent do private companies conduct record checks, what benefits do they provide, how are they regulated, and what challenges do they face?

Regarding the extent to which states conduct FBI record checks and related challenges, we assessed the extent to which states were conducting checks—either under state statutes or regulations, or under federal authorities—for employment and volunteer positions covered by three federal laws. Specifically, the National Child Protection Act of 1993,[1] the Edward M. Kennedy Serve America Act,[2] and the Private Security Officer Employment Authorization Act of 2004.[3] We selected these laws to represent a range of factors, including variation in whether the law requires or authorizes (permits) an FBI record check, different employment sectors covered (i.e., nonprofit, private, or public employment), and variation in paid versus volunteer positions.

In addition, we conducted a web-based survey of officials at agencies within all 50 states and the District of Columbia that maintain criminal history records (state repositories) to determine the extent to which states are conducting FBI checks for the employment sectors covered under the three federal laws. We conducted the survey from July 29, 2014, to September 30, 2014.

We received a response rate of 94 percent—47 states and the District of Columbia—which we collectively refer to as states throughout this report. Because this was not a sample survey, it has no sampling errors. However, the practical difficulties of conducting any survey may introduce errors, commonly referred to as nonsampling errors. We took steps in developing the questionnaire, collecting the data, and analyzing them to minimize such nonsampling error.

To ensure our survey questions were accurate, understandable, and unbiased, we pretested our survey instrument with officials in 3 states—California, Idaho, and Washington. An independent reviewer within GAO also reviewed a draft of the questionnaire prior to its administration. We made appropriate revisions to the content and format of the questionnaire after the pretests and independent review. To ensure the validity of the responses, we reviewed survey responses to ensure logic and consistency in the responses.

We also analyzed federal regulations and procedures for conducting criminal record checks and evaluated previously published reports from SEARCH, the Department of Justice (DOJ), and other organizations regarding the national availability of FBI background checks, solutions proposed to address access challenges, and what challenges remain.[4] To supplement information obtained through our national survey and our analysis of previously published reports, we conducted semistructured interviews with management officials from repositories and courts that maintain criminal history information in 4 case study states—California,

Florida, Idaho, and Washington—to determine the extent to which they conduct FBI checks, any challenges faced with conducting checks, and actions taken to address those challenges. We selected the 4 states based on geographic location and other factors, including participation in the Compact Council—the primary state and federal body for setting policy regarding the interstate sharing of criminal history records for noncriminal-justice purposes.

We interviewed FBI officials with responsibility for managing the Interstate Identification Index—the national system for the interstate sharing of criminal history records—to determine any challenges employers face in obtaining access to checks, and any challenges states face in adjudicating records on behalf of employers. Further, we interviewed management officials from the National Mentoring Organization, the National Center for Missing and Exploited Children, the Corporation for National and Community Service—the federal agency that oversees service programs such as AmeriCorps and Senior Corps—and the National Association of Security Companies—to obtain their views on the availability of FBI criminal record checks and any challenges in obtaining access. To better understand state legal and policy challenges regarding access to background checks, we interviewed officials with SEARCH and attended a November 2013 meeting of the Interstate Compact Council, where a wide range of issues related to the non-criminal-justice use of criminal history records were discussed.

Regarding the progress states have made in improving the completeness of criminal history records and related challenges, we analyzed data that states provided to DOJ via a survey from fiscal years 2006 through 2012 on the percentage of their arrest records that contained information on the disposition of those arrests.[5] We selected this time frame because 2006 was the year the Attorney General issued the criminal record background check report and 2012 was the year with the most current available survey data. To assess the reliability of the data, we analyzed the survey methodology, interviewed DOJ officials who conducted the surveys, and examined data for obvious errors. We determined that the data were sufficiently reliable for the purposes of this report.

We also analyzed the results of the FBI's most recent round of triennial state audits, which include assessing the completeness of state records and use of the records for non-criminal-justice purposes.[6] As of January 2014, the FBI had finalized 44 state audits that the FBI conducted from 2011 through 2013. Further, we interviewed officials who maintain criminal history records in our 4 case study states to determine challenges they face in maintaining complete records and related initiatives to improve record completeness. We also interviewed officials from the FBI and DOJ's Bureau of Justice Statistics (BJS) who have key roles in providing access to national criminal history records and providing assistance to states in maintaining complete records. In addition, we interviewed officials from the National Employment Law Project to discuss the potential impacts that incomplete criminal records have on job applicants. Further, we interviewed officials from the Office of Personnel Management (OPM) who collect disposition information as part of OPM background investigations.

Regarding what is known about the role of the private sector in conducting employment-related background checks, we reviewed relevant sections of the Fair Credit Reporting Act (FCRA)[7] and Title VII of the Civil Rights Act of 1964,[8] laws that govern the use of criminal history records and that regulate background checks conducted by private background screening companies.[9]

We analyzed SEARCH's 2005 report on the commercial sale of criminal justice record information and a 2006 Attorney General's report on criminal history background checks.[10] We analyzed guidance prepared by the Equal Employment Opportunity Commission on the use of criminal history record information in employment decisions in order to better understand what challenges employers, applicants, and consumer reporting agencies face in using criminal history record information. We also interviewed senior officials from associations that represent background screening companies, including the National Association of Professional Background Check Screeners and the Consumer Data Information Association, to determine the role of private sector agencies in providing criminal history information to employers. Further, we interviewed senior officials from federal agencies that regulate these private sector entities—including the Federal Trade Commission, the Equal Employment Opportunity Commission, and the Consumer Financial Protection Bureau—to determine how the industry is regulated as well as the size and scope of the industry.

We conducted this performance audit from October 2013 to February 2015 in accordance with generally accepted government auditing standards. Those standards require that we plan and perform the audit to obtain sufficient, appropriate evidence to provide a reasonable basis for our findings and conclusions based on our audit objectives. We believe that the evidence obtained provides a reasonable basis for our findings and conclusions based on our audit objectives.

APPENDIX II: EXAMPLES OF FEDERAL LAWS AUTHORIZING STATE ACCESS TO FBI-MAINTAINED CRIMINAL HISTORY RECORDS FOR NON-CRIMINAL-JUSTICE EMPLOYMENT AND LICENSING PURPOSES

Federal law	Description
Departments of State, Justice, and Commerce, the Judiciary, and Related Agencies Appropriation Act, 1973, Pub. L. No. 92-544	Allowing expenditure of funds for the Federal Bureau of Investigation (FBI) to be used for the exchange of identification records, including criminal history record information, with officials of state and local governments for purposes of employment or licensing if authorized by state statute and approved by the Attorney General.
Private Security Officer Employment Authorization Act of 2004, Pub. L. No. 108-458, § 6402, 28 U.S.C. § 534 Note	Allowing authorized employers to submit to the state identification bureau of a participating state, fingerprints or other means of positive identification, as determined by the Attorney General, of an employee or applicant for employment as a private security officer.
Edward M. Kennedy Serve America Act, Pub. L. No. 111-13, 42 U.S.C. § 12645g	For conducting criminal history checks of individuals selected to serve in a position in which the individuals receive a living allowance, stipend, national service educational award, or salary through a program receiving assistance under the national service laws.

Appendix II. (Continued)

Federal law	Description
National Child Protection Act of 1993, Pub. L. No. 103-209, amended by Volunteers for Children Act, Pub. L. No. 105-251, 42 U.S.C. § 5119a	Permitting states to have in effect procedures requiring qualified entities designated by the state to contact an authorized agency of the state to request a nationwide background check\for the purpose of determining whether an individual has been convicted of a crime that bears upon that individual's fitness to have responsibility for the safety and well-being of children, the elderly, or individuals with disabilities.
Interstate Transportation of Dangerous Criminals Act of 2000, Pub. L. No. 106-560, 42 U.S.C. § 13726b	Relating to promulgation of regulations by the Attorney General to address the minimum standards for background checks, including criminal background checks, and pre-employment drug testing for potential employees involved in the transportation of violent prisoners in or affecting interstate commerce in the private prisoner transport industry.
Crime Control Act of 1990, Pub. L. No. 101-647, 42 U.S.C. § 13041	Relating to the fingerprinting and criminal background check of individuals involved with the provision to children under the age of 18 of child care services for each federal agency or facility operated by the federal government that hires such individuals.
Adam Walsh Child Protection and Safety Act of 2006, Pub. L. No. 109-248, § 153, 42 U.S.C. § 16962	Provides for the Attorney General, upon request of the chief executive officer of a state, to conduct fingerprint-based checks of the national crime information databases pursuant to a request submitted by a private or public elementary or secondary school, a local educational agency, or state educational agency, on individuals employed by or under consideration for employment by, or otherwise in a position in which the individual would work with or around children in the school or agency.
Indian Gaming Regulatory Act, Pub. L. No. 100-497, 25 U.S.C. § 2701, et. seq.	For use of officials of the National Indian Gaming Commission in conducting background checks on key employees and primary management officials.
USA PATRIOT Act of 2001, Pub. L. No. 107-56, § 1012, 49 U.S.C. § 5103a	Upon the request of a state regarding the issuance of a license to operate a motor vehicle transporting in commerce a hazardous material to an individual, the Attorney General shall carry out a background records check, including a check of the relevant criminal history databases, regarding the individual and notify the Secretary of Homeland Secretary regarding the results.
Futures Trading Act of 1982, Pub. L. No. 97-444, 7 U.S.C. § 12a	The Commodity Futures Trading Commission is authorized to register futures commission merchants, associated persons of futures commission merchants, introducing brokers, associated persons of introducing brokers, commodity trading advisors, associated persons of commodity trading advisors, commodity pool operators, associated persons of commodity pool operators, floor brokers, and floor traders upon application in accordance with rules and regulations and in the form and manner to be prescribed by the commission, which may require the applicant, and such persons associated with the applicant as the commission may specify, to be fingerprinted and to submit, or cause to be submitted, such fingerprints to the Attorney General for identification and appropriate processing.
Omnibus Appropriations Act of 1999, Pub. L. No. 105-277, § 124, 28	A nursing facility or home health care agency may submit a request to the Attorney General (through the appropriate state agency or

Federal law	Description
U.S.C. § 534 Note	agency designated by the Attorney General) to conduct a search of the records of the Criminal Justice Information Services Division of the Federal Bureau of Investigation for any criminal history records corresponding to the fingerprints or other identification information submitted regarding an applicant for employment if the employment position is involved in direct patient care.
Aviation and Transportation Security Act, Pub. L. No. 107-71, 49 U.S.C. §§ 44935, 44936, and 44939	The Under Secretary of Transportation for Security shall require that an individual to be hired as a security screener undergo an employment investigation (including a criminal history record check) under 49 U.S.C. § 44936(a)(1).
Parimutuel Licensing Simplification Act of 1988, Pub. L. No. 100-413, 28 U.S.C. 534 Note	An association of state officials regulating pari-mutuel wagering, designated by the Attorney General, may submit fingerprints to the Attorney General on behalf of any applicant for a state license to participate in pari-mutuel wagering. In response to such a submission, the Attorney General may, to the extent provided by law, exchange, for licensing and employment purposes, identification and criminal history records with state governmental bodies to which such applicant has applied.
Securities Acts Amendments of 1975, Pub. L. No. 94-29, 15 U.S.C. § 78q(f)(2)	Every member of a national securities exchange, broker, dealer, registered transfer agent, registered clearing agency, registered securities information processor, national securities exchange, and national securities association, shall require that each of its partners, directors, officers, and employees be fingerprinted and shall submit such fingerprints, or cause the same to be submitted, to the Attorney General for identification and appropriate processing. In providing identification and processing functions, the Attorney General shall provide the Securities and Exchange Commission and self-regulatory organizations designated by the commission with access to all criminal history record information

Source: GAO analysis of federal laws authorizing state access to FBI-maintained criminal history records. | GAO-15-162.

Appendix III: Summary of Selected Federal Trade Commission (FTC) Complaints and Outcomes Involving Criminal History Record Information, Fiscal Years 2009 through 2014

Summary of federal complaint	Outcome
According to the FTC's complaint, a private background company failed to follow reasonable procedures to prevent the company from including the same criminal offense information in a consumer report multiple times, failed to follow reasonable procedures to prevent the company from providing obviously inaccurate consumer report information to employers, and in numerous cases even included the records of the wrong person to employers. The FTC alleged that these failures led to consumers being denied employment or other employment-related benefits.	The private background company agreed to settle with the FTC by paying a civil penalty and is barred from continuing the practices that the FTC identified as violating the Fair Credit Reporting Act (FCRA).

Appendix III. (Continued)

Summary of federal complaint	Outcome
According to the FTC's complaint, a private background company obtained, and provided employers with, information about job applicants, including possible criminal records of applicants on the National Sex Offender Registry. The FTC claimed the company violated the FCRA by failing to use reasonable procedures to assure maximum possible accuracy of the information and failing to provide written notices to applicants that the company reported public record information to prospective employers that may adversely affect the applicant's ability to obtain employment.	The private background company agreed to settle with the FTC by maintaining reasonable procedures to (1) assure the maximum possible accuracy of information provided in background checks, and (2) notify consumers when the company has provided public information about them that is likely to have an adverse affect upon their ability to obtain employment.
According to the FTC complaint, a private background company offered an online service allowing employers to purchase background reports that contain, among other information, arrest and conviction records. The FTC claimed that the background company violated several provisions of the FCRA, including failure to maintain reasonable procedures that the information provided was used for a permissible purpose and failure to use reasonable procedures to assure maximum possible accuracy of information provided to employers.	The private background company agreed to settle with the FTC and pay a civil penalty. In addition, the settlement barred the private background company from continuing the practices that the FTC identified as violating the FCRA.
According to the FTC's complaints, two employers contracted with a private background company to conduct background checks that included, among other information, criminal history records. The employers used the results of the background checks as a basis for hiring applicants or retaining employees, and throughout the course of a year, took adverse action against numerous job applicants by denying employment to them. The FTC claimed that the employers violated the FCRA by, among other things, failing to provide the employees and applicants with notices before taking adverse actions. Providing such notices would have allowed the applicants and employees to dispute the accuracy of the background checks.	The two employers agreed to settle with the FTC and both paid civil penalties. In addition, the settlements required the employers to provide FCRA-required notices to applicants and employees in the future. The settlements also contain record-keeping and reporting provisions to allow the FTC to monitor compliance.

Source: GAO analysis of FTC complaints from the agency's Legal Resources Database. | GAO-15-162.

End Notes

[1] 28 C.F.R. § 20.3(i).

[2] Pub. L. No. 92-544, 86 Stat. 1109.

[3] U.S. Department of Justice, The Attorney General's Report on Criminal History Background Checks (Washington, D.C.: June 2006).

[4] In general, a criminal history record is complete when it contains both the arrest charge and the disposition of the arrest (e.g., conviction or acquittal).

[5] In general, private sector companies that compile and sell background information do not have access to FBI record checks. Rather, these companies obtain criminal history information directly from states or other sources.

[6] Pub. L. No. 103-209, 107 Stat. 2490.

[7] Pub. L. No 103-209, § 3, 107 Stat. 2490, 2491 (codified, as amended by the Violent Crime Control and Law Enforcement Act of 1994, Pub. L. No. 103-322, § 320928, 108 Stat. 1796, 2131-2132 and the Volunteers for Children Act, Pub. L. No. 105-251, § 222, 112 Stat. 1885, at 42 U.S.C. § 5119a).

[8] Pub. L. No. 111-13, 123 Stat. 1460.

[9] Pub. L. No. 111-13, §§ 1612, 1614, 123 Stat. 1460, 1538-1541, 1541-1544 (codified at 42 U.S.C. § 12645g).

[10] Pub. L. No. 108-458, § 6402, 118 Stat. 3755, 3755-3758 (codified at 28 U.S.C. § 534 Note).

[11] The Compact Council was established by the National Crime Prevention and Privacy Compact Act of 1998, Pub. L. No. 105-251, 112 Stat. 1874.

[12] See, for example, U.S. Department of Justice, Bureau of Justice Statistics, Survey of State Criminal Justice Information Systems, 2012 (Washington, D.C.: 2012).

[13] The FBI audits each state's use of FBI-maintained criminal history records every 3 years.

[14] Pub. L. No. 91-508, 84 Stat. 1114.

[15] Pub. L. No. 88-352, 78 Stat. 241, 253-266.

[16] SEARCH, Report of the National Task Force on the Commercial Sale of Criminal Justice Information (Sacramento, CA: 2005). The task force included representatives from the law enforcement community, among others. The report resulted from a project funded by DOJ. SEARCH—the National Consortium for Justice Information and Statistics—is a non-profit organization governed by governor appointees from the 50 states and is a resource for information, best practices, services, and solutions for criminal justice information sharing.

[17] U.S. Department of Justice, The Attorney General's Report on Criminal History Background Checks (Washington, D.C.: June 2006).

[18] The Interstate Identification Index was developed in 1978 to coordinate the decentralized exchange of interstate criminal history record information among states and federal criminal justice agencies. All 50 states and the District of Columbia participate in the index.

[19] States generally charge a fee to cover the expenses related to conducting these checks, in addition to a fingerprint fee charged by the FBI.

[20] App. II contains examples of federal laws that authorize states to conduct FBI criminal history record checks for non-criminal-justice purposes.

[21] Under 15 U.S.C. § 1681a(f), "the term 'consumer reporting agency' means any person which, for monetary fees, dues, or on a cooperative nonprofit basis, regularly engages in whole or in part in the practice of assembling or evaluating consumer credit information or other information on consumers for the purpose of furnishing consumer reports to third parties, and which uses any means or facility of interstate commerce for the purpose of preparing or furnishing consumer reports."

[22] 15 U.S.C. § 1681(b).

[23] Pub. L. No. 88-352, 78 Stat. 241, 253-266.

[24] We surveyed officials at agencies within all 50 states and the District of Columbia that maintain criminal history records (state repositories), and received responses from 47 states and the District of Columbia. We collectively refer to survey respondents as states throughout this report.

[25] In general, states conduct FBI record checks using the authority of federal law or a state law that has been approved by the Attorney General under Public Law 92-544. States can establish suitability criteria for employment or licensing that are in addition to criteria that are established in federal law. This report focuses on the extent to which states conduct checks for selected employment sectors and generally does not distinguish between the use of federal or state authorities to conduct checks.

[26] 42 U.S.C. §§ 5119a, 5119c.

[27] Three states did not respond to our survey.

[28] In addition to the 3 states that did not respond to our survey, 1 state did not respond to our survey question about volunteers serving the elderly or individuals with disabilities.

[29] Pub. L. No. 108-21, § 108(a)(3), 117 Stat. 650, 656-658.

[30] The National Center for Missing and Exploited Children made determinations based on criteria that the center and other volunteer organizations jointly established.

[31] Subsequent legislation extended the Child Safety Pilot Program to a 104-month program and 200,000 criminal history record checks.

[32] 42 U.S.C. § 12645g(d)(3).

[33] Pub. L. No. 111-13, §§ 1612, 1614, 123 Stat. 1460, 1538-1541, 1541-1544 (codified at 42 U.S.C. § 12645g).

[34] Three states did not respond to our survey and officials from 4 of the 48 states that responded were unsure if their states conducted checks for grant recipients.

[35] Survey respondents could provide more than one reason for not conducting checks.

[36] Pub. L. No. 108-458, § 6402, 118 Stat. 3755. See 28 U.S.C. 534 Note.

[37] Pub. L. No. 108-458, § 6402(b)(1)-(3), 118 Stat. 3755, 3755.

[38] Three states did not respond to our survey and officials from 5 of the 48 states were unsure if their state conducted FBI checks for private security officers. It was beyond the scope of our review to assess the extent to which employers of private security officers used private companies to conduct criminal record checks.

[39] Under 28 C.F.R. § 105.27, an employer may take this step if the employer is prevented from submitting the fingerprints because the employment is in (1) a state that does not have an applicable Public Law 92-544 statute authorizing state and national fingerprint-based criminal history checks for private security officers and has elected to opt out of the PSOEAA, or (2) a participating state that has not yet established a process for receiving fingerprints and processing the checks in accordance with the established regulations.

[40] SEARCH, Report of the National Task Force on the Criminal Backgrounding of America (Sacramento, CA: 2005).

[41] U.S. Department of Justice, The Attorney General's Report on Criminal History Background Checks.

[42] We discuss the completeness of criminal history records and individuals' rights to correct inaccurate or incomplete information later in this report.

[43] In general, disposition refers to the result or conclusion of criminal proceedings, such as charge dismissed, acquittal, adjudication withheld, probation, or conviction.

[44] U.S. Department of Justice, Bureau of Justice Statistics, Survey of State Criminal History Information Systems (Washington, D.C.: 2006). U.S. Department of Justice, Bureau of Justice Statistics, Survey of State Criminal History Information Systems, 2012, (Washington, D.C.: January 2014).

[45] Florida's Criminal and Juvenile Justice Information Systems Council's mission is to develop standards and policies that will promote and enhance the sharing of criminal and juvenile justice information throughout the state. The council is composed of representatives from many different state agencies, including Florida's Attorney General's office, local law enforcement officials, court administrators, a public defender, and criminal justice information users.

[46] U.S. Department of Justice, Bureau of Justice Statistics, Improving Access to and Integrity of Criminal History Records (Washington, D.C.: 2005).

[47] The mission of the National Center for State Courts is to promote the rule of law and to improve the administration of justice in the state courts and courts around the world.

[48] See, for example, U.S. Department of Justice, Bureau of Justice Statistics, Improving Access to and Integrity of Criminal Records, (Washington, D.C.: 2005), and SEARCH– National Consortium for Justice Information and Statistics, Report of the National Taskforce on the Criminal Backgrounding of America (Sacramento, CA: 2005).

[49] We have previously reported on DOJ efforts to assist states. See, GAO, Bureau of Justice Statistics Funding to States to Improve Criminal Records, GAO-08-898R (Washington, D.C.: July 8, 2008), and National Criminal History Improvement Program: Federal Grants Have Contributed to Progress, GAO-04-364 (Washington, D.C.: Feb. 27, 2004).

[50] For additional information on state challenges making records available for the National Instant Criminal Background Check System, see GAO, Gun Control: Sharing Promising Practices and Assessing Incentives Could Better Position Justice to Assist States in Providing Records for Background Checks, GAO-12-684 (Washington, D.C.: July 16, 2012).

[51] It was beyond the scope of our review to assess DOJ's grant-monitoring efforts.

[52] According to National Center for State Courts officials from the Technology and Research divisions, the web-based tool kit is scheduled for completion in 2015, but the National Center for State Courts has been posting information to the website as activities are completed.

[53] The FBI's Advisory Policy Board is responsible for reviewing appropriate policy, technical, and operational issues related to the FBI's Criminal Justice Information Services Division programs.

[54] The task force's initial goals were to (1) develop strategies to improve the flow of disposition information with little or no funding, (2) increase the electronic transfer of information from the courts to the state repositories, and (3) educate decision makers on the importance of allocating resources for disposition improvement.

[55] The task force's revised goals are to (1) refine disposition rate calculations, (2) identify existing federal and state requirements for collecting and reporting disposition information, (3) identify and recommend best practices for collecting and reporting disposition information, (4) examine and recommend improvements to the

national standards for collecting and reporting disposition information, and (5) promote the adoption of national standards for sharing dispositions by state judicial systems.

[56] Project Management Institute, A Guide to the Project Management Body of Knowledge (PMBOK® Guide), Fifth Edition, (Newton Square, PA: 2013). We have used this guide to provide criteria in previous reports, including GAO, Nonproliferation and Disarmament Fund: State Should Better Assure the Effective Use of Program Authorities, GAO-13-83 (Washington, D.C.: Nov. 30, 2012).

[57] 28 C.F.R. § 20.37.

[58] The FBI is to conduct an audit of each state once every 3 years to ensure that the state complies with Interstate Identification Index participation requirements, including disposition reporting requirements. As of January 2014, the FBI had finalized 44 state audits that the FBI conducted from 2011 through 2013.

[59] The prosecutor is the principal representative of the state in all matters related to the adjudication of criminal offenses.

[60] U.S. Department of Justice, Bureau of Justice Statistics, Reporting by Prosecutors' Offices to Repositories of Criminal History Records, (Washington, D.C.: 2005). The results of this survey are not representative of state prosecutors nationwide.

[61] National Conference of State Legislatures, "Citation in Lieu of Arrest" (Denver, CO: National Conference of State Legislatures, 2013).

[62] The disposition-reporting focus group was conducted as part of the Warrant and Disposition Toolkit project under a DOJ grant to the National Center for State Courts.

[63] OPM conducts approximately 2.5 million investigations each year, and each investigation is to include a fingerprint-based check of FBI criminal history records.

[64] One individual's FBI record check could result in multiple records if the individual had criminal records from multiple locations and law enforcement agencies.

[65] GAO, Managing for Results: Key Considerations for Implementing Interagency Collaborative Mechanisms, GAO-12-1022 (Washington, D.C.: Sept. 27, 2012). Agencies can enhance and sustain their collaborative efforts by engaging in several practices, including defining and articulating a common outcome through having clear goals.

[66] The FBI is to audit each state once every 3 years to ensure that the state complies with requirements on the use of criminal history records, including applicant notification requirements. As of January 2014, the FBI had finalized 44 state audits that the FBI conducted from 2011 through 2013.

[67] 28 C.F.R. § 50.12(b).

[68] It was beyond the scope of our review to assess the states' corrective actions.

[69] According to FBI officials, both of these documents largely track the language of the relevant regulations.

[70] GAO, Standards for Internal Control in the Federal Government, GAO-AIMD-00-21.3.1 (Washington, D.C.: Nov. 1, 1999).

[71] SEARCH, Report of the National Task Force on the Commercial Sale of Criminal Justice Information. The task force included representatives from the law enforcement community and the private background check industry, among others. The report was produced as a product of a project funded by DOJ.

[72] U.S. Department of Justice, The Attorney General's Report on Criminal History Background Checks.

[73] 15 U.S.C. § 1681e.

[74] 15 U.S.C. § 1681b(b)(3)(A).

[75] 15 U.S.C. § 1681p. We did not assess the extent to which consumers file complaints with state regulators or through private litigation because this was outside the scope of this review.

[76] App. III contains a summary of the 4 FTC complaints.

[77] EEOC Enforcement Guidance, Enforcement Guidance on the Consideration of Arrest and Conviction Records in Employment Decisions Under Title VII of the Civil Rights Act of 1964, as amended, 42 U.S.C. § 2000e et seq., 2012.

[78] EEOC and FTC. Background Checks: What Employers Need to Know, 2012.

[79] GAO, Terrorist Watchlist Screening: Efforts to Help Reduce Adverse Effects on the Public, GAO-06-1031 (Washington, D.C.: Sept. 29, 2006).

[80] 15 U.S.C. § 1681k(a). Items of public record relating to arrests, indictments, convictions, suits, tax liens, and outstanding judgments are considered up to date if the current public record status of the item at the time of the report is reported.

End Notes for Appendix I

[1] Pub. L. No. 103-209, 107 Stat. 2490.

[2] Pub. L. No. 111-13, 123 Stat. 1460.

[3] Pub. L. No. 108-458, § 6402, 118 Stat. 3755, 3755-3758 (codified at 28 U.S.C. § 534 Note)

[4] SEARCH, the National Consortium for Justice Information and Statistics, is a nonprofit organization governed by appointees from the 50 states that shares best practices and solutions for criminal justice information sharing.

[5] See, for example, U.S. Department of Justice, Bureau of Justice Statistics, Survey of State Criminal Justice Information Systems, 2012 (Washington, D.C.: January 2014).

[6] The FBI audits each state's use of FBI-maintained criminal history records every 3 years.

[7] Pub. L. No. 91-508, 84 Stat. 1114.

[8] Pub. L. No. 88-352, 78 Stat. 241, 253-266.

[9] Private sector agencies that conduct background checks do not have access to FBI record checks. Rather, these agencies obtain criminal history information directly from states or other sources.

[10] SEARCH, Report of the National Task Force on the Commercial Sale of Criminal Justice Information (Washington, D.C.: 2005). The task force included representatives from the law enforcement community and the private background check industry, among others. The report was produced as a product of a project funded by DOJ; U.S. Department of Justice, The Attorney General's Report on Criminal History Background Checks (Washington, D.C.: June 2006)

In: Criminal History Records and Background Checks
Editor: Brian Wilkins
ISBN: 978-1-63483-438-4

Chapter 3

In Search of a Job: Criminal Records as Barriers to Employment*

Amy L. Solomon

"I am writing this letter ... out of desperation and to tell you a little about the struggles of re-entering society as a convicted felon." Thus began a letter that made its way to me at the U.S. Department of Justice (DOJ). The letter came from a 30-year-old man who — in 2003, at age 21 — lost control of his car after a night of drinking, killing his close friend. "Jay" was convicted of involuntary manslaughter and sentenced to 38 months in state prison.

"I have worked hard to turn my life around. I have remained clean for nearly eight years, I am succeeding in college, and I continue to share my story in schools, treatment facilities and correctional institutions, yet I have nothing to show for it. ... I have had numerous interviews and sent out more than 200 resumes for jobs which I am more than qualified. I have had denial after denial because of my felony." Jay ends the letter saying, "I do understand that you are not responsible for the choices that have brought me to this point. Furthermore, I recognize that if I was not abiding by the law, if I was not clean, and if I was not focusing my efforts toward a successful future, I would have no claim to make."

Jay's story is not unusual.

A Substantial Share of the U.S. Population Has Arrest Records

A new study shows that nearly one-third of American adults have been arrested by age 23.[1] This record will keep many people from obtaining employment, even if they have paid their dues, are qualified for the job and are unlikely to reoffend. At the same time, it is the chance at a job that offers hope for people involved in the criminal justice system, as we

* This is an edited, reformatted and augmented version of an article which appeared in the National Institute of Justice Journal, Issue 270, June 2012. The article is an adaptation of the author's July 26, 2011 testimony before the Equal Employment Opportunity Commission.

know from research that stable employment is an important predictor of successful re-entry and desistance from crime.[2]

Criminal records run the gamut — from one-time arrests where charges are dropped to lengthy, serious and violent criminal histories. Most arrests are for relatively minor or nonviolent offenses. Among the nearly 14 million arrests recorded in 2009, only 4 percent were considered among the most serious violent crimes (which include murder, rape, robbery and aggravated assault).[3] (See Figure 1.) Another 10 percent of all arrests were for simple assault; these do not involve a weapon or aggravated injury but often include domestic violence and intimate partner violence. The remainder of the arrests in 2009 were for:

- Property crimes, which accounted for 18 percent of arrests. These include burglary, larceny-theft, motor vehicle theft, arson, vandalism, stolen property, forgery and counterfeiting, fraud, and embezzlement.
- Drug offenses, which accounted for 12 percent of arrests. These include production, distribution and use of controlled substances.
- Other offenses, which accounted for 56 percent of all arrests. These include disorderly conduct, drunkenness, prostitution, vagrancy, loitering, driving under the influence and weapons violations.

Although many of these "other" offenses are for behaviors that harm the community, they do not constitute the most serious violent offenses of murder, rape, robbery and aggravated assault.

Furthermore, what is often forgotten is that many people who have been arrested — and, therefore, technically have a criminal record that shows up on a background check — were never convicted of a crime. This is true not only among those charged with minor crimes, but also for many individuals arrested for serious offenses. A snapshot of felony filings in the 75 largest counties, for example, showed that approximately one-third of felony arrests did not lead to conviction.[4]

People of Color Are Disproportionately Impacted

The impact of having a criminal record is exacerbated among African Americans, who may already experience racial discrimination in the labor market and are more likely than whites to have a criminal record. Two prominent studies by Devah Pager involved employment audits of men in Milwaukee and New York City. Both studies, funded by NIJ, found that a criminal record reduces the likelihood of a job callback or offer by approximately 50 percent. This criminal record "penalty" was substantially greater for African Americans than for white applicants. The more recent study included Latinos in the test pool and showed they suffered similar "penalties" in the employment market.[5]

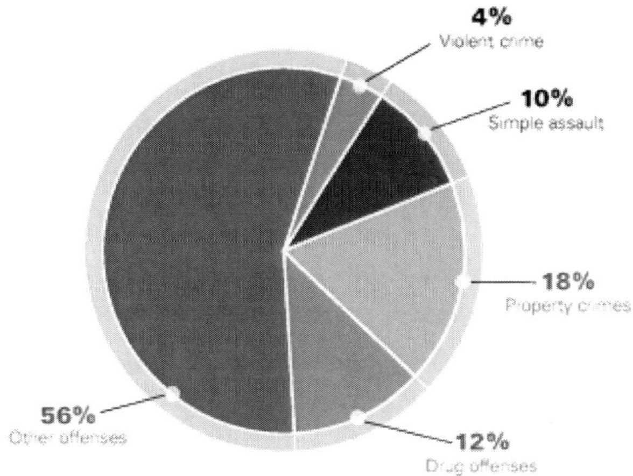

Source: Crime in the United States, 2009, Washington D.C.: U.S. Department of Justice, Federal Bureau of Investigation, 2010.

Figure 1. Arrests in 2009 by Offense.

Nearly 75 percent of arrestees are male. African Americans account for less than 14 percent of the U.S. population[6] but 28 percent of all arrests. They are even more highly represented in the incarcerated population, comprising almost 40 percent of those behind bars.[7]

Although many arrests do not lead to conviction, and many convictions do not result in imprisonment, the incarcerated population is substantial. Each year, there are almost 13 million people admitted to — and released from — local jails[8] and more than 700,000 admitted to/released from state and federal prisons.[9] Incarceration rates in the United States are higher than in any other country in the world. The United States has less than 5 percent of the world's population but almost a quarter of the world's prisoners.[10] Over the last 30 years, the incarcerated population has more than quadrupled, and today, just under 2.3 million men and women are held in prisons and jails.[11]

In 2008, the Pew Center on the States brought heightened public attention to our nation's incarceration rate when it reported that 1 in 100 U.S. adults was behind bars on any given day.[12] (See Figure 2.) One in 100 is substantial, but it is also an average that does not hold evenly across all populations. One in 54 men is incarcerated, compared to 1 in 265 women. Looking just at men, we see that 1 in 106 white men is behind bars, compared to 1 in 36 Hispanic men and 1 in 15 African American men. When we consider young African American men (ages 20-34), the ratio lowers further to 1 in 9. In fact, young, male African American high school dropouts have higher odds of being in jail than being employed.[13] As these numbers make clear, incarceration is heavily concentrated among men, particularly young men of color.

There is also an intergenerational component at work. Forty-six percent of jail inmates have a family member who was incarcerated.[14] On any given day, 1 in 28 children has a parent behind bars. Again, communities of color are most acutely affected; 1 in 9 African American children has an incarcerated parent.[15] One recent study estimates that 25 percent of

African Americans born after 1990 will witness their father being sent to prison before their 14th birthday.[16]

Incarceration is also a geographically concentrated phenomenon. A large number of prisoners come from — and return to — a relatively small number of already disadvantaged neighborhoods.[17] In many neighborhoods around the country, incarceration is no longer an unusual occurrence but a commonplace experience, especially for young men of color.

Incarcerated Populations Face a Broad Set of Challenges

The corrections population consists largely of men who have for many years exhibited a consistent pattern of criminal involvement, a lack of attachment to mainstream institutions of social integration and a multiplicity of interconnected problems. Among jail inmates:

- Sixty-eight percent meet the criteria for substance abuse or dependence.[18]
- Sixty percent do not have a high school diploma or general equivalency diploma.[19]
- Thirty percent were unemployed in the month before arrest, and almost twice as many were underemployed.[20]
- Sixteen percent are estimated to have serious mental health problems.[21]
- Fourteen percent were homeless at some point during the year before they were incarcerated.[22]

The need for treatment, training and assistance is great.[23] It is critical that individuals entering prisons and jails be screened and assessed to determine their criminogenic risks and needs, and that appropriate evidence-based interventions be applied during incarceration and after release to produce the best outcomes.[24]

Collateral Consequences Create Additional Barriers

In addition to these significant and often overlapping challenges, an extra set of punishments, or "collateral consequences," is imposed on individuals as a direct result of their criminal convictions. NIJ is funding a national study, conducted by the American Bar Association's Criminal Justice Section, which has catalogued more than 38,000 statutes that impose collateral consequences on people convicted of crimes, creating barriers to jobs, housing, benefits and voting.[25] More than 80 percent of the statutes operate as a denial of employment opportunities.

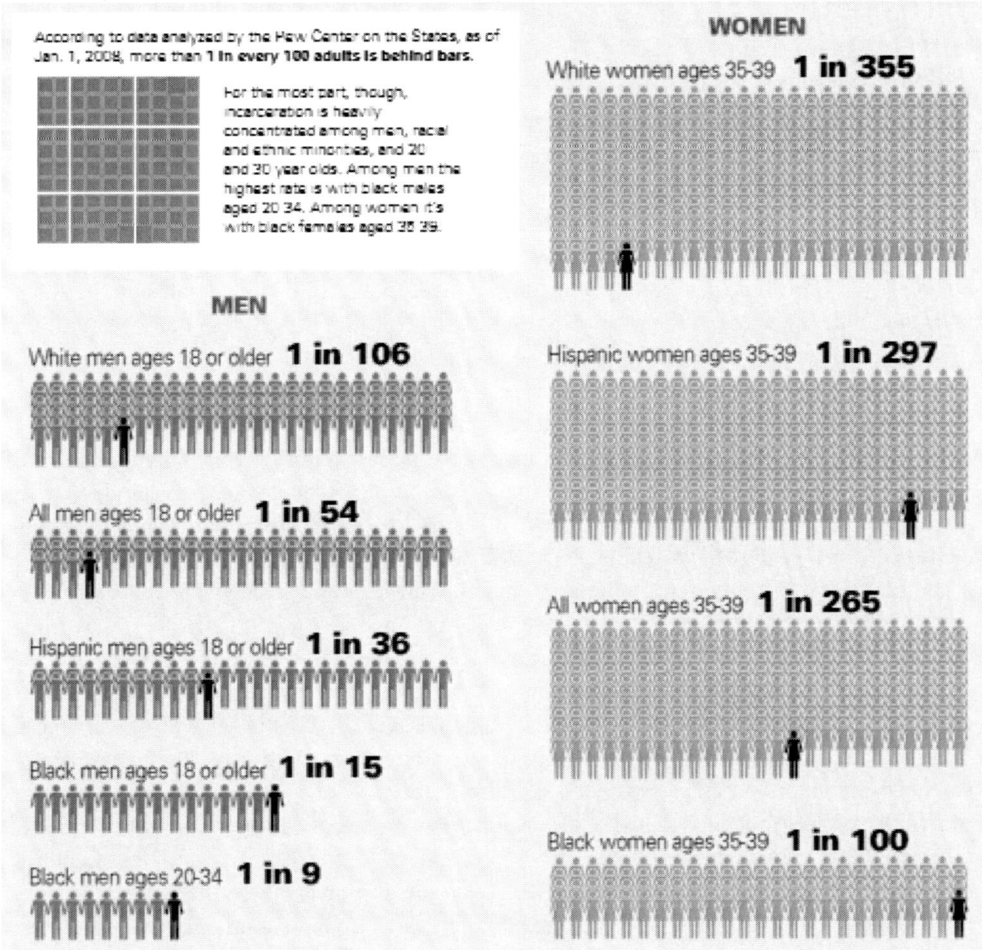

Source: The Pew Center on the States, One in 100: Behind Bars in America 2008, Washington, D.C.: The Pew Charitable Trusts, 2008, http://www.pewstates.org/uploadedFiles/PCS_Assets/2008/one%20in%20100.pdf.

Figure 2. U.S. Incarceration Rates by Race and Sex.

Although some of these consequences serve important public safety purposes, others may be antiquated and create unnecessary barriers to legitimate work opportunities. A commonly cited example is that in some states, formerly incarcerated people who were trained as barbers cannot hold those jobs after release because state laws prohibit felons from practicing the trade, presumably because their access to sharp objects makes them a threat to the public.[26]

U.S. Attorney General Eric Holder recently wrote to every state Attorney General, with a copy to every Governor, asking them to assess their state's collateral consequences and determine if any should be eliminated "so that people who have paid their debt to society are able to live and work productively."[27] The Attorney General's letter also said the federal government would assess the federal collateral consequences — and through the auspices of the interagency Reentry Council, we are doing just that.

The Attorney General's Reentry Council

In January 2011, U.S. Attorney General Eric Holder established a Cabinet-level federal interagency Reentry Council, representing a significant executive branch commitment to coordinating re-entry efforts and advancing effective reentry policies. The Reentry Council is premised on a real recognition that many federal agencies — not just the Department of Justice (DOJ) — have a major stake in re-entry. The re-entry population is one with which we are all already working — not only in prisons, jails and juvenile facilities, but in emergency rooms, homeless shelters, unemployment lines, child support offices, veterans hospitals and elsewhere. When we extend out to the children and families of returning prisoners, the intersection is even greater.

At its first meeting, the council adopted a mission statement to advance public safety and well-being through enhanced communication, coordination and collaboration across federal agency initiatives that: (1) make communities safer by reducing recidivism and victimization, (2) assist those who return from prison and jail in becoming productive citizens, and (3) save taxpayer dollars by lowering the direct and collateral costs of incarceration. The council has empowered staff — now representing 20 federal departments and agencies — to work toward a number of goals organized around coordinating and leveraging federal resources for re-entry; removing federal barriers to re-entry; and using the bully pulpit to dispel myths, educating key stakeholders about federal policies, resources and effective reentry models.

Regarding employment and reentry, the council has an active working group composed of staff from the Department of Labor (DOL), DOJ, the Office of Personnel Management, the Equal Employment Opportunity Commission (EEOC), the Federal Trade Commission and the Small Business Administration, among others. The council has developed public education materials, a website and a set of "Reentry MythBusters" to clarify federal policy on a number of issues. Five MythBusters focus on employer responsibilities and incentives as well as worker rights in this area. On the incentives side, DOL offers both tax credits and federal bonding protection for employers that hire ex-offenders. On the employer-responsibility and worker rights side, an EEOC-authored MythBuster provides guidance to employers about the appropriate use of a criminal record in making hiring decisions.[1]

The EEOC has long-standing guidance on this issue and is doing enhanced, extensive training and outreach. In July 2011, the Commission held a meeting focused exclusively on arrest and conviction records as barriers to employment. After substantial consideration and review of the information presented both at the meeting and during the public comment period, the EEOC voted 4-1 to issue updated enforcement guidance. The revised guidance, issued April 25, 2012, calls for employers to assess applicants on an individual basis rather than excluding everyone with a criminal record through a blanket policy. It provides new detail and direction for employers in how to consider three key factors — the nature of the job; the nature and seriousness of the offense; and the length of time since it occurred — in writing a hiring policy and in making a specific hiring decision. The updated guidance also emphasizes that employers should not reject a candidate because of an arrest without a conviction, as arrests are not proof of criminal conduct. "The ability of African-Americans and Hispanics to gain employment after prison is one of the paramount civil justice issues of our time," said Commissioner Stuart J. Ishimaru in his statement at the April 25 meeting.

Additionally, in January 2012, the EEOC announced an important settlement agreement with Pepsi regarding its use of arrest and conviction records in employment.[2] The company's policy excluded applicants arrested for any crime — even if they had never been convicted of any offense — from permanent employment. The EEOC found that the criminal background check policy discriminated against African Americans in violation of Title VII of the Civil Rights Act of 1964. This was the first public conciliation concerning the use of arrest and conviction records and is already raising awareness among employers. During fiscal year 2010 and fiscal year 2011, the Commission received more than 1,200 charges alleging job discrimination involving criminal background checks.

DOL is also playing a critical role in this area. In addition to substantial investments in re-entry programs and research, DOL is making important commitments to educate its broad network of employment and training entities on these issues. In June 2010, Secretary Hilda L. Solis hosted a roundtable on workforce development and employment strategies for people with criminal records, and she has gone on record with strong statements on the topic. As she stated at the June roundtable, "When someone serves time in our penal system, they shouldn't face a lifetime sentence of unemployment when they are released. Those who want to make amends must be given the opportunity to make an honest living."[3]

Notes

1 Reentry MythBusters and additional information about the Reentry Council are available at http://www.nationalreentryresourcecenter.org/reentry-council.

2 See Equal Employment Opportunity Commission, "Pepsi to Pay $3.13 Million and Made Major Policy Changes to Resolve EEOC Finding of Nationwide Hiring Discrimination Against African Americans," press release, January 11, 2012, http://www.eeoc.gov/eeoc/newsroom/release/1-11-12a.cfm; and Hananel, Sam, "Pepsi Beverages Pays $3M in Racial Bias Case," USA Today (January 11, 2012), http://www.usatoday.com/money/industries/food/ story/2012-01-11/pepsi-racial-bias-case/52498132/1.

3 Remarks of Hilda L. Solis, Secretary of Labor, "Workforce Development and Employment Strategies for the Formerly-Incarcerated," June 21, 2011, https:// www.dol.gov/_sec/media/speeches/20110621_EX.htm.

Regardless of the legal restrictions, the majority of employers indicate that they would "probably" or "definitely" not be willing to hire an applicant with a criminal record, according to a study by Harry Holzer and colleagues.[28] In fact, a recent report by the National Employment Law Project found frequent use of blanket "no-hire" policies among major corporations, as evidenced by their online job ads posted on Craigslist.[29] The employer motivation is understandable. Employers do not want to hire individuals who might commit future crimes and who may be a risk to their employees' and customers' safety. The assumption, of course, is that a prior record signals higher odds that the individual will commit more crimes in the future. A key question is: If a person who has been arrested stays *arrest-free* for some period of activity go down? A recent study sheds light on just this issue.

Alfred Blumstein and Kiminori Nakamura conducted the NIJfunded "Redemption Study." They were looking for a way to empirically determine when it is no longer necessary for an employer to be concerned about a criminal record in a prospective employee's past.[30]

The researchers examined the criminal records of everyone who was arrested for the first time in 1980 in the state of New York. They then tracked those criminal records forward to find who was arrested again, who wasn't and how long people "stayed clean." In general, once a person had stayed clean for a certain period of time, his chances of being arrested for a new crime were substantially reduced. This is what the researchers refer to as the "point of redemption" — when a prior arrest no longer distinguishes that person from a similar person in the general population in terms of the risk of future criminal arrests.

For individuals who commit their first crime at a very young age or who are first arrested for a more serious crime, it takes longer — about eight years — to reach the point of redemption; but for those who are older when first arrested or who commit less serious crimes, the point of redemption can come in as little as three or four years. After staying clean for this period of time, these individuals become indistinguishable from the general population in terms of their odds of another arrest.[31]

This research has important practical implications. Blumstein and Nakamura suggest that "forever rules be replaced by rules that provide for the expiration of a criminal record." They continue, in an op-ed published by *The New York Times,* that "it is unreasonable for someone to be hounded by a single arrest or conviction that happened more than 20 years earlier — and for many kinds of crimes, the records should be sealed even sooner."[32]

Some states are taking steps in exactly this direction.[33] Thirteen states enacted laws in their 2010- 2011 legislative sessions to expunge and seal low-level offenses after a discrete number of years. Three states passed laws to limit the liability of employers that hire people with criminal records.[34]

This is not to say that criminal background checks serve no purpose. They give employers a tool — albeit an imperfect one — for helping assess risk to their employees, customers, assets and reputations when making hiring decisions. In fact, some of the same research cited earlier indicates that the use of criminal history records and the practice of performing background checks can, in some cases, *reduce* racial discrimination in hiring. The Holzer study, in particular, suggests that employers that perform background checks may end up hiring more African American workers (especially African American men) than those that do not perform them. This is because some employers may assume young African American men have criminal records, and a background check may actually dispel that assumption and increase their chances of being hired.

It is also important to note that criminal records are often incomplete and inaccurate. A DOJ report states that "no single source exists that provides complete and up-to-date information about a person's criminal history."[35] Even the best-maintained record systems are incomplete, often lacking final disposition information in 50 percent or more of the records.[36] If criminal records were a perfect reflection of a person's criminal history, the need for this discussion would be less critical.

Focusing on Prisoner Re-Entry

As noted earlier, incarceration rates are high, and nearly everyone in prison will eventually be released. When re-entry fails, the costs — both societal and economic — are high. More than two-thirds of state prisoners are rearrested within three years of their release, and half are reincarcerated.[37] High rates of recidivism mean more crime, more victims and more pressure on federal, state and municipal budgets. In the past 20 years, state spending on corrections has grown at a faster rate than nearly any other state budget item. The United States now spends more than $74 billion annually on federal, state and local corrections.[38]

The good news is that the response being mounted to meet these challenges is robust. Because re-entry intersects with issues such as health, housing, education, employment, family, faith and community wellbeing, many federal agencies are focusing on the re-entry population with initiatives that aim to improve outcomes in each of these areas (see sidebar, "The Attorney General's Reentry Council"). Congress has supported re-entry efforts as well. The Second Chance Act was passed by Congress with strong bipartisan support and then signed into law by President Bush in 2008. Senators Patrick Leahy (D-VT) and Rob Portman (R-OH) introduced S. 1231, the Second Chance Reauthorization Act of 2011. Re-entry efforts are under way all over the country, and strong bipartisan support is found in state houses and city halls, on county commissions, and in community forums.

Moving Forward

These issues are large-scale and impact an increasingly sizable share of our population. In some distressed communities, arrest and incarceration are commonplace occurrences and part of daily life. Getting a job is arguably the most important step toward successful re-entry for people who have broken the law and paid their debt to society. Yet too many people are barred from job opportunities and thus denied a critical chance to succeed.

Guidance to Employers and Job Seekers on the Use of Criminal Records in the Hiring Process

A 2010 survey by the Society for Human Resource Management reported that 92 percent of employers conduct background checks on job applicants. According to the Equal Employment Opportunity Commission (EEOC), if an employer is aware of a conviction or incarceration, that information should bar someone from employment only when the conviction is closely related to the job, after considering: (1) the nature of the job, (2) the nature and seriousness of the offense, and (3) the length of time since it occurred. Because an arrest alone does not necessarily mean that someone has committed a crime, an employer should allow the person to explain the circumstances of the arrest and again assess whether the circumstances of the arrest are closely related to the job. In the vast majority of cases, employers may not automatically bar everyone with an arrest or conviction record from employment because it could have a disparate impact on communities of color, violating Title VII of the Civil Rights Act of 1964. The EEOC's guidance in this area was revised in April 2012. It now provides greater detail and direction to employers on the appropriate use of arrest and conviction records in hiring decisions.

It is important that job applicants know their rights. The Fair Credit Reporting Act (FCRA) requires employers to receive an applicant's permission, usually in writing, before asking a background screening company for a criminal history report. If the applicant does not give permission, the application for employment may not get reviewed. If a person does give permission but does not get hired because of information in the report, the potential employer has several legal obligations. Specifically, they must tell the individual:

- The name, address and telephone number of the company that supplied the criminal history report
- That the company that supplied the criminal history information did not make the decision to take the adverse action and cannot give specific reasons for it
- About his or her right to dispute the accuracy or completeness of any information in the report, and his or her right to an additional free report from the company that supplied the criminal history report, if requested within 60 days of the adverse action

For more information:

- Reentry MythBusters on the EEOC guidance: http://www. National reentryresourcecenter.org/documents/0000/1082/Reentry_Council_Mythbuster_ Employment.pdf
- FCRA and criminal background checks: http://www. Nationalreentryresource center.org/documents/0000/1176/Reentry_Council_Mythbuster_ FCRA_Employment.pdf
- Revised EEOC guidance, issued April 25, 2012: http://www.eeoc. gov/laws/ guidance/arrest_ conviction.cfm

The argument here is not about giving preference to this population when it comes to jobs. And employers certainly have a right to consider a person's criminal history in making a hiring decision. The concern is that some employers cast an overly broad net banning this population altogether. What is important is that people have an opportunity to apply and be considered for jobs when they are qualified and when their criminal record is not relevant or occurred long enough in the past to no longer be a significant factor in predicting future behavior.

In following up with Jay, I learned that he now has two part-time jobs at local broadcasting companies. He holds himself accountable for his crime, but is also encouraged that he can make positive contributions and is eager to help others. It is critical that we, as a society, provide a path for individuals who have served their time and paid their debts to compete for legitimate work opportunities.

It is, in fact, our only choice if we want people with past criminal involvement to be able to support themselves and their families, pay their taxes, and contribute to our communities.

About the Author

Amy L. Solomon is a Senior Advisor to the Assistant Attorney General in the Office of Justice Programs at the U.S. Department of Justice.

FOR MORE INFORMATION

- n Learn more about Devah Pager's research on the impact of conviction status on the employment prospects of young men at http://www.nij.gov/topics/ corrections/ reentry/employment.htm.
- n Read "'Redemption' in an Era of Widespread Criminal Background Checks," by Alfred Blumstein and Kiminori Nakamura, at http://www.nij.gov/journals/ 263/redemption.htm.

End Notes

[1] Barnes, Robert, Michael G. Turner, Raymond Paternoster, and Shawn D. Bushway, "Cumulative Prevalence of Arrest From Ages 8 to 23 in a National Sample," *Pediatrics* (January 2012): 21-27, http:// pediatrics. aappublications.org/ content/129/1/21.abstract.

[2] Visher, Christy A., Laura Winterfield, and Mark B. Coggeshall, "Ex- Offender Employment Programs and Recidivism: A Meta-Analysis," *Journal of Experimental Criminology* 1 (2005): 295-316. See also Laub, John H., and Robert J. Sampson, "Understanding Desistance from Crime," *Crime & Justice* 28(1): 17-24, http://www.wjh.harvard. edu/soc/ faculty/sampson/articles/2001_C&J_ Laub.pdf.

[3] *Crime in the United States, 2009,* Washington, D.C.: U.S. Department of Justice, Federal Bureau of Investigation, 2010, http://www2.fbi.gov/ucr/cius2009/ index.html.

[4] Cohen, Thomas H., and Tracey Kyckelhahn, *Felony Defendants in Large Urban Counties, 2006,* Bulletin, Washington, D.C.: U.S. Department of Justice, Bureau of Justice Statistics, 2010, NCJ 228944, http://bjs.ojp.usdoj.gov/content/pub/ pdf/fdluc06.pdf.

[5] Pager, Devah, "The Mark of a Criminal Record," *American Journal of Sociology* 108 (2003): 957-960, http://www.princeton.edu/~pager/ pager_ajs.pdf; Pager, Devah, Bruce Western, and Bart Bonikowski, "Discrimination in a Low-Wage Labor Market: A Field Experiment," *American Sociological Review* 74 (October 2009): 777-779, http:// www.princeton.edu/~pager/ASR_ pager_etal09.pdf.

[6] Rastogi, Sonya, Tallese D. Johnson, Elizabeth M. Hoeffel, and Malcolm P. Drewery, Jr., *The Black Population: 2010,* 2010 Census Briefs, Washington, D.C.: U.S. Department of Commerce, U.S. Census Bureau, 2011, http://www.census.gov/prod/ cen2010/briefs/c2010br-06.pdf.

[7] Sabol, William J., Todd D. Minton, and Paige M. Harrison, *Prison and Jail Inmates at Midyear 2006,* Bulletin, Washington, D.C.: U.S. Department of Justice, Bureau of Justice Statistics, 2011, NCJ 217675, http://bjs.ojp.usdoj.gov/content/pub/ pdf/pjim06.pdf.

[8] Minton, Todd D., *Jail Inmates at Midyear 2010,* Statistical Tables, Washington, D.C.: U.S. Department of Justice, Bureau of Justice Statistics, April 2011, NCJ 233431, http://bjs.ojp.usdoj.gov/content/pub/ pdf/jim10st.pdf.

[9] Guerino, Paul, Paige M. Harrison, and William J. Sabol, *Prisoners in 2010,* Bulletin, Washington, D.C.: U.S. Department of Justice, Bureau of Justice Statistics, December 2011, NCJ 236096, http://bjs.ojp.usdoj.gov/ content/pub/pdf/p10.pdf.

[10] Walmsley, Roy, *World Prison Population List,* 8th ed., London: King's College, 2008.

[11] Glaze, Laura, *Correctional Population in the United States, 2010,* Bulletin, Washington, D.C.: U.S. Department of Justice, Bureau of Justice Statistics, December 2011, NCJ 236319, http://www.bjs.gov/content/ pub/pdf/cpus10.pdf.

[12] The Pew Center on the States, *One in 100: Behind Bars in America 2008,* Washington, D.C.: The Pew Charitable Trusts, 2008, http://www.pewstates.org/ uploadedFiles/PCS_Assets/2008/ one%20in%20100.pdf.

[13] The Pew Charitable Trusts, *Collateral Costs: Incarceration's Effect on Economic Mobility,* Washington, D.C.: The Pew Charitable Trusts, 2010, http:// www.pewstates.org/uploadedFiles/PCS_Assets/2010/Collateral_ Costs(1).pdf.

[14] James, Doris J., *Profile of Jail Inmates, 2002,* Special Report, Washington, D.C.: U.S. Department of Justice, Bureau of Justice Statistics, 2004, NCJ 201932, http://bjs.ojp.usdoj.gov/content/ pub/pdf/pji02.pdf.

[15] The Pew Charitable Trusts, *Collateral Costs: Incarceration's Effect on Economic Mobility.*

[16] Western, Bruce, "Reentry: Reversing Mass Imprisonment," *Boston Review* (July/August 2008), http://www. bostonreview.net/BR33.4/ western.php.

[17] Visher, Christy A., Jennifer Yahner, and Nancy LaVigne, "Life After Prison: Tracking the Experiences of Male Prisoners Returning to Chicago, Cleveland, and Houston Washington, D.C.: Urban Institute, 2010; Cadora, Eric, "Criminal

Justice and Health and Human Services: An Exploration of Overlapping Needs, Resources, and Interests in Brooklyn Neighborhoods," Washington, D.C.: Urban Institute, 2002.

[18] Karberg, Jennifer, and Doris James, *Substance Dependence, Abuse, and Treatment of Jail Inmates, 2002,* Special Report, Washington, D.C.: U.S. Department of Justice, Bureau of Justice Statistics, 2005, NCJ 209588, http://bjs.ojp.usdoj.gov/ content/pub/pdf/sdatji02.pdf.

[19] Harlow, Caroline Wolf, *Education and Correctional Populations,* Special Report, Washington, D.C.: U.S. Department of Justice, Bureau of Justice Statistics, 2003, NCJ 195670.

[20] James, Doris J., *Profile of Jail Inmate, 2002,* Special Report, Washington D.C.: U.S. Department of Justice, Bureau of Justice Statistics, 2004, NCJ 201932, http://bjs.ojp.usdoj.gov/content/ pub/pdf/pji02.pdf.

[21] Ditton, Paula, *Mental Health and Treatment of Inmates and Probationers,* Special Report, Washington, D.C.: U.S. Department of Justice, Bureau of Justice Statistics, 1999, NCJ 174463.

[22] James, Doris J., *Profile of Jail Inmates, 2002.*

[23] Federal Interagency Reentry Council, *Reentry in Brief: A Product of the Federal Interagency Reentry Council,* May 2011, http://www. nationalreentryresourcecenter.org/ documents/0000/1059/Reentry_ Brief.pdf.

[24] For a more thorough discussion of the challenges facing the incarcerated population and re-entry models to address these challenges, see Solomon, Amy L., Jenny W.L. Osborne, Stefan F. LoBuglio, Jeff Mellow, and Debbie A. Mukamal, *Life After Lockup: Improving Reentry From Jail to the Community,* Washington, D.C.: Urban Institute, 2008, http://www.urban.org/ UploadedPDF/411660_life_after_ lockup.pdf.

[25] Available at: American Bar Association, "Adult Collateral Consequences Project," July 2011, http://isrweb.isr. temple. edu/projects/accproject. See also, Blumstein, Alfred, and Kiminori Nakamura, "'Redemption' in an Era of Widespread Criminal Background Checks," *NIJ Journal* 263 (June 2009): 10-17, http://www.nij.gov/ journals/263/redemption.htm.

[26] Haberman, Clyde, "Ex-Inmate's Legacy: Victory Over Bias and Catch-22 Bureaucracy," *New York Times* 29 (August 2008): B5.

[27] Holder, Eric H., Jr., Letter, April 18, 2011, National Reentry Resource Center, http://www. Nationalreentry resourcecenter.org/ documents/0000/1088/Reentry_ Council_AG_Letter.pdf.

[28] Holzer, Harry J., Steven Raphael, and Michael A. Stoll, "Perceived Criminality, Criminal Background Checks, and the Racial Hiring Practices of Employers," *The Journal of Law and Economics* 49 (2006): 451, 453-454.

[29] Rodriguez, Michelle N., and Maurice Emsellem, *65 Million 'Need Not Apply': The Case for Reforming Criminal Background Checks for Employment,* New York: National Employment Law Project, March 2011.

[30] Blumstein, Alfred, and Kiminori Nakamura, "'Redemption' in an Era of Widespread Criminal Background Checks," *NIJ Journal* 263 (June 2009): 10-17, http://www.nij.gov/ journals/263/redemption.htm. It is worth emphasizing that this research was based on first-time arrests, and the subjects were rarely incarcerated or were incarcerated for short periods of time. First-time arrestees rarely go to prison. Blumstein and Nakamura were recently awarded a new grant to examine "redemption" times for re-entering prisoners.

[31] To test the general applicability of their results, Blumstein and Nakamura have conducted additional research in two other states and with two other sampling years. Their results are consistent, especially after the first five years after initial arrest. NIJ is currently funding Blumstein and Nakamura to test the robustness of the previous findings and to look at out-of-state arrests and racial differences.

[32] Blumstein, Alfred, and Kiminori Nakamura, "Paying a Price, Long After the Crime," *New York Times* (January 9, 2012), http://www.nytimes.com/2012/01/10/opinion/paying-a-price-long-after-the-crime. html?_r= 2&ref= opinion.

[33] National Employment Law Project, *State Reforms Promoting Employment of People With Criminal Records: 2010-11 Legislative Round-Up,* Legislative Update, December 2011, http://www.nelp.org/page/-/ SCLP/2011/PromotingEmploymentof PeoplewithCriminalRecords. pdf?nocdn=1.

[34] Ibid.

[35] U.S. Department of Justice, Office of the Attorney General, *The Attorney General's Report on Criminal History Background Checks,* Washington, D.C.: U.S. Department of Justice, Office of the Attorney General, June 2006, http://www.justice.gov/olp/ ag_bgchecks_report.pdf. The report states that approximately 50 percent of the records in the FBI's criminal history record repository are missing final disposition information. More recent arrest records, however, have a higher rate of completeness.

[36] Also note that even after a criminal record has been expunged, the record can still appear in private database searches. See SEARCH Group, *Report of the National Task Force on the Commercial Sale of Criminal Justice Record Information,* SEARCH Group: Sacramento, Calif., 2005, http://www.search.org/files/ pdf/RNTFCSCJRI.pdf.

[37] Beck, A.J., "The Importance of Successful Reentry to Jail Population Growth," presented at the Urban Institute's Jail Re-Entry Roundtable, Washington, D.C., June 27, 2006, http://www.urban.org/projects/ reentry-

roundtable/upload/beck.PPT. Bureau of Justice Statistics, "BJS Expenditure and Employment Data Collections,"

[38] Washington, D.C.: U.S. Department of Justice, Bureau of Justice Statistics, http://bjs.ojp. usdoj.gov/ index.cfm?ty=tp&tid=5; Kyckelhahn, Tracey, *Justice Expenditures and Employment, FY 1982-2007,* Statistical Tables, Washington, D.C.: U.S. Department of Justice, Bureau of Justice Statistics, December 2011, NCJ 236218, http://www.bjs.gov/content/ pub/pdf/jee8207st.pdf.

INDEX

D

E

F

G

H

I

J

L

X